D0146475

ESSAYS IN
THE HISTORY
OF ECONOMICS

ESSAYS IN THE HISTORY OF ECONOMICS

GEORGE J. STIGLER

THE UNIVERSITY OF CHICAGO PRESS
CHICAGO AND LONDON

HB
171
.S86

Library of Congress Catalog Card Number: 65-14426

THE UNIVERSITY OF CHICAGO PRESS, CHICAGO & LONDON
The University of Toronto Press, Toronto 5, Canada

© *1965 by The University of Chicago. All rights reserved. Published
1965. Composed and printed by* THE UNIVERSITY OF CHICAGO
PRESS, *Chicago, Illinois, U.S.A.*

Preface

The study of the history of economics has escaped all the forces that have transformed the character of economic research in the twentieth century. Neither foundation nor government is at all interested in intellectual history, so it is perhaps the last unsubsidized research area in economics. It has escaped any serious quantification, and research assistants can seldom be used—why, even committees are scarce in the field! I therefore apologize to my fellow workers in the field for the lapse from old-fashionedness in the previously unpublished essay in this volume, "Statistical Studies in the History of Economics," and promise not to sin again, often.

GEORGE J. STIGLER

September 1964

v

Alma College Library
Alma, Michigan

Contents

1

The Nature and Role of Originality in Scientific Progress

We set great store on originality in economics. Cournot was a great economist because he was original; Mill was not a great economist—only a great expositor—because he was not original. At times the attitude is carried to such extremes that we admire a man for his original and ingenious absurdities: he has a seminal mind. Even when we stop short of this curious perversity, we like to associate each eminent economist with the doctrine he originated. Jevons—marginal utility; Walras—general equilibrium; Marshall—quasi-rents, long and short run; Wicksteed—Euler's theorem; Pigou—private and social marginal products; Thünen— $\sqrt{ap}$; and so it goes on. If we cannot associate a catchword with the man, we are inclined to deny him originality.

Originality is decidedly a fine virtue, and I have no desire to praise the mind that devotes itself exclusively to an almost incestuous admiration of earlier wisdom. But originality is a

Reprinted from *Economica*, Vol. XXII (November, 1955).

more complicated virtue than most discussion seems to recognize, and its role in the progress of science is not easy to state or to assess. It is to these matters that this essay is devoted.

I. THE MEANING OF ORIGINALITY

Originality has as its simplest meaning the temporal priority in the statement of an idea. Marshall was the first man to write that

$$\text{elasticity of demand} = -\frac{dq}{dp}\frac{p}{q},$$

and hence he is the originator of this concept. Cournot was the first man to analyze the two-firm industry: he is the originator of duopoly theory. Bowley originated the generalization of this analysis, by introducing the rate of change of one duopolist's output with respect to his rival's output.

Even at the level of specificity of these examples, however, we should notice the extreme difficulty of ascertaining the earliest statement. Marshall was the first to write the equation defining elasticity, but Cournot almost wrote it,[1] and the whole literature of the pre-Marshallian period teems with discussions of it.[2] Bowley's generalization of Cournot had previously been made

---

[1] "Suppose that when the price becomes $p + \Delta p$, the annual consumption as shown by statistics, such as custom-house records, becomes $D - \Delta D$. According to as:

$$\frac{\Delta D}{\Delta p} < \text{ or } > \frac{D}{p}$$

the increase in price, Δp, will increase or diminish the product $pF(p)$; . . ." *Mathematical Principles of the Theory of Wealth* (New York, 1929), pp. 53–54.

[2] For example, Gossen made the elasticity of unity the dividing line between luxuries and necessities; *Entwickelung der Gesetze des menschlichen Verkehrs* (3rd ed., Berlin, 1927), p. 136. For a crude definition of elasticity, see W. Whewell, "Mathematical Exposition of Some Doctrines of Political Economy," *Transactions of the Cambridge Philosophical Society*, III (1830), pp. 201 *et seq.*

by Kotany.[3] I do not know a respectable discussion of duopoly before Cournot's but not all the returns are in.

And when an idea is more than a technical definition or highly specific analysis, the temporal priority is hopelessly obscure. Who first discovered diminishing marginal utility, or diminishing returns, or the quantity theory, or the theory of underemployment equilibrium? I do not know, but it is common knowledge that all such ideas have long histories before they are stated by the men who made them important.

It is not an accident that one can find anticipations of every "discovery" that was important in the sense of influencing the course of scientific thought. At any time there is a sort of frequency distribution of the scientific views of members of a science. Some men hold to the ideas of the past, most have a more or less similar position—which is therefore the current view—and a few are in diverse ways radical. (At closer view, a man often falls in all three classes, being radical in some branches of the discipline, with the crowd in others, and behind it in still others. Malthus was a leader in population theory, a Ricardian of sorts in value theory, and a physiocrat on agriculture.) Great economists are those who influence the profession as a whole, and this they can do only if their doctrines do not involve too great a change from the views and knowledge of the rank and file of the science. It is simply impossible for men to apprehend and to adopt wholly unfamiliar ideas. If it be true that science, like nature, moves at most by short jumps, it is highly probable that the great new ideas of any period will have found an earlier and neglected statement.

Originality may also be subjectively first in time. (A few years ago when one of my friends remarked that output was at a maximum under competition, a young French economist replied: "I proved that in 1940.") Great economists usually discover their leading ideas rather than excavate them from the

---

[3] "Suggestion on the Theory of Value," *Quarterly Journal of Economics,* XIX (1904–5), 583–84.

literature. This is an interesting problem for the students of the psychology of invention, but it makes no difference to the science whether its new ideas come from current or past originality.

Scientific originality in its important role should be measured against the knowledge of a man's contemporaries. If he opens their eyes to new ideas or to new perspective on old ideas, he is an original economist in the scientifically important sense. It is in this sense that all great economists are necessarily original. Smith, Ricardo, Jevons, Walras, Marshall, Keynes—they changed the beliefs and interests of economists and thus changed economics.

It is conceivable for an economist to be ignored by contemporaries and yet exert considerable influence on later generations, but this is a most improbable event. He must have been extraordinarily out of tune with (in advance of) his times, and rarely do first-class minds throw themselves away on the visionary. Perhaps Cournot is an example of a man whose work skipped half a century, but normally such men become famous only by reflecting the later fame of the rediscovered doctrines.

Originality, then, in its scientifically important role, is a matter of subtle unaccustomedness—neither excessive radicalism nor statement of the previously unformulated consensus.

II. THE TECHNIQUE OF PERSUASION

Suppose I get a "new" idea and gradually work it (and myself) into the state where I believe that it is scientifically important. I may then find it in earlier writers, for now I am sensitive to the subject and look more searchingly and sympathetically at the relevant writings. Then I take up my pen and write:

> I submit for critical appraisal my recent thoughts
> on linear oligopoly. These thoughts, which were

first presented by Süssmilch in 1745, by Say in 1811, and then became so common as to reach the United States by 1870, are by no means of major significance. In fact if they are improperly utilized they will probably lead to serious error. Yet under certain conditions, which I am not fully able to specify, they offer promise of a minor usefulness.

Will my fellow economists read on—once they get used to the novelty of this approach?

No. New ideas are even harder to sell than new products. Inertia and the many unharmonious voices of those who would change our ways combine against the balanced and temperate statement of the merits of one's "original" views. One must put on the best face possible, and much is possible. Wares must be shouted—the human mind is not a divining rod that quivers over truth.

The techniques of persuasion also in the realm of ideas are generally repetition, inflated claims, and disproportionate emphases, and they have preceded and accompanied the adoption on a large scale of almost every new idea in economic theory. Almost, but not quite, every new idea. A few men have such unusual powers that their contemporaries recognize their claims without the usual exaggerations: Smith and Marshall are the only economists who seem to me indisputably to belong in this supreme class.

The rest have employed in varying degrees the techniques of the huckster. Consider Jevons. Writing a *Theory of Political Economy,* he devoted the first 197 pages of a book of 267 pages to his ideas on utility! Or consider Böhm-Bawerk. Not content with writing two volumes, and dozens of articles, in presenting and defending his capital theory, he added a third volume (to the third edition of his *Positive Theorie des Kapitals*) devoted exclusively to refuting, at least to his own satisfaction, every criticism that had arisen during the preceding decades.

Although the new economic theories are introduced by the

technique of the huckster, I should add that they are not the work of mere hucksters. The sincerity of Jevons, for example, is printed on every page. Indeed I do not believe that any important economist has ever deliberately contrived ideas in which he did not believe in order to achieve prominence: men of the requisite intellectual power and morality can get bigger prizes elsewhere. Instead, the successful inventor is a one-sided man. He is utterly persuaded of the significance and correctness of his ideas and he subordinates all other truths because they seem to him less important than the general acceptance of his truth. He is more a warrior against ignorance than a scholar among ideas.

Nor do I argue that a strong conviction of the validity of one's ideas and energetic dissemination are sufficient to alter significantly a science's work. It is possible by mere skill of presentation to create a fad, but a deep and lasting impression on the science will be achieved only if the idea meets the more durable standards of the science. Among these standards is truth, but of course it is not the only one.

III. THE CASE OF MILL

John Stuart Mill is a striking example with which to illustrate the foregoing remarks. He is now considered a mediocre economist of unusual literary power; a fluent, flabby echo of Ricardo. This judgment is well-nigh universal: I do not believe that Mill has had a fervent admirer in the twentieth century.

I attribute this low reputation to the fact that Mill had the perspective and balance, but not the full powers, of Smith and Marshall. He avoided all the tactics of easy success. He wrote with extraordinary balance, and his own ideas—considering their importance—received unbelievably little emphasis. The bland prose moved sedately over a corpus of knowledge organized with due regard to structure and significance, and hardly at all with regard to parentage.

One must search carefully in Mill's *Principles* to discover his own ideas. The only one of which he boasts—the immutability of the laws of production vs. the social plasticity of the laws of distribution—is at least unhappy. The rest receive no fanfare: Mill devoted some seven pages to summarizing the work of John Rae on capital accumulation and one paragraph to his own important idea of non-competing groups.

Yet however one judges Mill, it cannot be denied that he was original. In terms of identifiable theories, he was one of the most original economists in the history of the science. I shall list his major contributions, each of which was at least original to him as any important theory is to the person with whom it is chiefly associated. The list is restricted to value theory—although we must remember that what shreds of originality Mill is commonly credited with were in international trade theory—because I can be more confident of the priorities.

1. Non-Competing Groups

> So complete, indeed, has hitherto been the separation, so strongly marked the line of demarcation, between the different grades of labourers, as to be almost equivalent to an hereditary distinction of caste; each employment being chiefly recruited from the children of those already employed in it, or in employments of the same rank with it in social estimation, or from the children of persons who, if originally on a lower rank, have succeeded in raising themselves by their exertions.[4]

Smith's illustrious discussion of differences in wages was limited to differences consistent with full occupational mobility of the labour force in the long run. Mill made the first major

---

[4] *Principles of Political Economy* (Ashley, ed.; New York: Longman's, Green and Company, 1929), p. 393.

advance beyond this theory by his recognition of the barriers to mobility erected by the costs of education.

2. JOINT PRODUCTS

Mill clearly formulated the problem of joint production, i.e., production of two or more products in fixed proportions. He gave the complete and correct solution: the sum of the prices of the products must equal their joint cost, and the price of each product is determined by the equality in equilibrium of quantity supplied and quantity demanded.[5]

3. ALTERNATIVE COSTS

> Land is used for other purposes than agriculture, especially for residence; and when so used, yields a rent, determined by principles similar to those already laid down. The ground rent of a building, and the rent of a garden or park attached to it, will not be less than the rent which the same land would afford in agriculture. . . .
>
> But when land capable of yielding rent in agriculture is applied to some other purpose, the rent which it would have yielded is an element of the cost of production of the commodity which it is employed to produce.[6]

This was a frank and clear recognition of the fact that rent is a cost of production even from the social viewpoint when land has alternative uses. Marshall was unwilling to depart thus far from Ricardian theory.

4. THE ECONOMICS OF THE FIRM

Mill's chapter (Bk. I, Chap. IX), "Of production on a large, and production on a small, scale," is the first systematic dis-

---

[5] *Ibid.*, p. 570.   [6] *Ibid.*, pp. 475, 479.

cussion of the economies of scale of the firm to be found in a general economic treatise. It would take us afield to analyze this chapter in detail, but we may point out that Mill was the first economist to notice that one can deduce information on the costs of firms of different sizes from their varying fortunes through time.[7]

5. SUPPLY AND DEMAND

Mill introduced into English economics the concept of demand as a schedule or function, and hence was able to state the "law of supply and demand" clearly and with substantial accuracy:

> Demand and supply, the quantity demanded and the quantity supplied, will be made equal. If unequal at any moment, competition equalizes them, and the manner in which this is done is by an adjustment of the value. If the demand increases, the value rises; if the demand diminishes, the value falls: again, if the supply falls off, the value rises, and falls if the supply is increased. . . . the value which a commodity will bring in any market is no other than the value which, in that market, gives a demand just sufficient to carry off the existing or expected supply.[8]

This is, to be sure, very obvious once announced, but its explicit development was a highly useful addition to the Ricardian economics. Mill used the apparatus very competently in dealing with Thornton's absurd objections to the "law."[9] (I do not assert that Mill's discussion was superior to all earlier discussion; Cournot in particular was more precise.)

---

[7] *Ibid.*, p. 134.   [8] *Ibid.*, p. 448.

[9] "Thornton on Labour and Its Claims," in *Dissertations and Discussions*, Vol. 5.

6. Say's Law

Mill's discussion of the limitations to the proposition that there cannot be an overproduction of all commodities was penetrating as well as original:

> This argument is evidently founded on the supposition of a state of barter; and, on that supposition, it is perfectly incontestable. . . .
>
> If, however, we suppose that money is used, these propositions cease to be exactly true. . . . Interchange by means of money is therefore, as has been often observed, ultimately nothing but barter. But there is this difference—that in the case of barter, the selling and the buying are simultaneously confounded in one operation; you sell what you have and buy what you want, by one indivisible act, and you cannot do the one without doing the other. Now the effect of the employment of money, and even the utility of it, is, that it enables this one act of interchange to be divided into two separate acts or operations, one of which may be performed now, and the other a year hence, or whenever it shall be most convenient.[10]

It follows that at a given time people may wish to hasten sales and to postpone purchases, and this is then a period of "general excess."

> In order to render the argument for the impossibility of an excess of all commodities applicable to the case in which a circulating medium is employed, money must itself be considered as a commodity. It

---

[10] *Essays on Some Unsettled Questions of Political Economy* (London, 1844), pp. 69–70.

must undoubtedly be admitted that there cannot
be an excess of all other commodities, and an excess of money at the same time.[11]

Say's law therefore is not inconsistent with the existence of
periods of general excess and general deficiency, which arise
out of the "unreasonable hopes and unreasonable fears (which)
alternately rule with tyrannical sway over the minds of a
majority of the mercantile public."[12] Is this essay, written
about 1830, the work of an unoriginal mind?

This is a very respectable list of contributions. But it is also
a peculiar list: any one of the contributions could be made
independently of all the others. Mill was not trying to build
a new system but only to add improvements here and there
to the Ricardian system. The fairest of economists, as Schumpeter has properly characterized Mill, unselfishly dedicated his
abilities to the advancement of the science. And, yet, Mill's
magisterial quality and conciliatory tone may have served less
well than sharp and opinionated controversy in inciting his
contemporaries to make advances.

IV. ORIGINALITY AND SCIENTIFIC PROGRESS

What do we mean by scientific progress? An empirical science is a body of related generalizations with empirical content, as it is known to the group of competent students of the
science.[13] The generalizations must be of a known degree of
reliability or precision; otherwise the predictions based upon
them are acts of faith rather than of analysis. The science is
what the scientists know, not the storehouse of books which
record all that past and present scientists have ever known.

---

11 *Ibid.*, p. 71.   12 *Ibid.*, p. 68.

13 A case can be made for the view that a science includes also a body
of techniques, but more persuasively for the alternative view that the techniques are servants of the generalizations.

Knowledge can be and has been forgotten, but I shall pass over the problems of professional literacy and memory. A science progresses, then, when a new generalization is discovered, or is made more discoverable, when an existing generalization is refined analytically, or when an existing hypothesis is "confirmed" or shown to be false.

If these are the major components of scientific progress, it is demonstrable that progress may take place without any important originality.[14] Three kinds of work, requiring no more than diligence and professional competence (but of course allowing high originality), contribute to scientific progress.

The first kind of work is the testing of hypotheses. The numerous predictions of the level of employment which were shattered in 1946 were not original work, but served to test the widely accepted hypothesis that the consumption function was stable in the short run. The demonstration of error in a widely held hypothesis is an important part of scientific progress. Similarly, Kuznets' study of savings in relation to national product since 1869, which was also more courageous than original,[15] served to test the hypothesis that the consumption function was stable in the long run. This role of empirical work is too familiar to require elaboration.

The second kind of work is the accumulation of knowledge. It is excessively easy to start a quarrel by appearing to praise unmotivated collections of facts or by implying that one should collect only those facts which are specified by a heaven-inspired hypothesis, but I hope to avoid both quarrels. All that need be asserted here is that streams of empirical work, frequently

---

[14] No doubt every non-repetitive act has some element of novelty, and the highest flights of originality incorporate much well-known information, but both truths do not destroy the distinction between the two kinds of work. The basic tests are whether the work can be assigned to a merely competent economist and whether a merely competent economist would assign it.

[15] Kuznets' basic work on national income, however, was of a high order of constructive analysis.

but not necessarily embodying much critical and analytical originality, have given rise to major theoretical innovations. An example would be the inductive studies of prices initiated by Jevons and Laspeyres,[16] which played a major role in the development of monetary theory. Indeed I think one can predict that theoretical systems will eventually appear in areas where much empirical work is going on: for example, we may expect a number of new theories of income distribution in the next decade.

The third kind of useful but unoriginal work will serve to remind us that empirical work is not the only unoriginal work. The refinement or elaboration of a theory is often an essentially routine task. Indeed, any reader of the journals knows that most theoretical work is essentially repetitive, and dominated by fashion. One must look to accidental personal circumstances, and not to nature's distribution of high intellectual gifts, to explain who first applies monopolistic competition theory to foreign trade, or who first applies input-output analysis to regions, or who generalizes price discrimination theory from 2 to n markets, or who first puts income distribution into a consumption function. Not the least of the useful purposes served by such work is that of allowing respectable reiteration of a basic idea until everyone who can read has learned it.

These not very original kinds of empirical and theoretical work are sufficient to allow indefinite progress in a science. One is entitled to conjecture, however, that although the progress could be indefinite, it would not be large. Unless a science is thoroughly shaken up from time to time, its practitioners tend to become a spiritless and stultifying lot. They drift into a rigid orthodoxy, and fail to maintain even the kinds of

---

16 Jevons, "A Serious Fall in the Value of Gold Ascertained, and Its Social Effects Set Forth," reprinted in *Investigations in Currency and Finance* (London, 1909); and Laspeyres, "Hamburger Waarenpreise," *Jahrbücher für Nationalökonomie und Statistik*, Vol. III (1864).

progress of which they are capable. Significantly original work, with its consequent controversies, feuds, victories, and defeats, appears necessary to maintain the esprit of a science.

If scientific progress can continue, at least for a time, without originality, originality may also impair progress. Originality means difference, not improvement, and one may invent new errors as well as new truths. The equations of Keynes's *Treatise on Money* were original but not useful; the work on business cycles by Henry Moore was highly original but not useful; the statistical work on the 200 largest non-financial corporations was original but not useful.

Quite aside from the fact that much original work is mistaken, an excessive rate of production of original work may retard scientific progress. It may appear a paradox to assert that progress, consisting in large part of "good" originality, can be impaired by an excess of such originality, but the explanation lies in the fact that a high rate of innovation in a science reacts upon the quality of the innovations.

A new idea does not come forth in its mature scientific form. It contains logical ambiguities or errors; the evidence on which it rests is incomplete or indecisive; and its domain of applicability is exaggerated in certain directions and overlooked in others. These deficiencies are gradually diminished by a peculiar scientific ageing process, which consists of having the theory "worked over" from many directions by many men. This process of scientific fermentation can be speeded up, and it has speeded up in the modern age of innumerable economists. But even today it takes a considerable amount of time, and when the rate of output of original work gets too large, theories are not properly aged. They are rejected without extracting their residue of truth, or they are accepted before their content is tidied up and their range of applicability ascertained with tolerable correctness. A cumulative slovenliness results, and is not likely to be eliminated until a more quiescent period allows a full resumption of the ageing process.

Yet it would probably be unwise, as it would certainly be

futile, to wish for a steady rate of innovation in a science—the unpredictable course of scientific work is an element of its adventure. But it seems to be of the nature of original work to come and go in surges: economics was stuffy from 1850 to 1870 and sedate from 1900 to 1914, and there was possibly an excess of originality in the 1930's. The members of a science are also more receptive to new ideas at one time than at another, but this is a large separate problem in its own right.

These reflections on the nature and role of originality, however, have no utilitarian purpose, or even a propagandistic purpose. If I have a prejudice, it is that we commonly exaggerate the merits of originality in economics—that we are unjust in conferring immortality upon the authors of absurd theories while we forget the fine, if not particularly original, work of others. But I do not propose that we do something about it.

2

The Influence of Events and Policies on Economic Theory

The full range of subjects and problems which have attracted economists' attention throughout our history has been both extraordinarily wide and tolerably stable. The great multitude of modern economists do not work on a broader terrain than did Adam Smith and his sprinkling of contemporaries. True, some minor areas have been yielded up to younger sciences; for example, the economics of primitive peoples is now handled or mishandled by anthropologists. True, some minor additions have been made to our present-day agenda; for example, certain types of statistical problems are generally treated only by economists. But in the broad, the boundaries of the discipline have not varied much.

Within these wide-flung boundaries, however, the problems which arouse active interest and the variables which are deemed most significant have fluctuated greatly over time. In 1830, no general work in economics would omit a discussion

Reprinted from *The American Economic Review,* Vol. L (May, 1960).

of population, and, in 1930, hardly any general work said any-thing about population. The problem of economic growth was at the forefront of discussion in 1825, it was almost ignored in 1900, and today it is again *haute mode*. And the question which has been posed to me is: To what extent have the areas of active work and the lines of attack been influenced by contem-porary economic events and economic policies?

I

To be sane, one must recognize at least a portion of the physical and social world in which he lives; so the sane eco-nomic theories have always had at least a possible connection with the world in which they were written. It is not surprising, therefore, that many historians have explained and even justi-fied past economic theories by the special circumstances of the time and place in which they were written.

An example both contemporary and extreme is afforded by W. Stark, who has said that "modern economics immediately appears as a simple product of historical development, as a mirroring of the socio-economic reality within which it took its origin, not unlike the various theories which have preceded it."[1] Literally read, Stark seems to assert even that the growth of mechanization between 1817 and 1820 forced Ricardo to quali-fy the labor theory of value published in the former year.[2]

No such detailed reconciliation of economic theories with their environments, however, is even remotely tenable. When two Englishmen, named Mill and Cairnes, found themselves on opposite sides with respect to the validity of the wages-fund doctrine, both theories could not be mirroring the same real-ity. If their mirrors were turned to different realities, the en-

---

[1] *The History of Economics* (New York: Oxford University Press, 1944), p. 2.

[2] *Ibid.*, p. 37. Actually Ricardo had the same value theory at both dates and also in 1819.

vironmental explanation of economic theories becomes too
flexible to be useful.

Wesley C. Mitchell presented the same general viewpoint in
a much more qualified version:

> The passing on of ideas from one to another and
> the development of these ideas by successive gener-
> ations as an intellectual stunt has been in economics
> a secondary rather than a primary factor. The thing
> which has most of all stimulated the minds of suc-
> cessive generations of economists has been to en-
> deavor to contribute to the understanding of the
> problems with which their generation as a whole
> was concerned. . . .
>
> . . . .
>
> These economic problems were caused primarily
> by changes in the economic life of the people,
> changes that were coming about through a cumula-
> tive process.[3]

Thus Mitchell finds the leitmotiv of Smith in the emergence of
individualism, of Ricardo in the problems raised by the Napoleonic Wars, of Marx in the growth of an urban proletariat,
etc.

That major economic problems sometimes become matters
of paramount interest to economists is not debatable. But this
is not enough to make the environmental theory useful; i.e., to
make it more than a platitude. To be useful in explaining the
subject matter of economics, the environmental theory must be
given a more specific content. The theory could be developed
in various directions. Let me discuss three.

First, it could be asserted that every truly major economic
development leaves its imprint on economic theory, at least in

---

[3] *Lecture Notes on Types of Economic Theory* (New York: A. M. Kelley,
1949), pp. 45–46.

the choice of subject matter of the theory and possibly in its major empirical hypotheses. Although some historians approach this view (e.g., Leo Rogin in a special policy oriented version), it seems to me clearly untenable. At the height of the industrial revolution, when great technological advances were crowding hard upon one another, the main tradition of classical economics treated the state of the arts as a datum. The arts were held to be subject to sporadic improvements, but not of a magnitude comparable to the force of diminishing returns in agriculture. Here, then, the almost overwhelming characteristic of economic life was excluded from economic theory. Again, perhaps the second most influential development (or a special form of the first) in economic life in the nineteenth century was the improvement of transportation, which never played a strategic and usually not even an explicit role in economic theory.

Second, it could be maintained that even though not all major social and economic developments left their imprint on economic theory, every important element of economic theory sprang from this source. And this, too, would be untenable. The prolific analyses of utility theory from 1870 to 1915 and from 1932 on reflect no detectable environmental influence. The doctrine of non-competing groups emerged centuries after it would have been most realistic. The economic system did not become linear until about 1946. Of course, after the event one can always find something in the environment—especially if we include the intellectual environment—that may be related to the development in economic theory, but this is an exercise in erudition, not in explanation.

At this point we may pause to observe that a basic distinction must be drawn between the period in which a field of study is dominated by controversies over policy (applications) and the period in which it is a discipline pursued by professional scholars. In the age of mercantilism, all economics was oriented toward contemporary problems and institutions. Some of the writers analyzed problems more deeply than the immediate policy needs dictated, but their work was highly personal and mostly non-cumulative. Beginning with the Physiocrats, economics began to be cultivated increasingly by scholars, and scholarly values such as consistency, generality, precision, and elegance began to be introduced.

In the period of the classical economics, this disciplinary aspect of economic study became increasingly more prominent. Hume, Smith, Malthus, Senior, Whately, Longfield, and Cournot all had scholarly, and usually academic, orientations toward economics, and after 1870 this orientation became not merely dominant but well-nigh exclusive.

Thus it is a sign of the maturity of a discipline that its main problems are not drawn from immediate, changing events. A genuine and persistent separation of scientific study from the real world leads to sterility, but an immediate and sensitive response to current events stultifies the deepening and widening of analytical principles and techniques. The leading theoretical chemists are not working on detergents or headache remedies and the leading economic theorists need not be concerned with urban renewal or oil embargoes.

There remains a third interpretation of the environmental theory: that economic problems and developments can be classified into groups which impinge very differently upon economics. This seems to me both correct and potentially fruitful, and I shall attempt a tentative classification of economic problems from this viewpoint.

The vast majority of all current—I shall call them popular—social economic problems are routine from the viewpoint of economic theory. This excise or that central banking policy, this farm subsidy or that housing program, this stock pile or that form of wage bargain—all are essentially routine in their demands on the theory. The facts of the case may vary, or the juxtaposition of two policies may offer complications, but fundamentally no new demands are put on the theory.

This is not to say that the theory is necessarily adequate to the demands one would like to put on it. The theory may have deficiencies in logic, or be ambiguous with respect to significantly different outcomes, or its predictions may even be contradicted in certain respects by events. But imperfection is as inevitable in theory as it is in man, and one does not need new incidents to document it.

A second class consists of events of major economic significance: the colonization of a continent, major wars, basic technological advances such as the railroad, and great depressions. It is more remarkable that most of these events leave economic theory essentially unaffected. Since Ricardo's time, wars have had little effect upon the basic theory, although many illustrious economists (among them Edgeworth, Pigou, and Wicksell) have been stimulated to write about the economics of war. The current popularity of the economic theory of development has not yielded important theoretical results. It may be (though I somewhat doubt it) that Keynes's *General Theory* was the product of the Great Depression, but if so it is one of the very few great events that have affected the basic theory.

One reason for the impotence of great events is that from the viewpoint of economic theory they are also usually routine. A war may ravage a continent or destroy a generation without posing new theoretical questions. And even the theoretically challenging catastrophes are not likely to be influential, for a simple reason: the great event is a poor stimulus to anything except a basic reconstruction of the science. Minor changes in a theory hardly seem appropriate—let alone adequate—to great new problems, and extensive reconstructions of economic theory are usually the result, not of a frontal assault on the traditional theory, but of the systematic elaboration of a single basic and pervasive idea which previously had been ignored or given only *ad hoc* recognition.

And this suggests the third and theoretically influential type of economic problem: that which is pervasive. It is not enough that a problem be of vast importance, if that importance is momentary; it is not enough that the problem be persistent, if it is local to a particular market. A theory is a statement of general relationships: a theory of unique events is a contradiction in terms, and a theory of local events is simply uninteresting from the scientific viewpoint. The most pervasive problem of economic life is of course that of value, and this is why the routine and undramatic problem of value has elicited the supreme efforts of the greatest theorists.

On this view, one can predict that certain problems will affect economic theory and others will not. The problem of personal income distribution will eventually receive much theoretical atention, since it is a problem of all economies and all times. On the other hand, the economic problems of cold wars will not influence economic theory unless such wars become general and persistent—and this will probably not happen because cold wars seem intrinsically unstable situations.

Since neither popular economic problems nor heroic events influence much the development of economic theory—and please notice that I distinguish economic theory from discussion by economists, and deal only with the former—do theoretical changes come only from, as Mitchell puts it, "the development of these ideas by successive generations"?

My answer is, proximately, yes. The dominant influence upon the working range of economic theorists is the set of internal values and pressures of the discipline. The subjects for study are posed by the unfolding course of scientific developments. With the introduction of mathematical technique it became inevitable that there be a theory of general equilibrium. The marginal utility theory must sooner or later—the great surprise is that it took two decades—lead to the general marginal productivity theory. The untidiness in the theory of the firm was bound to attract a Sraffa and a Viner.

This is not to say that the environment is without influence, for every great economist injects some portion of it into the developing theoretical corpus. This element of realism, however, need have no simple or direct connection with the contemporary scene. Menger, Jevons, and Walras took the most pedestrian, even vulgar, "fact" of diminishing marginal utility of objects to man as their element of realism, and with it reconstructed a large part of the theory of value. Marshall took an equally pedestrian fact—that it takes time to do things thoroughly—and constructed his theory of short- and long-run normal prices.

Whether a fact or development is significant depends primarily on its relevance to current economic theory. There is no intrinsic basis for saying that the fact (1) people spend a lesser fraction of their income on food as they become richer is less important than the fact (2) people save about the same share of their income as they become richer. Yet Engel's law (now a century old) had no effects on economic theory for a long time, and no direct influence to this day, but Kuznets' finding has contributed substantially to the excitement and controversy over the consumption function. Kuznets' fact was an ostensible contradiction of the ruling theory whereas Engel's fact was and is outside the domain of the ruling theory.

Every major development in economic theory in the last hundred years, I believe, could have come much earlier if appropriate environmental conditions were all that were needed. Even Keynes's *General Theory* could have found an evident empirical basis in the post-Napoleonic period or the 1870's or the 1890's. Perhaps this amounts only to saying—what is surely true and almost tautological—that the elements of an economic system which economists believe to be basic have been present for a long time. The nature of economic systems has changed relatively little since Smith's time.

Thus I assign a minor, and even an accidental, role to the contemporary economic environment in the development of economic theory since it has become a professional discipline. Even where the original environmental stimulus to a particular analytical development is fairly clear, as in Ricardo's theory of rent, the profession soon appropriates the problem and reformulates it in a manner that becomes increasingly remote from current events, until finally its origin bears no recognizable relationship to its nature or uses.

The channel through which economic events are reaching

economic theorists is undergoing change. Specialization has created the empirical research economist, who collects and systematizes the (some) facts of economic life. He is becoming substantially the only source of information for the specialized theorists: the only things the theoretical economist knows about economic life are those things the empirical economist tells him. All other sources (the theorist must increasingly assume) are unreliable or unrepresentative—in short, unscientific.

It does not follow that the theorist is the slave of the empirical economist, for the latter usually collects data recommended by the ruling theories. The national income accounts, for example, are a creature of economic theory. But the empirical economist also collects many facts not dictated by the theory, some because of his own intuitions (be they theoretical, propagandistic, or what), some because policy enforcement makes the data available.

Whether this specialization will increase the sensitivity of theory to events is an open question. The statistical work of Gardiner Means on administered prices has had an extensive effect on theoretical literature,[4] but it can hardly be said (and indeed Means expressly denies) that the phenomena he found were new phenomena. The work of John Kendrick and others will undoubtedly influence the theorizing on technical progress, but again the underlying phenomena are not new. My guess is that most empirical research economists will possess the professional values, and hence will seek pervasive and stable empirical uniformities rather than seek to detect quickly any new economic phenomena. If so, the specialization will not affect greatly the relationship between theory and contemporary events.

---

[4] Much of this work was also done earlier by Frederick Mills, however, without a comparable effect—partly because Mills did not use it as a springboard for extreme policy insinuations.

II

Public policy is no doubt a part of the environment broadly construed, but it is a separable part. Policies and policy proposals are not closely geared to events. Policies designed to lessen income inequality emerged during a period when market forces were making substantial contributions to this end, and a similar relationship between policy and events is found in hours of labor, provision of education, the development of domestic manufacturing, etc. Here policy rides on the wave of events, although often it makes impudent claims to leadership. Often, too, policies are initiated in one country to deal with problems which are more serious in other countries: American antitrust policy is an example.

Nor should we forget that few policies, even successful policies, change the basic nature of the economy. The fact that our country had a protective tariff before 1932, but England did not, was not enough to make the basic theories of economics less applicable to one of the countries. Reformers and deformers of economic life dare not take the Olympian stance of economic theory, but neither dare economic theory become academic journalism with its excitement over fundamentally unimportant changes.

The classical problems of public policy have always provided much of the standard fare of economic theory: tariffs and monetary standards; monopoly; control of business fluctuations; the role of government and unions in labor markets; the incidence of taxes; banking structure; the treatment of the indigent—these have been persistent problems of policy and therefore of economic theory. The efforts of economists to understand these problems have led to advances in every branch of theory, including the most abstract branches.

It should not be necessary to retrace in detail the argument of the previous section, which is fully applicable: only general and persistent policy questions are likely to call forth permanent advances in the theory. The unending train of ephem-

eral or local policy questions is of no more significance for economic theory than the corresponding types of economic developments.

But continuity and pervasiveness of policy are not enough
to command influence on theory. We have been regulating
railroads for seventy-two years, but neither this instance nor a
hundred others of governmental regulations have brought
forth even the rudiments of a theory of regulation. Nor has a
century of protectionism called forth a substantive theory of
the content and level of tariffs. On the other hand, our antitrust policy has been a main source of continued interest in
monopoly, and it may be more than coincidence that the
interest of English economists in industrial organization has
been reviving since a monopoly policy was adopted in England. Like empirical facts, policies must be directly relevant to
the main topics of traditional theory if they are to achieve
easy influence.

Policies have better press agents than events; so a com-
manding policy controversy—such as that on full employment
in the thirties or the rapid attainment of terrestrial prosperity
today—captures the interest of a large number of economists.
This tendency is now reinforced by the foundations, which are
headed by men who (like all sensible people) find a headline
more comprehensible and persuasive than a vague prospectus
for a scientific expedition. But important, basic theory is not
very responsive to explicit demands. A great many facts will be
found or fabricated, and a literature will be amassed and then
tidied up, but a basic development awaits a man of vision. He,
likely as not, is wholly preoccupied with something which only
he will make important. The marginal utility theory owed
nothing to immediate policy problems, nor did the marginal
productivity theory, the theory of capital, the theory of imperfect competition, game theory, etc. Conversely, all the disin-
terested and avaricious attention lavished upon business cycles
has not yielded a useful short-run theory, and the ratio of
cliché to analytical creativity in the literature of economic
development is awesome to contemplate.

Often, of course, the explicit policy desires of economists have had a deleterious effect upon the theory itself. The bending of theories to views of tax justice popular with economists as well as the public has been chronic. Ever since Mill recanted the wages-fund doctrine ostensibly for unimportant analytical reasons, much of labor economics has had a flavor easier to explain by economists' policy preferences than elaboration of their general economic analysis. Almost always, I conjecture, the effect of policy views on the general theory (and not merely one man's version) has stemmed from a feeling that the theory must adapt to widely held humanitarian impulses.

Yet economic theory often takes a hostile stance toward policies of great political popularity. For long periods the tradition of economic theory has been opposed to protectionism, minimum wage legislation, price and production controls, and "just" (non-rational) prices. When I say that the policies are hostile to the theory, I mean of course only that the traditional use of the theory led to policy views contrary to those adopted.[5]

This audience does not need to be told that under these conditions the economists have not simply altered the theory to suit the policy. The policy views of the ruling theory have generally not catered to popularity. The general theory still says that these policies are inefficient and hence undesirable. There are many defenses of these policies by economists, but they are almost invariably antitheoretical: the main theoretical results are repudiated as "unrealistic." The chief effect of continued adversity of policy has been resignation, and it is fair to say that indignation and outrage have disappeared from economics. This is no doubt the reason economics is at the moment highly respectable and—if I may transgress on Professor Wilcox' subject—lacking in promise of basic influence on policy in the future. I do not know whether it is an occasion for pride or for regret that the economist is using Marquis of

---

[5] For some remarks on this point, see "The Politics of Political Economists," *Quarterly Journal of Economics*, Vol. LXXIII (November, 1959).

Queensbury arguments in an arena where emotional brass knuckles continue in fashion.

III

On a broad interpretation, the development of related disciplines is also a part of the environment within which economic theory evolves. The influence upon economics of other disciplines is a large subject on which only a few tentative observations can be offered here.

If one were to seek a major economic theory whose existence depended directly and essentially upon prior work in another field, he would find few likely candidates. Putting aside for a moment the methodological fields of statistics and mathematics, there is in fact no important candidate. A theory of behavior, such as our profit maximizing assumption implies, could have come from psychology, but of course it did not. In fact Smith's professional work on psychology (in the *Theory of Moral Sentiments*) bears scarcely any relationship to his economics, and this tradition of independence of economics from psychology has persisted despite continued efforts from Jennings (1855) to Herbert Simon and George Katona to destroy it. Again, the theory of production could be the economist's summary of the technological sciences, but of course it has never been. Economists have produced whatever laws of production they have.

The methodological discplines are in a different relationship to economics: obviously we use mathematics and statistics with all our might. The effects of methodology, in this instrumental sense, are pervasive: it affects our choice of problems, our methods of analyzing them, and—since a good theory is at least as reliable as a report of facts—our view of the nature of the economic system. It may well be that a superlative algebraist could make better predictions of the future directions of economic theory than any economist. But it may also be that the algebraist could not: the branches of mathematics seem to have their turns at popularity in economics, and in a longer run may really be servants of the discipline. For surely statistics has had this role: it has had immense influence on the nature of economic investigation but (as yet) almost none on the nature of economic theory. The extensive use of these disciplines in economics, however, still covers too short a period to disentangle relationships from wishes.

The developments in other substantive fields have had a general effect upon what Schumpeter called our "scientific vision." Although we have made frequent verbal use of Darwin's theory, for example, in our economics, we have made almost no substantive use of it, but by analogy it has increased our awareness of the malleability of economic institutions and men (as has Marx's theory of history). The ascendancy of positivism in the natural sciences has had a large effect upon the methodology, and a minor one upon the content, of economics. Most of the effects of these other fields, however, have been subtle and indirect; so it is virtually impossible to point to a single important theory in economics that is plausibly the direct consequence of developments in neighboring fields.

There are many voices that tell us that this is a deplorable state of affairs: that our insularity has kept us from solving many problems (or even seeing them). We are told that political science is obviously important to a study of political economy, that organization and learning theory are essential to (e.g.) a successful theory of oligopoly, that only a sociology of groups can illuminate fully the behavior of labor unions, etc. And how chemistry was revivified by modern physics.

Many of the claims in this direction rest on deep conviction, and the promises of large success support professional position and hopes; so no cavalier comment upon any one would be appropriate. Yet I would emphasize here, as I have with respect to events and policies, the immense degree of autonomy that any successful science must apparently possess. A theory whose continual progress demands the association of very different specialists is outside the historical experience of economics, and—I conjecture—that of other sciences as well.

This autonomy of a science is surely essential to its existence.

A discipline which was in intimate and continuous dependence upon the current output of events or other disciplines would simply not be a discipline; it would be a temporary collection of subjects. It could have no specialists—who would be pathetically obsolete in a few years—nor any accumulated theoretical corpus, for its theory would change with each new liaison or external development. It would be not a science but an edition of the encyclopedia of knowledge. Why, even its professors could not have tenure!

3

Statistical Studies in the History of Economic Thought

The history of economics is, from a sheer quantitative viewpoint, simply immense. It consists of the works of literally thousands of men: books and articles without number. Even if one snobbishly restricts himself to the traditional core of value theory, the materials exceed what any man can read, let alone read carefully; and of course much of the most important literature lies outside the core, whether one measures importance by impact upon the science or impact upon the world.

The material invites statistical treatment, and I shall report two statistical studies of the development of economics. The first is devoted to tracing the professionalization of economics —the gradual rise and eventual complete dominance of economic literature by the full-time economist. This study centers on the nineteenth century. The second study is devoted to the evolution of American economics since 1890.

I. THE PROFESSIONALIZATION OF ECONOMICS

A professional is a man who supports himself by the activity in question. Until late into the nineteenth century the opposite of the professional was the independent gentleman, who has since been displaced (or taxed away) by the amateur.

The income derived from an activity is not a direct index of the single-minded pursuit of that activity. Ricardo, the retired bond broker, was as diligent in the pursuit of economics (and of fame as an economist) as most hungry assistant professors of today. Ricardo's friend, James Mill, who was long an unprosperous journalist, roamed much more widely in his work.

There are in fact at least two attributes of the "professionalization" of a field in which we should be interested. One is specialization: the professional, in contrast to the dilettante, concentrates his efforts in a defined area, within which he acquires expertise of technique and accumulated knowledge. The second is persistence: continued application to this defined area. If we waived this second attribute, we should be compelled to treat the lazy dilettante who completes only one book or article as a professional. In fact, only an adequate time span will reveal the professional. This time span, of course, creates its own ambiguities: if Adam Smith had died in 1760, we would probably call him a specialist in philosophy, rather than, as we now do, a non-specializing economist.

Persistence and specialization are not easily measured. The traditional input measure is the way in which a man spends his time, and this is, of course, how income enters the scene. The sources of income are related to the extent to which a man becomes a professional scholar. There are few activities which yield substantial incomes for less than a substantial fraction of a man's time, so it is difficult to be a professional outside, and easy to be one inside, the field of one's livelihood. Inherited wealth weakens the relationship, but with the great growth of the learned occupations the gentleman scholar would in any event be declining in relative importance, and the competition

of the specialists forces even the gentleman scholar to special-
ize. But of course the sources of income are an imperfect
measure of either persistence or specialization.

The traditional outputs of scholarly activity are publications
and educated students. We all place much greater value on the
publications than the students, although we (especially the
less prolific of us) assert the great importance of instruction.
The pre-eminence of publication has various bases. It is
deemed a greater achievement to produce knowledge than to
communicate it; although most publications produce precious
little knowledge. The publication is capable of professional
appraisal in a way teaching is not. The publication may reach
a wider audience; but here I venture that the average journal
article is extremely fortunate to have 100 careful readers, and
most teachers have many more tolerably attentive students for
each article they write. The publication more or less clearly
belongs to the author alone; an able student belongs to several
teachers in this sense, and we all recognize the point in Leslie
Stephen's remark that he could not understand why schools
were credited with producing the men they had not succeeded
in suppressing.

A. Economists Important to the Science

I begin with the economists who are important to the development of economics. They are generally (and in fact only
then genuinely) important to the development of economics
when they have had a substantial influence upon the economists of their times. I have departed from this principle only
to the extent of including some brilliant theorists who did not
achieve contemporary influence (Lloyd, Longfield). The English economists who meet these subjective criteria over the
period from 1766 to 1915 are listed in Table 1.[1] Historians of

---

[1] The dates are set by the mid-date of publications in economics. The
initial year is accidental: economists were included if they published after
1776.

TABLE 1

Important English Economists, 1766-1915

Name	Birth	Death	Publications in Economics			Occupation	Economics Main Source of Income	Appreciable Income from Economics		Appreciable Publication outside Economics
			Begin	End	Major			Writing	Teaching	
Anderson, James	1739	1808	1777	1801	1777	Farmer; journalist	.....	.....	.....	x
Ashley, W. J.	1860	1927	1888	1928	1908*	Professor	x	x	x	.....
Babbage, Charles	1792	1871	1832	1856	1832	Gentleman; professor (mathematics); inventor	.....	x	.....	x
Bagehot, Walter	1826	1877	1860	1877	1868*	Journalist	.....	x	.....	x
Bailey, Samuel	1791	1870	1825	1837	1825	Merchant	.....	x	.....	x
Bentham, Jeremy	1748	1832	1787	1821	1804*	Gentleman; philosopher	.....	x	.....	x
Cairnes, John	1823	1875	1857	1874	1866*	Professor	x	x	x	x
Cannan, Edwin	1861	1935	1888	1929	1908*	Professor	x	x	x	.....
Chalmers, George	1742	1825	1782	1812	1797*	Lawyer; civil servant	.....	x	.....	x
Cunningham, William	1849	1919	1882	1916	1882	Divine; professor	.....	x	x	x
DeQuincey, Thomas	1785	1859	1824	1844	1844	Gentleman; writer	.....	x	.....	x
Eden, Frederick	1766	1809	1797	1802	1797	Finance	.....	.....	.....	x
Edgeworth, F. Y.	1845	1926	1881	1925	1903*	Professor	x	x	x	x
Foxwell, Herbert S.	1849	1936	1886	1927	1906*	Professor	x	.....	x	.....
Giffen, Robert	1837	1910	1872	1904	1888*	Journalism; civil servant	.....	x	.....	.....
Hodgskin, Thomas	1787	1869	1825	1857	1825	Naval officer; journalist	x	x	.....	.....
Hobson, John	1858	1940	1889	1938	1914*	Teacher; author	.....	x	.....	x
Ingram, John K.	1823	1907	1863	1899	1888	Professor (oratory, Greek)	.....	x	.....	x

* Mean year of publication.

TABLE 1—Continued

Name	Birth	Death	Publications in Economics			Occupation	Economics Main Source of Income	Appreciable Income from Economics		Appreciable Publication outside Economics
			Begin	End	Major			Writing	Teaching	
Jenkin, Fleeming	1833	1885	1868	1871	1870*	Professor (engineering)				x
Jevons, William S.	1835	1882	1859	1882	1870*	Professor	x	x	x	x
Jones, Richard	1790	1855	1831	1852	1831	Divine; professor; civil servant			x	
Joplin, Thomas	1790	1847	1822	1845	1838*	Banker				
Keynes, J. N.	1852	1949	1890	1907	1890	Professor (logic)	x		x	x
Lauderdale (Maitland)	1759	1839	1796	1829	1804	Gentleman		x		
Leslie, T. E. Cliffe	1827	1882	1855	1878	1866*	Professor; lawyer			x	x
Longfield, Mountifort	1802	1884	1833	1870	1833	Professor (law); judge			x	
Lloyd, William F.	1794	1853	1833	1837	1834	Professor; gentleman			x	
Malthus, Thomas R.	1766	1834	1798	1830	1816*	Professor	x	x	x	
Marshall, Alfred	1842	1924	1872	1923	1890	Professor	x	x	x	
McCulloch, John R.	1789	1864	1816	1864	1840*	Journalist; civil servant		x		x
Mill, James	1773	1836	1804	1823	1814*	Journalist; civil servant		x		x
Mill, John Stuart	1806	1873	1825	1871	1848	Civil servant		x		x
Newmarch, William	1820	1882	1853	1862	1858*	Insurance; banking				
Place, Francis	1771	1854	1822	1822	1822	Tailor		x		
Porter, George R.	1792	1852	1836	1851	1844*	Merchant; civil servant		x		
Price, Richard	1723	1791	1769	1780	1744*	Divine				x
Ricardo, David	1772	1823	1809	1824	1817	Broker				

TABLE 1—*Continued*

| NAME | BIRTH | DEATH | PUBLICATIONS IN ECONOMICS | | | OCCUPATION | ECONOMICS MAIN SOURCE OF INCOME | APPRECIABLE INCOME FROM ECONOMICS | | APPRECIABLE PUBLICATION OUTSIDE ECONOMICS |
			Begin	End	Major			Writing	Teaching	
Rogers, James E. T.	1823	1890	1866	1892	1879*	Divine; professor	x	....	x	x
Scrope, G. Poulett	1797	1876	1833	1874	1833	Gentleman	....	x	....	x
Senior, Nassau	1790	1864	1821	1852	1836*	Lawyer; professor	....	x	x	x
Sidgwick, Henry	1838	1900	1883	1901	1883	Professor (philosophy)	....	x	....	x
Smart, William	1853	1915	1890	1910	1900*	Manufacturer; professor	x	x	x	....
Smith, Adam	1723	1790	1776	1789	1776	Professor (moral philosophy); civil servant	....	x	x	x
Spencer, Herbert	1820	1903	1850	1892	1871*	Engineer; writer	....	x	....	x
Steuart, James	1712	1780	1761	1783	1770	Lawyer; exile; gentleman	....	x	....	x
Thornton, Henry	1760	1815	1802	1811	1802	Banker	....	....	....	....
Thornton, William	1813	1880	1845	1874	1860*	Civil servant	....	....	....	x
Tooke, Thomas	1774	1858	1823	1857	1840*	Merchant	....	....	....	....
Torrens, Robert	1790	1864	1804	1858	1831*	Soldier	....	....	....	....
Tucker, Josiah	1712	1799	1750	1782	1766*	Divine	....	....	....	x
Wakefield, Edward G.	1796	1862	1829	1849	1839*	Colonialist	....	....	....	....
Webb, Sidney	1859	1947	1887	1935	1911*	Gentleman	....	x	....	x
West, Edward	1782	1828	1815	1826	1820*	Lawyer	....	....	....	....
Whately, Richard	1787	1863	1831	1847	1839*	Divine	....	....	....	x
Wicksteed, Philip	1844	1927	1884	1922	1903*	Divine; teacher (economics)	....	....	x	x
Young, Arthur	1741	1820	1767	1815	1791*	Farmer; civil servant	....	x	....	x

economics will inevitably quarrel with a few inclusions and exclusions,[2] but it is most improbable that their lists would display significantly different characteristics.

The income sources ignore inherited wealth (as in the case of Cannan, who had independent means) except where the man did not consistently pursue some remunerative occupation, in which case he is a "gentleman." The occupations are those of substantial duration, and "professor" denotes all teaching at the collegiate level. Some of the early professorships were of minor economic and professional significance (the early Drummond professorships at Oxford paid £100 a year and could be held for only five years) and even the first Cambridge professorship, established in 1863, paid only £300 and required Fawcett (an easy exclusion) to spend only 16 weeks a year at the University.

The expected drift toward professionalization is clear when the data are summarized by periods (Table 2). In the late eighteenth century not one man specialized in economics; in the early twentieth century there were only four who wrote outside the field (Hobson and Webb in political science, Edgeworth in statistics, Wicksteed in literature). Before 1850 only Malthus was supported primarily by teaching and writing in economics (McCulloch could be added for a decade or more); after 1900 only Hobson and Webb and Wicksteed were not professors.[3] If we had continued our survey after 1915, I believe that only Lord Stamp and Hawtrey would be numbered among the non-professors. One may conclude that the special-

---

2 The chief group I was tempted to include was the unusual collection of monetary writers: Fullarton, Horner, Overstone, Parnell, and Pennington. Parnell was, in my terminology, a gentleman, Horner a lawyer, Pennington a civil servant, the others bankers. Only Horner of this group wrote appreciably outside of economics.

3 It is worth noting that of these three persistent exceptions, only Wicksteed was important in theoretical economics. The mid-date of his *important* writings comes before 1900.

ized writer on economics, with a professional base, was dominant after 1900.

Certain other characteristics of these leading economists are worth noticing, even though they are not part of our problem of professionalization. They began to publish in economics at what would now be considered advanced ages: even in the final group (1900–1915), the mean age at the first publication

TABLE 2

CHARACTERISTICS OF IMPORTANT
ENGLISH ECONOMISTS, 1766–1915

MEAN DATE OF PUBLICATION	NO. OF ECONOMISTS	No. WITH INCOME FROM ECONOMICS			NO. WITH APPRECIABLE PUBLICATIONS OUTSIDE ECONOMICS	PROFESSORS OF ECONOMICS
		Major	Appreciable			
			Writing	Teaching		
1766–1800......	8	0	4	1	8	0
1800–1825......	7	1	2	1	2	1
1825–1850......	14	0	7	4	6	0
1850–1875......	10	3	6	4	8	3
1875–1900......	7	2	5	4	5	2
1900–1915......	8	6	6	6	4	5
Total......	54	13	30	20	30	11

was 33. The only striking exception was John Stuart Mill, who began at 19.

It is seldom possible to identify a single major work, a fact of some interest in itself. Malthus' essay on population preceded his discovery of the rent theory by 17 years; Edgeworth's *Mathematical Psychics* preceded the great articles on the laws of return by 30 years. Even where a single major performance can be dated, it is seldom at an early age:

Longfield...............	31 years old
J. S. Mill...............	42 years old
Henry Thornton.........	42 years old
Ricardo...............	45 years old
Marshall...............	48 years old
Smith.................	53 years old

In the lesser men, the range is from 31 (Eden) to 65 (Ingram).

The span of the writing life of these men lengthened greatly over time: from 24 years before 1800 to 40 years in 1900–1915 (Table 3). The publication began 7 years younger, and with the 6 year longer life span, publications continued three years closer to death. The lengthening writing span is due in good part to the process of professionalization: the professional has

TABLE 3

PUBLISHING HABITS OF IMPORTANT
ENGLISH ECONOMISTS, 1766–1915

PERIOD	No.	AVERAGE AGE WHEN WRITINGS OF ECONOMICS		AVERAGE No. OF YEARS FROM LAST WRITING ON ECONOMICS TO DEATH
		Begin	End*	
1766–1800........	8	40	64	8
1800–1825........	7	38	59	11
1825–1850........	14	36	63	10
1850–1875........	10	32	56	7
1875–1900........	7	38	67	9†
1900–1915........	8	33	73	5

* Posthumous works are treated as written in the year of death.
† Three years if we exclude J. N. Keynes (42 years).

stronger inducements to earlier publication, and his close-knit fraternity urges him on to later efforts with its paraphernalia of annual meetings, symposia, lectures, revised books, etc. Whether the span of scientifically important writing has lengthened is a more difficult question which I shall not try to answer.

B. REPRESENTATIVE WRITERS

It would be useful to supplement this survey of English economists important in the development of economics by a more representative group of writers on economic subjects. If "representative" is interpreted in any respectable statistical sense, this proves to be an impossible task for reasons which I shall discuss immediately.[4] But repectability and interesting-ness are not the best of friends, so some unrepresentatively representative writers will be surveyed.

The very lack of specialization in the earlier periods creates the impossibility of a comprehensive survey of the nature of economic writers and economic literature in those times. Consider the first half of the nineteenth century.

First, the journals were not specialized into scientific and popular types, so an article in the *Edinburgh Review* could be an important analytical essay or it could be a political tract on some current economic issue or a description of some foreign land. The first semi-professional journal of importance in English economics was the *Journal of the Royal Statistical Society,* begun in 1838. The first fully professional journal was the *Royal Economic Journal* (1891); the *Quarterly Journal of Economics* of course preceded it by five years in the United States, and there were still earlier continental journals.

Second, the channels of publication were more varied. The pamphlet played an enormously larger role than at present, when indeed it has almost vanished in the United States and is unimportant in England. The pamphlet could be produced with extraordinary speed, so Ricardo's "Essay on the Profits of Stock," published February 24, 1815, contains page references to Malthus' "Inquiry into Rent," published February 3, and his "Grounds of an Opinion," published February 10. The average period between completion of a journal article and its publication was also shorter by many months than it is today, and book publishing, which now would bore a glacier, was then an efficient industry.

For this early period only the authorship of the economic

---

4 Indeed, I do not believe that a fully comprehensive list of writers on economics would be interesting: newspaper reporters would jostle poli-ticians and learned savants, and Marco Polo would join the less talented writers on underdeveloped economies.

essays in the major English literary journals is surveyed. This task would have been quite impossible if Professor Frank Fetter had not identified most of the anonymous authors.[5] The complementary task of analyzing the scope of the writings of men we now view as primarily economists will not be undertaken, but it would reinforce the picture of non-specialization.

The number of articles on economic subjects (Professor Fetter's criterion was not stringent) is reported by 5-year periods for the first half of the century in Table 4. There was

TABLE 4

ARTICLES ON ECONOMICS IN ENGLISH JOURNALS, 1802–1853

Period	Edinburgh Review	Quarterly Review	Blackwood's	Westminster Review	Total
1802–05	16				16
1805–10	33	2*			35
1810–15	16	20			36
1815–20	25	22	26†		73
1820–25	34	30	24	12‡	100
1825–30	31	48	64	32	165
1830–35	38	35	42	73	188
1835–40	27	22	26	42	117
1840–45	26	24	46	39	135
1845–50	14§	24	41	43	122
1850–53		21	62	10‖	93
					1,190

* Begins 1809.   § To 1847.
† Begins 1817.   ‖ To 1852.
‡ Begins 1824.

5 He performs this valuable task in:

"The Authorship of Economic Articles in the *Edinburgh Review*, 1802–47," *Journal of Political Economy*, June, 1953.

"The Economic Articles in the *Quarterly Review* and Their Authors, 1809–52, II," *Journal of Political Economy*, April, 1958.

"The Economic Articles in *Blackwood's Edinburgh Magazine*, and Their Authors, 1817–53," *Scottish Journal of Political Economy*, November, 1960.

"Economic Articles in the *Westminster Review* and Their Authors, 1824–51," *Journal of Political Economy*, December, 1962.

a marked peak in interest in economics from 1825 to 1835,
and the decline which then set in was not even fully reversed
by the Corn Law agitation a decade later.

If we turn to the more prolific authors of these articles
(Table 5), we find only one name familiar to economists in
Blackwood's, DeQuincey, and only one such name also in the
Quarterly Review, Scrope (who would be better known if his
proposal of a certain index number were not labeled the
Laspeyre index). The *Edinburgh Review* favored the econo-

TABLE 5

MOST FREQUENT CONTRIBUTORS ON ECONOMIC SUBJECTS
IN ENGLISH JOURNALS, 1802–1853

	No.	Occupation	Main Interest
Blackwood's			
Archibald Alison......	47	Lawyer; sheriff	History
David Robinson......	45	Political writer	....
W. E. Aytoun........	$43\frac{5}{8}$	Lawyer; professor (rhetoric)	Poetry
Alfred Mallalieu......	12	Journalist	....
John Galt..........	12	Unsuccessful smuggler; journalist	Non-economic
William Johnstone....	12	Journalist	....
Thomas DeQuincey...	11	Gentleman; writer	Literature
John Wilson........	10	Professor (moral philosophy)	Literature
Quarterly Review			
John Barrow........	33	Civil servant	Adventure
John Croker.........	$23\frac{1}{2}$	Civil servant	Politics
Robert Southey......	$16\frac{1}{2}$	Author	Poetry; literature
G. P. Scrope........	12	Gentleman	Geology; economic
Edward Edwards.....	11	Clergy	....
George Ellis.........	10	Gentleman; diplomat	Poetry; literature
Edinburgh Review			
John McCulloch......	78	Civil servant	Economics
Henry Broughman....	$24\frac{1}{2}$	Lawyer	Politics
Nassau Senior........	9	Lawyer	Economics
Francis Horner.......	8	Lawyer	Politics; economics
Westminster Review			
T. Perronet Thompson	$45\frac{1}{2}$	Soldier; journalist; politician	Economics
J. S. Mill...........	$12\frac{1}{2}$	Civil servant	Intellectual
William Ellis........	$10\frac{1}{2}$	Manager of insurance company	Economics

mists, and especially the prodigious McCulloch. The *West-minster Review* was the one journal dominated by economists if we include, as we should, General Thompson in their ranks. The great majority of the articles in the first three journals were written by part-time journalists, whose major occupation was most commonly politics.

TABLE 6

ECONOMISTS WRITING IN THE ENGLISH
JOURNALS, 1802–1853

Name	No. of Articles
McCulloch	78
T. Perronet Thompson	$45\frac{1}{2}$
Scrope	14
J. S. Mill	$13\frac{1}{2}$
DeQuincey	11
Senior	10
J. Mill	8
Horner	8
Malthus	8
T. Chalmers	4
Merivale	4
Buchanan	$3\frac{1}{2}$
Whately	2
Fullarton	1
Playfair	1
Torrens	1
Martineau	1
Total	$216\frac{1}{2}$

The economists are segregated in Table 6, and the list includes most of the famous economists of the first half-century, although there are notable exceptions; Lauderdale, Bailey, and above all, Ricardo. The relative infrequency of the contributions of economists is itself evidence of the unspecialized nature of the journals—they felt it necessary to present their serious works as pamphlets or books. The comparison of the totals in Tables 4 and 6 is instructive: 82 out of every 100 articles on economics were written by non-economists, and if that prolific pair, McCulloch and Thompson, had chosen another field, 91 out of every 100 would have been written by non-economists.[6]

No comparable study has been undertaken of the modern period, chiefly because the changing nature of the publication media makes it difficult to contrive a fair comparison. If learned journals are chosen, almost all authors are professional economists (as we shall see below). If specialized financial and business publications are chosen, an entirely different type of economic literature (one that scarcely existed in 1825) is encountered. The general literary journals have lost their eminence as a forum for economic discussion. This very specialization of media of communication documents the professionalization of economics.

II. THE JOURNAL LITERATURE IN AMERICAN ECONOMICS

The periodical has been the main outlet for professional economic writing, especially of a theoretical tendency, since its first appearance in the 1880's. It offers (in principle!) the speed of the pamphlet, and does not suffer the latter's great disability: that each pamphlet appeals to a different set of readers so no good machinery of distribution is possible. A journal is, in fact, a set of pamphlets, sufficiently varied in subject matter to appeal to numerous readers. The journal is the channel for serious professional conversation.

The number of economic journals has grown substantially, although perhaps less rapidly than the number of economists, and the growth of numbers has led to the usual increase in specialization. Nevertheless, there are several "general" journals and they have been chosen to study several developments

---

[6] These ratios are biased upward to the uncertain (but surely minor) extent that some of the articles whose authorship would not be ascertained were written by economists.

in American economics. The study is based upon 1,726 articles appearing in pairs of years (1892–93 through 1962–63).[7]

If we tarry a moment with the professionalization of economics, we find that the journals have been in the almost exclusive possession of the academic economists from the outset (see Table 7). One aspect of this dominance is a trifle surprising: despite the substantial increase in the share of economists in governmental employment, their share of the articles

TABLE 7

OCCUPATIONS OF AUTHORS OF ECONOMIC ARTICLES*

Year	Academic	Government	Other	Total
1892–93	54	5	7	66
1902–03	57	4	16	77
1912–13	123	16	32	171
1922–23	181	9	8	198
1932–33	229.2	6.5	4.3	240
1942–43	221.8	47.1	10.1	279
1952–53	267.8	23.6	9.7	301
1962–63	367.8	17.1	9.1	394

* In the case of multiple authors, each author is credited with a proportionate fraction of the article.

in the journals has not risen to an important extent. Governmental economists contribute to more specialized journals (including several published by the federal government), of course, but apparently governmental service is unfavorable to participation in the main issues and controversies of professional economics.

American economics was, of course, unimportant and derivative at the beginning of our period. Walker, Taussig, Irving

---

[7] The journals are: *Quarterly Journal of Economics,* since 1892; *Journal of Political Economy,* since 1892; *American Economic Review,* since 1912; *Review of Economics and Statistics,* since 1922; and *Econometrica,* since 1932. The analysis of the articles was made by Gwendolyn Dietmann, to whom I must express my indebtedness.

Fisher, and J. B. Clark were the first American economists to achieve an international standing. There was no major training center at home: until World War I at least a year in Germany was the proper background for a proper young economist. The gradual development of American economics, which continued until the center of world economics moved from England to the United States after World War II, could be documented (statistically!), but we shall look only at certain domestic effects of our scientific prosperity.

TABLE 8

THE NATIONALITY OF AUTHORS OF ARTICLES

YEARS	PERCENTAGE DISTRIBUTION*		
	American	European	Other
1892–93.......	83	15	2
1902–03.......	94	2	4
1912–13.......	94	4	2
1922–23.......	88	9	3
1932–33.......	88	10	2
1942–43.......	97	2	1
1952–53.......	88	9	3
1962–63.......	88	6	6

* *Econometrica* is not an exclusively American journal, and, if we exclude it, the percentage of European authors falls to 5 in 1932–33, to 0.4 in 1942–43, to 4 in 1952–53, and to 3 in 1962–63.

One modest effect of our rise is a substantial decline in the share of articles written by European economists (see Table 8). We identify contributors by residence, so the numerous contributions of economists who have migrated here from Europe (the Austrians in particular) escape our measure of indebtedness. Yet a study of American contributions to foreign journals would undoubtedly confirm the fact that we have a favorable balance of trade in economic articles.

A stronger indication of our rise is the sharp decline in the citation of foreign language literature (Table 9).[8] At the be-

---

[8] The citations exclude newspapers, statistical reports, etc.

ginning of the period over 40 per cent of the citations were to other languages: half German, one-fourth in the Romance languages, and the remainder scattered (but largely Scandinavian). The total foreign language citations have fallen to less

TABLE 9

LANGUAGE OF PROFESSIONAL LITERATURE
CITED IN ARTICLES

Language	1892–93	1902–03	1912–13	1922–23	1932–33	1942–43	1952–53	1962–63
	Percentage Distribution							
English.........	61	79	83	78	85	86	85	96
German.........	19	14	11	14	9	7	3	......
French.........	10	7	4	5	5	4	7	1
Spanish.........	2	......	1	......	......	......	......	......
Italian.........	4	1	......	......	1	1	1	......
Scandinavian.....	5	......	......	......	......	1	......	......
Russian.........	......	......	......	......	......	1	3	1
Other.........	......	......	1	2	......	......	......	1
	Total Citations							
English.........	160	371	541	950	1940	2274	2940	5096
German.........	50	64	71	174	196	189	103	18
French.........	25	31	29	65	109	115	257	66
Spanish.........	4	......	5	......	1	7	2	5
Italian.........	11	7	1	2	27	18	25	16
Scandinavian.....	12	2	......	......	5	17	11	15
Russian.........	......	......	......	......	2	26	113	52
Other.........	1	......	4	24	8	6	7	38*

* Six Dutch, 31 Czechoslovakian, one Hungarian.

than four per cent in recent years, and German has almost vanished as a language from American economics.

If references to Schmoller and Pantaleoni are now rare, references to differentials and matrices have made some sort of compensation. Only one article in twenty used even graphs or simple algebra at the beginning of our period; today only one article in three still finds the language of words sufficient (Table 10).[9] The shift to more mathematical techniques began in the decade of the 1920's and shows no sign of retardation. The science will have become completely mathematical by 2002–3, when (as Aaron Director has remarked) editors will be unable to read a non-mathematical article.

I had contemplated use of the *Index of Economic Periodicals* for a study of the role of fashion in economics. One would

TABLE 10

THE LEVEL OF TECHNIQUE IN ARTICLES

YEARS	PERCENTAGE DISTRIBUTION			
	No Special Techniques	Geometry	Algebra	Calculus or More
1892–93	95	3	2	
1902–03	92	1	6	
1912–13	98	1	1	
1922–23	95	1	2	2
1932–33	80	1	8	10
1942–43	65	8	6	21
1952–53	56	6	7	31
1962–63	33	8	13	46

trace out, for example, the cycle of interest in monopolistic competition in the 1930's, the sweep of linear programming through the journals in the 1950's, and similar episodes. Alas, the index does not allow such analysis: the categories are broad, and the index itself recognizes only the categories of subjects which were fashionable in 1960!

Accepting the *Index* classification, much the largest change has been in economic theory (class 2), which started at 18 per

---

[9] An article is ranked by its most elaborate technique, so the use of geometry in 7 per cent of the articles in 1962–63 means that only this share used geometry without also using algebra or calculus.

cent of all articles, fell to half that level by 1912–13, and recently has been nearly 40 per cent of the total. To a large degree this high and rising share of theory is a result of bias in our selection of journals—articles on labor, taxation, economic history, and agricultural economics (to name only a few) are increasingly published in specialized journals. The *Index of Periodicals* itself reveals a much smaller trend in this direction (although it is not restricted to the United States):

	Per Cent of Articles on Theory
1886–1924	8.1
1925–1939	11.4
1940–1949	11.1
1950–1954	14.9
1955–1959	16.3

The rise of interest in mathematical and statistical techniques and in social accounting (classes 8 and 9), however, is a real phenomenon: an obvious counterpart of the increasing sophistication of technique. (See Table 11.)

In the substantive fields, the most striking development was the virtual disappearance of monetary economics from the 1930's through the 1950's. This was the great era of Keynesian economics, and the extent to which it drew attention away from traditional monetary economics is truly remarkable. The changes in the comparative attention to the other substantive fields were wholly minor.

III. CONCLUSION

These small studies illustrate what I take to be a potentially large role for the statistical method in intellectual history. Quetelet astonished his contemporaries by showing empirical regularities in the commission of crimes and even in suicides; we should be less surprised to learn that we can trace the international propagation of economic theories, or the relationship of specialization of economists to the number of economists. The traditional analytical treatment of predecessors is appropriate to the understanding of the work of individual economists, but only the statistical method can reveal the typical positions and relationships within a science.

TABLE 11

PERCENTAGE DISTRIBUTION OF SUBJECT AREAS OF ARTICLES

Area	1892–93	1902–3	1912–13	1922–23	1932–33	1942–43	1952–53
1. Scope and Method of Economics	2	1	3	4	3	1	2
2. Economic Theory	18	14	9	14	20	34	36
3. Economic Systems	.....	.....	.....	3	2	2	1
4. History of Economic Thought	8	1	2	3	6	3	5
5. Economic History	3	.....	1	4	2	1	1
6. General Contemporary Conditions	3	.....	2	6	5	3	1
7. Mathematical, Statistical, and Other Tools of Analysis	.....	2	1	2	7	7	15
8. Social Accounting	.....	.....	.....	.....	.....	.....	.....
9. Money, Credit, and Banking	24	12	15	8	18	3	2
10. Public Finance	6	2	5	7	3	8	5
11. International Economics	11	10	8	12	7	5	9
12. Economic Fluctuations	2	.....	1	4	4	2	2
13. War and Defense Economics	.....	1	.....	1	.....	12	1
14. Business Organization	.....	1	5	11	1	1	1
15. Industrial Organization	4	23	23	8	9	7	7
16. Agriculture	6	8	4	2	2	.....	1
17. Natural Resources	.....	4	2	.....	.....	.....	.....
18. Population	.....	2	4	.....	1	.....	1
19. Labor Economics	9	10	14	11	6	7	5
20. Consumer Economics	.....	1	.....	.....	.....	2	1
21. Health, Education, Welfare	4	.....	1	.....	1	2	2
22. Regional Planning and Development	.....	.....	1	.....	1	.....	1
23. Unclassified	.....	4	1	.....	.....	.....	.....

4

The Politics of Political Economists

The professional study of a discipline no doubt has a variety of effects upon the beliefs and attitudes of a person. Not only is he subjected to an intensive and more or less standardized discipline, but he is also subjected to the influence of a set of practitioners who share distinctive beliefs.

One interesting, if minor, example of this is the aversion economists display toward employment in business—even those economists (like me) who think a good entrepreneur is worth three good bureaucrats. I do not recall ever hearing or giving a lecture on the Nobility of Pure Scholarship contrasted with the Sordidness of Commercial Applications, and yet in innumerable instances I have seen young economists spurn handsome positions in business for devotion to an academic life in which often they will not prosper greatly. Somehow, by a mysterious intellectual osmosis, they absorb the values of the professional academic economist.

This paper was prepared for a lecture at Harvard University, whence its informality and *ad hominem* illustrations.

Reprinted from *The Quarterly Journal of Economics,* Vol. LXXIII (November, 1959).

I direct my remarks on this occasion, however, to only one effect of professional economic training: the effect on the political views of economists. It does not seem necessary to retread familiar ground to show that economics as a positive science is ethically—and therefore politically—neutral. The corpus of economic analysis can be turned to a thousand contradictory ends. But by and large it is not: my thesis is that the professional study of economics makes one politically conservative.

The support of this thesis is a formidable task. Among laymen it would be formidable because they nurture a stereotype of the economist as the wild-eyed visionary, whispering absurd schemes to Franklin Roosevelt. Among academicians it is formidable because they do not relish this designation. But let me try.

I. WHAT IS A CONSERVATIVE?

Before we embark upon the argument that the professional economist tends to be politically conservative, we must establish the usage of the key word, conservative.

A conservative, the dictionary tells us, is an individual who wishes to maintain or preserve the existing social system, and the dictionary also tells us that this meaning of the word is only a little over a century old. The use of language in areas such as this is notoriously lax, and the word is used to denote a much wider range of views than simply the maintenance of the status quo. Those men who wish to undo recent changes are also called conservative, and indeed it is clear that in a period of considerable social change there is hardly anyone who wishes to preserve the state of affairs of the moment—the anti-conservatives have achieved only half their desired changes, and the conservatives possess less than they want of the past. The concept of a conservative or a radical can be applied unambiguously only in a very stable social setting.

But the language stretches even farther. Since no thinking

man ever finds his society completely ideal, the conservative is held to be the one who accepts the state of society (current or recent past) as desirable in its *basic* outlines, not necessarily in every detail. Since every society has some inconsistent institutions and practices, this element of flexibility is essential.

Once the concept of a conservative is enlarged so that he need support only the basic structure of the society, a new problem arises: what are the basic institutions of the country? Is the gold standard a basic institution of private enterprise societies? It is possible to find economists who quarrel over the answer, although not so easily as it once was. Is an agricultural price support system a basic violation of such a system? What system of progressive—or for that matter, proportional—taxes destroys a private enterprise system? These examples suggest that it is possible for a man to be an inadvertent radical, by proposing policies which are basically in conflict with his general preferences without realizing their fundamental nature. A layman who professes conservatism might possibly propose that the interest rate be held at zero, although this would be no compliment to his intelligence; a professional economist could not make a proposal that has such radical implications for saving and investment under the banner of conservatism. Our examples also show why it is possible, in the absence of complete knowledge of the effects of a policy or institution, for sincere men to disagree whether a given proposal is conservative or radical.

These various difficulties in the substantive definition of a conservative are enough to make it a treacherous tool of analysis. For my purposes, however, a fairly definite content is essential. I shall mean by a conservative in economic matters a person who wishes most economic activity to be conducted by private enterprise, and who believes that abuses of private power will usually be checked, and incitements to efficiency and progress usually provided, by the forces of competition. A gradually increasing role has been assigned to the democratic state even by the conservatives, but they have retained the belief that the individual is normally to be free of public as well as private controls over consumption patterns, occupational choice, and the allocation of privately-owned resources. One would have to specify some limitations on the role of competition, even where it is effective, and upon the freedom of the individual in a variety of activities, but some disagreement about the details of these limitations would be compatible with a generally conservative position.

This sketchy outline of the conservative position on economic policy is sufficiently definite to suggest, what I believe to be true, that the profession of economists has become more conservative in recent decades in the sense of being hostile to an increasing number of innovations in economic policy. But in the last century and a half this conservative position has been widely held in both Western European and North American countries, and substantial as the disagreements within the conservative position have been and are, they are smaller than the disagreements between the conservative and the collectivistic or socialistic position.

II. THE INFLUENCE OF THE STUDY OF ECONOMICS UPON POLICY VIEWS

The isolation of the net effect of scientific training upon the policy views of a man is a most difficult task. Economists are subject to the coercion of the ruling ideologies of their times, and if they wholly resist them they would lose all rapport with their societies—the expression would become "the visitor from economics" not from Mars. If the discipline of economics has a net effect upon the views of its practitioners, it is only a moderate effect.

Yet I would assert that it has a significant effect, and the effect is to make the economist conservative in the sense I have discussed above. This is not a bold claim, but it may encounter instant objection. It will be asked: what, precisely, is the conservative element common to the views of Hansen, who believes that the marginal utility of a public dollar far exceeds that of a private dollar; Seymour Harris, who adds to this viewpoint a request for protective tariffs for New England; and Galbraith, whose non-conservative proposals would constitute a fairly complete bibliography of his works—and, please notice, all of Harvard. Or Mitchell, with inclinations toward central planning, or the numerous proponents of widespread public housing, minimum wage legislation, federal financing of research, etc.? If these people are all conservative, who besides Karl Marx is not conservative?

I have quite possibly stated this criticism so strongly that my answer will seem unconvincing, but I believe that the economics profession has been basically more conservative than the educated classes generally. Even the extremes of professional opinion have been less than those outside the profession. In the 1930's, when admiration of private enterprise was at low ebb, no economist participated in the more extreme popular movements, such as technocracy and the Townsend plan. As a group, economists were hostile to the farm program, the extreme forms of pro-unionism of the period, and after a brief period of stunned silence, they became outspoken critics of the NRA.

More broadly, one can say that economists have not been among the leaders of any important movement for the adoption of policies incompatible with the conservative position. They have not been leaders in the sense of being active public propagandists for the non-conservative policies or in the sense of providing a blueprint of reform or even a trenchant indictment of the real or alleged failures of conservative economic policy. They have been camp followers, when not critics, in the area of egalitarian policies, in the areas of state intervention in competitive markets, including agriculture, labor, and housing. In fact they have been leaders only in the areas of freer trade policy and antitrust policy, two traditional elements of the conservative position, and in the fields of monetary and fiscal policy, where the paramount role of the state has always been acknowledged although the script for that role has been much debated.

This generally conservative record is all the more remarkable because there are two forces making for radicalism in the members of the economics profession.

The first and much the stronger of these forces is the interest of economists in social reform. Economics has seldom attracted to its ranks the detached and unemotional intellectual who finds the posing and solving of difficult problems satisfying even in the absence of immediate or perhaps even eventual usefulness of the solution. On the contrary, individuals have chosen this field because they wished to solve live economic problems and felt a need to master the weapons provided by the science which deals with these problems.

The policy orientation of the classical economists does not need to be argued. Indeed there was only one, and he a part-time, economist of importance before 1870 whose interest in economics was predominantly scientific, and he was Cournot. The story has not been greatly different since the study of economics became an academic discipline.

Marshall, for example, had started as a mathematician. He has recounted the shifting of interests which led him to economics:

> From Metaphysics I went to Ethics, and thought that the justification of the existing condition of society is not easy. A friend, who had read a great deal of what are now called the Moral Sciences, constantly said: "Ah! if you understood Political Economy you would not say that." So I read Mill's *Political Economy* and got much excited about it. I had doubts as to the propriety of inequalities of *opportunity*, rather than of material comfort. Then, in my vacations I visited the poorest quarters of several cities and walked through one street after another, looking at the faces of the poorest people.

Next, I resolved to make as thorough a study as I could of Political Economy.[1]

A more striking example is Knut Wicksell. Those who have read Torsten Gårdlund's fine biography will know how radical and even undisciplined he was. At thirty-seven he refused to go through a marriage ceremony when he and Anna Bugge "married"; at forty-eight he endangered his career by refusing to sign a petition to the King for a permanent professorship with the traditional phrase, "Your Majesty's most obedient servant"; and at fifty-six he went to prison for satirizing the doctrine of the Immaculate Conception in a public lecture. He (like Marshall) started as a mathematician, but a deep commitment to neo-Malthusianism led him to economics. I consider it highly suggestive that Wicksell's policy positions in economics—and only in economics—were conservative. In a less dramatic way, the life of Philip Wicksteed seems equally persuasive.

This selectivity of economics is reinforced by a second factor: the science equips its members with a larger knowledge of the deficiencies of existing economic arrangement than the layman is likely to possess. The young graduate student is thoroughly drilled in the iniquities of monopoly in all its myriad forms. He is taught of the variety of special privileges sought and often obtained by particular groups, through tariffs, percentage depletion, exemptions from regulatory laws, and plain and subtle subsidies. He is acquainted with the existence of a poverty class, and in general his humanitarian colleagues—the profession has been consistently humanitarian throughout its history—are more prone to exaggerate than to minimize the sufferings of particular classes.

It could be argued that there is one powerful factor making for conservatism: the inability of a very radical young econ-

---

1 Keynes, *Essays in Biography* (London: Macmillan and Company, 1933), pp. 165–66.

omist to get a desirable university post. It is indeed true that a believer in the labor theory of value could not get a professorship at a major American university, although the reason would be that the professors could not bring themselves to believe that he was both honest and intelligent, and I hope they are not improper in their demand that a professor be at least tolerably honest and presumptively intelligent. But this argument is invalid, and not merely because one can be an economist without being a professor. It is improper because it concedes the case: it concedes that economists are conservative, and this is precisely my thesis.

This same conclusion, that economists have been politically conservative, can also be reached by another route, the examination of the authors of economically radical programs.

In the United States, which has not been an important source of movements of economic reform, only two economic programs of fairly radical import have made something of an impact in the last hundred years. The first was the program of land nationalization, bearing the now nostalgic label of "single tax," proposed by Henry George. His knowledge of economics, which never became excessively profound, was acquired after arriving at his basic viewpoint. The second was a series of hostile sketches of our economy and society by Thorstein Veblen, and although they never culminated in a definite program of economic reform they did contribute to the milieu of dissatisfaction with private enterprise which paved the way for some non-conservative policies of the 1930's. It is uncertain whether Veblen's basic viewpoint was formed before he entered (at the age of thirty-four) upon the serious study of economics—his dissertation was in philosophy.

In England the story is much the same. I do not know whether Marx's long exile in England qualifies him for inclusion here, but in any event he is not an exception to the general rule. His general position was developed in the 1830's and 1840's, and it was only shortly before the writing of the *Manifesto* that he began the serious study of economics. The study of economics affected many details of his position, and suggested lacunae, but it did not come early enough to make him approach a problem the way a trained economist would have done.

The later British socialists of the Fabian School fall into much the same pattern. Bernard Shaw and the Webbs, or perhaps I should say Sidney, acquired some fluency in the language of economics, but for them it was mostly a troublesome set of doctrines, to be twisted to their ends when possible and otherwise ignored.

I cannot speak with even faint authority on the role of economists in the radical movements of the Continent. It should be noted, however, that only in select European nations such as Austria, Sweden, and Italy was economic analysis, in the sense in which almost all modern economists use the term, an actively taught and generally understood discipline, in contrast with historical or sociological approaches.

A final word. There have, of course, been well-trained young economists who have become Marxists, communists, socialists, guild socialists, and the like. The fact to be noticed, however, is that they have been relatively few despite the natural selectivity of the study of economics.

III. THE CAUSE OF PROFESSIONAL CONSERVATISM

The conservatism of the economists cannot be explained by the vulgar argument of venality: that economists have sold their souls to the capitalists. The current rates of pay for good economists are much below what I would assume to be the going rate for a soul.

The main reason for the conservatism surely lies in the effect of the scientific training the economist receives. He is drilled in the problems of *all* economic systems and in the methods by which a price system solves these problems. It becomes impossible for the trained economist to believe that a small group of selfish capitalists dictates the main outlines of the allocation of resources and the determination of outputs. It becomes impossible for him to believe that men of good will can by their individual actions stem inflation, or that it is possible to impose changes in any one market or industry without causing problems in other markets or industries. He cannot unblushingly repeat slogans such as "production for use rather than for profit." He cannot believe that a change in the *form* of social organization will eliminate basic economic problems.

The impact of economic analysis upon one's *Weltanschauung* is well illustrated by a piece of analysis given by a fine Irish economist, Mountifort Longfield, over a century ago. At that time, wealthy Englishmen sometimes bought wheat in years of high price and resold it to the needy poor at half price. This was pure humanitarianism, and on its face an effective method of aiding the poor. But Longfield pointed out that it did not help the poor at all, and might even injure them. The poor would have a given demand function for grain, and the lower the price the more they would wish to buy. But the total supply was by hypothesis unusually small so, in their attempts to consume the large quantity the subsidized price encouraged, they drove up the price themselves, and of course drove up the price to the rich benefactors to twice this higher level. The whole scheme amounted only to a gift from the wealthy to the grain dealers. Only a knowledge of economic analysis, as Longfield argued, would teach the inevitability of some form of rationing in a period of short supply.

An equally apt example of the effect of economic analysis was given by Edwin Cannan. Consider the perennial charge of profiteering that is levied at the producers or owners of commodities in relatively short supply. As Cannan pointed out, this is a singularly perverse distribution of blame. The only way in which the supplier can benefit by a high price is by selling the commodity, that is, by making the supply larger. If there is a shortage of meat, then we should blame everyone except the members of the livestock industry, for everyone else is not producing the meat which we desire in larger quantities.

These instances illustrate the strong influence a training in economics analysis exerts upon the economist and the way in which he sees the economic world. The intricate elaboration of the basic logic of a competitive price system is the dominant element of this viewpoint, and even if one believes that the existing economy departs far from the ideals of abstract theory, the problems of allocation of resources dwell in the mind of the economist and make him an imaginative and realistic critic of economic nostrums.

Professor Mises, whom many regard as of conservative persuasion, would, I believe, accept the main tenor of the foregoing remarks, but he has argued that it is economic statistics, or more generally quantitative economics, which generates a radical political viewpoint. And I in turn believe that this view is precisely wrong.

The quantitative, or better, empirical study of economic life is the only way in which one can get a real feeling for the tasks and functioning of an economic system. The completely formal theorist does not know the range or subtlety of the economic problems that arise each day, for a man is not as resourceful or imaginative as a society of men. The formal theorist therefore has a much simplified picture of the world and of the complexity of the scientific theorems required to explain its operation. He fails to realize the extent to which the successful explanation of the workings of the economy demands an enlarged scientific technique, judgment, and information, whereas the experienced empirical worker has had the complexities of the economy burned into his soul. It is not a coincidence that the theorists who have turned socialist or communist have usually been completely abstract theorists, and the more radical wing of the New Dealers was not distinguished for its empirical knowledge of the American economy.

IV. THE SCIENTIFIC EFFECTS OF
CONSERVATISM

Let us grant—or at least, let me grant—that the professional study of economics increases one's political conservatism in the sense in which I have defined it. The question then arises: what effects, if any, does this political attitude have upon the scientific work of economists?

The policy position has first of all a pronounced effect upon the *direction* of scientific work. It poses a set of problems, integral to the logic of the conservative position, and economists devote to these problems an amount of attention that would be quite inexplicable on any other ground than their policy relevance. Let me give a few examples.

The field of industrial organization is devoted to the analysis of the structure of industries, their behavior with respect to variables such as price and variety of product, and the changes in structure and behavior over time. In actual fact, something like 98 per cent of the general literature is concerned, explicitly or implicitly, with the question of monopoly.

This emphasis is surely attributable to the conservative position of economists, which places great value upon dispersion of economic power and determination of resource allocation by impersonal markets. Were it not for this orientation, it would be hard to explain the attention given to competition and monopoly in the analyses of questions such as innovation and vertical integration, and the comparative neglect of questions such as the influence of consumers and cyclical fluctuations upon industrial structure, and the international flow of technology.

The theory of international trade is almost equally appropriate as an example. If one takes a standard treatise in this area, he finds that the larger part of the field is directly or indirectly concerned with free trade. That is, it is concerned with the operation of international trade in the absence of state intervention, and the determination of effects—one can even say, distortions introduced by this intervention. In the absence of the conservative influence, much larger attention might have been paid to the effects of differences in natural resource endowments, the use of foreign trade policies to re-distribute income, and similar topics, which have only recently been receiving attention.

Not only has the conservative tradition influenced the direction of economic research, it has also given economics much of its *substance*. I mean this in a very special sense. The apparatus of economics is very flexible: without breaking the rules of the profession—by being illogical or even by denying the validity of the traditional theory—a sufficiently clever person can reach *any* conclusion he wishes on any *real* problem (in contrast to formal problems). This was impressed upon me immediately after the war when Milton Friedman and I wrote a little piece, based strictly upon elementary economics, against rent controls. Our plentiful critics reached the opposite conclusion by a variety of paths. Some denied the quantitative importance of the functional relationships we used, others simply argued that rent decontrol would lead to great wage increases and these to extensive inflation, which even conservatives think is bad.

In general there is no position, to repeat, which cannot be reached by a competent use of respectable economic theory. The reason this does not happen more often than it does is that there is a general consensus among economists that some relationships are stronger than others and some magnitudes are larger than others. This consensus rests in part, to be sure, on empirical research. Empirical evidence, and not his conservative bias, is what keeps Seymour Harris from proposing establishment of a banana-growing industry in Vermont.

But some of the consensus stems also from the general acceptance of the same political preference. I ask you to do three things.

1. Write down a list of propositions in economics having substantive content and policy relevance. For example, free

housing (or rather, housing provided without price by the federal government) would lead to an inappropriately large expansion of this sector of consumption.

2. Write down all the empirical relationships relevant to each argument.

3. Write down the places where these empirical relationships are rigorously established.

Rigor being what the econometricians have made it, I am confident that hardly any conclusions will survive beyond a 2 per cent confidence interval. And yet when an economist plays the game of withholding judgments on the ground that a freshly laundered scientist cannot stake the life of his first-born on the results, we are invariably and properly highly suspicious of the stance.

Of course, I have asserted and not proved that our generally conservative position underlies some of the consensus on the orders of magnitude of empirical relationships and effects. It is not easy to devise a proof, other than a mere mathematical proof, but some support is found in a comparison of American economists with those of other nations. The typical Latin American or Indian economist, for example, appears to differ more from our estimates of empirical magnitudes than one would expect if only empirical evidence underlaid them, and the same is true in some degree even with respect to Swiss or French or German economists.

V. CONCLUDING REMARKS

If we are politically conservative, it is not surprising that ours is known as a dismal science in a period when the trend of policy has been strongly anti-conservative. And it is not without relevance that this characterization did not emerge and become popular until what Dicey called the age of collectivism had begun.

Our conservatism, giving the term the special meaning of attachment to private enterprise, has been attenuated. Once violent debates over questions like the propriety of free public libraries have vanished from discussion, and once absurd heresies like governmental support of an agricultural class have won, if not our support, at least a measure of tolerant resignation. We shall no doubt continue to bend before a strong wind, but I consider it a remarkable effect of our professional discipline that we shall not be contributing to the wind.

5

The Development of
Utility Theory

But I have planted the tree of utility. I have
planted it deep, and spread it wide.—BENTHAM.

The history of economic thought can be studied
with many purposes. One may trace the effects of contemporary economic and social conditions on economic theory or—
rather more bravely—the effects of economic theories on economic and social developments. One may study the history to
find the original discoverers of theories, spurred on by the
dream of new Cantillons; or one may compare the economics
of the great economists with that of the rank and file, as a
contribution to the structure and process of intellectual change.
Or one may, and most often does, simply set forth the major
steps in the development of a branch of economic theory,
hoping that it can be justified by its contribution to the understanding of modern economics. This history of utility theory
is offered primarily with this last purpose, although in the

Reprinted from *The Journal of Political Economy*, Vol. LVIII (August
and October, 1950).

final section I review the history to answer the question, "Why do economists change their theories?"

The scope of this study is limited in several respects. First, it covers primarily the period from Smith to Slutsky, that is, from 1776 to 1915. Second, the study is limited to certain important topics and to the treatment of these topics by economists of the first rank. The application of utility theory to welfare economics is the most important topic omitted. An estimate of the part played by utility theory in forming economists' views of desirable social policy is too large a task, in the complexity of issues and volume of literature involved, to be treated incidentally. The omission is justified by the fact that most economists of the period used utility theory primarily to explain economic behavior (particularly demand behavior) and only secondarily (when at all) to amend or justify economic policy.[1]

I. THE CLASSICAL BACKGROUND

ADAM SMITH

Drawing upon a long line of predecessors, Smith gave to his immediate successors, and they uncritically accepted, the distinction between value in use and value in exchange:

> The word VALUE, it is to be observed, has two different meanings, and sometimes expresses the utility of some particular object, and sometimes the power of purchasing other goods which the posses-

---

[1] I have also omitted consideration of the criticisms raised by the antitheoretical writers, who played no constructive part in the development of the theory. For a discussion of some of their views see J. Viner, "The Utility Theory and Its Critics," *Journal of Political Economy*, XXXIII (1925), 369–87.

I wish to acknowledge the helpful suggestions of Arthur F. Burns, Milton Friedman, and Paul A. Samuelson.

sion of that object conveys. The one may be called "value in use"; the other, "value in exchange." The things which have the greatest value in use have frequently little or no value in exchange; and on the contrary, those which have the greatest value in exchange have frequently little or no value in use. Nothing is more useful than water: but it will purchase scarce any thing; scarce any thing can be had in exchange for it. A diamond, on the contrary, has scarce any value in use; but a very great quantity of other goods may frequently be had in exchange for it.[2]

The fame of this passage rivals its ambiguity.

The paradox—that value in exchange may exceed or fall short of value in use—was, strictly speaking, a meaningless statement, for Smith had no basis (i.e., no concept of marginal utility of income or marginal price of utility) on which he could compare such heterogeneous quantities. On any reasonable interpretation, moreover, Smith's statement that value in use could be less than value in exchange was clearly a moral judgment, not shared by the possessors of diamonds. To avoid the incomparability of money and utility, one may interpret Smith to mean that the ratio of values of two commodities is not equal to the ratio of their total utilities.[3] On such a reading, Smith's statement deserves neither criticism nor quotation.

---

2 *The Wealth of Nations* (New York: Modern Library, 1937), p. 28.

3 Or, alternatively, that the ratio of the prices of two commodities is not equal to the ratio of their total utilities; but this also requires an illegitimate selection of units: The price of what quantity of diamonds is to be compared with the price of one gallon of water? Smith makes such illegitimate statements; for example, "The whole quantity of a cheap commodity brought to market, is commonly not only greater, but of greater value, than the whole quantity of a dear one. The whole quantity of bread annually brought to market, is not only greater, but of greater value than the whole quantity of butcher's-meat; the whole quantity of butcher's meat, than the whole quantity of poultry; and the whole quantity of poultry,

This passage is not Smith's title to recognition in our history of utility. His role is different: it is to show that demand functions, as a set of empirical relationships, were already an established part of economic analysis. The negatively sloping demand curve was already axiomatic; for example, "A competition will immediately begin among [the buyers when an abnormally small supply is available], and the market price will rise more or less above the natural price."[4] The effect of income on consumption was not ignored:

> The proportion of the expence of house-rent to the whole expence of living, is different in the different degrees of fortune. It is perhaps highest in the highest degree, and it diminishes gradually through the inferior degrees, so as in general to be lowest in the lowest degree. The necessaries of life occasion the great expence of the poor. They find it difficult to get food, and the greater part of their little revenue is spent in getting it. The luxuries and vanities of life occasion the principal expence of the rich; and a magnificent house embellishes and sets off to the best advantage all the other luxuries and vanities which they possess. A tax upon house-rents, therefore, would in general fall heaviest upon the rich; and in this sort of inequality

---

than the whole quantity of wild fowl. There are so many more purchases for the cheap than for the dear commodity, that, not only a greater quantity of it, but a greater value, can commonly be disposed of" (*ibid.*, p. 212; see also p. 838).

Nevertheless, this statement can be reformulated into a meaningful and interesting hypothesis: Order commodities by the income class of consumers, using the proportion of families in the income class that purchase the commodity as the basis for choosing the income class. Then does aggregate value of output fall as income class rises?

4 *Ibid.*, p. 56. Substitution is illustrated by the effects of a royal death on the prices of black and colored cloth (*ibid.*, p. 59).

there would not, perhaps, be any thing very unreasonable.[5]

This type of demand analysis was continued and improved by
Smith's successors, but his example should suffice to remind us
that a history of utility is not a history of demand theory.

BENTHAM

Jeremy Bentham brought the principle of utility (to be understood much more broadly than is customary in economics)
to the forefront of discussion in England at the beginning of
the nineteenth century. In his *Introduction to the Principles
of Morals and Legislation* (1789) he suggested the measurement of quantities of pleasure and pain (primarily for the
purpose of constructing a more rational system of civil and
criminal law). Four dimensions of pleasure and pain were distinguished for the individual: (1) intensity, (2) duration, (3)
certainty, and (4) propinquity.[6]

The first two dimensions are clearly relevant to the measurement of a pleasure, but the latter two are better treated as
two of the factors which influence an individual's response to
a particular pleasure or pain.[7] Bentham did not give explicit
directions for calculating a given pleasure and indeed devoted
a long chapter (vi) to "Circumstances Influencing Sensibility,"

---

[5] *Ibid.*, pp. 793–94. This is of course the opposite of modern budgetary
findings, but near-contemporary budget studies seem to me indirectly to
support Smith.

[6] *Op. cit.*, chap iv. In addition, two further "dimensions" were added for
the appraisal of the total satisfaction of an "act": the consumption of a
loaf of bread might be the pleasure to which the first four dimensions refer;
the theft of the loaf might be the act. These additional dimensions were
fecundity and purity; respectively, the chance of one pleasure leading to
another and the chance of a pleasure not being followed by a pain.

[7] As Bentham indicated elsewhere (see *Works of Jeremy Bentham* [Edin-
burgh: Tait, 1843], I, 206; III, 214).

which listed no less than thirty-two circumstances (such as age, sex, education, and firmness of mind) that must be taken into account in carrying out such a calculation.

The theory was much elaborated with respect to economic applications in *Traités de legislation* (1802), a lucid synthesis of many manuscripts made by his disciple, Étienne Dumont.[8] Bentham was particularly concerned with the problem of equality of income, and this raised the question of comparisons of the utilities of persons who might differ in thirty-two circumstances:

> It is to be observed in general, that in speaking of the effect of a portion of wealth upon happiness, abstraction is always to be made of the particular sensibility of individuals, and of the exterior circumstances in which they may be placed. Differences of character are inscrutable; and such is the diversity of circumstances, that they are never the same for two individuals. Unless we begin by dropping these two considerations, it will be impossible to announce any general proposition. But though each of these propositions may prove false or inexact in a given individual case, that will furnish no argument against their speculative truth and practical utility. It is enough for the justification of these propositions—1st, If they approach nearer the truth than any others which can be substituted for them; 2nd, If with less inconvenience than any others they can be made the basis of legislation.[9]

---

8 The reliability of the presentation of Bentham's views has been attested by Élie Halévy, *La Formation du radicalisme philosophique* (Paris: Germer Baillière, 1901), Vol. I, Appendix I. Here the Hildreth translation of the *Traités* is used (London: Trübner, 1871).

9 *Theory of Legislation*, p. 103.

Thus, he achieved interpersonal comparisons, not by calculation, but by assumption, justified by the desirability (somehow determined) of its corollaries. This resort to a question-begging assumption was a fundamental failure of his project to provide a scientific basis for social policy: the scientific basis was being justified by the policies to which it led. In one of his manuscripts he argued that this assumption was merely an abbreviation and that the conclusions he deduced could be reached (more laboriously) without it,[10] which is not in general true.

Having surmounted this obstacle no better than subsequent economists, Bentham proceeded to establish a set of propositions on the utility of income:[11]

> 1st. Each portion of wealth has a corresponding portion of happiness.
> 2nd. Of two individuals with unequal fortunes, he who has the most wealth has the most happiness.

---

[10] " 'Tis in vain to talk of adding quantities which after the addition will continue distinct as they were before, one man's happiness will never be another man's happiness; a gain to one man is no gain to another: you might as well pretend to add 20 apples to 20 pears, which after you had done that could not be 40 of any one thing but 20 of each just as there was before. This addibility of the happiness of different subjects, however, when considered rigorously it may appear fictitious, is a postulatum without the allowance of which all political reasoning is at a stand: nor is it more fictitious than that of the equality of chances to reality, on which that whole branch of the Mathematics which is called the doctrine of chances is established. The fictitious form of speech (expression) in both cases, which, fictitious as it is, can give birth to no false consequences or conclusions, is adopted from a necessity which induces the like expedient in so many other instances, merely for the sake of abbreviation: as it would be endless to repeat in every passage where it was used, what it was it wanted to be rigorously true" (Halévy, *op. cit.*, III, 481).

[11] *Theory of Legislation,* pp. 103 ff.; all statements italicized by Bentham.

3rd. The excess in happiness of the richer will not
be so great as the excess of his wealth.[12]

Each of these propositions was elaborated, and the utility calculus was used to defend equality ("The nearer the actual proportion approaches to equality, the greater will be the total
mass of happiness"), although equality was finally rejected in
favor of security of property. As corollaries, gambling was
utility-decreasing and insurance utility-increasing.[13]

In a manuscript written about 1782, Bentham attempted to
set forth more clearly the precise measurement of utility.[14] We
are given a definition of the unit of intensity:

> The degree of intensity possessed by that pleasure
> which is the faintest of any that can be distin-
> guished to be pleasure, may be represented by unity.
> Such a degree of intensity is in every day's experi-
> ence: according as any pleasures are perceived to
> be more and more intense, they may be represented
> by higher and higher numbers: but there is no fix-
> ing upon any particular degree of intensity as be-
> ing the highest of which a pleasure is susceptible.[15]

---

12 The use of marginal analysis was even more explicit in his *Pannomial
Fragments:*

"But the quantity of happiness will not go on increasing in anything near
the same proportion as the quantity of wealth:—ten thousand times the
quantity of wealth will not bring with it ten thousand times the quantity
of happiness. It will even be matter of doubt whether ten thousand times
the wealth will in general bring with it twice the happiness.

". . . the quantity of happiness produced by a particle of wealth (each
particle being of the same magnitude) will be less and less at every particle;
. . ." (*Works*, III, 229; see also IV, 541).

13 *Theory of Legislation*, pp. 106–7.

14 Lengthy extracts are given by Halévy, *op. cit.*, Vol. I, Appendix II.

15 *Ibid.*, p. 398.

(This suggested measure will be discussed in connection with the Weber-Fechner literature.) Then, shifting ground, Bentham argues that, although utility does not increase as fast as income, for small changes the two move proportionately,[16] so we may measure pleasures through the prices they command:

> If then between two pleasures the one produced by the possession of money, the other not, a man had as lief enjoy the one as the other, such pleasures are to be reputed equal. But the pleasure produced by the possession of money, is *as* the quantity of money that produces it: money is therefore the measure of this pleasure. But the other pleasure is equal to this; the other pleasure therefore is as the money that produces this: therefore money is also the measure of that other pleasure.[17]

Unfortunately, this procedure is illegitimate; we cannot use an equality (or, more strictly, a constancy of the marginal utility of money) that holds for small changes to measure total utilities.[18] These suggestions are important chiefly in revealing Bentham's awareness of the crucial problems in his calculus and his ingenuity in attempting to solve them.[19]

Bentham had indeed planted the tree of utility. No reader could overlook the concept of utility as a numerical magni-

---

16 *Ibid.*, p. 408.

17 *Ibid.*, p. 410.

18 Bentham appears to have recognized this difficulty when, in a passage following a discussion of diminishing marginal utility, he wrote: "[Intensity] is not susceptible of precise expression: it *not* being susceptible of measurement" (*Codification Proposal* [1822], in *Works*, IV, 542).

19 For more general discussions of Bentham see W. C. Mitchell, "Bentham's Felicific Calculus," in *The Backward Art of Spending Money* (New York: McGraw-Hill Book Co., 1937); and J. Viner, "Bentham and J. S. Mill," *American Economic Review*, XXXIX (1949), 360–82.

tude; and the implications for economic analysis were not obscure. But they were overlooked.

THE RICARDIANS

The economists of Bentham's time did not follow the approach he had opened. One may conjecture that this failure is due to the fact that Ricardo, who gave the economics of this period much of its slant and direction, was not a Benthamite. It is true that he was the friend of Bentham and the close friend of James Mill, Bentham's leading disciple. Yet there is no evidence that he was a devout utilitarian and much evidence that he was unphilosophical—essentially a pragmatic reformer.[20]

It is clear, in any event, that Ricardo did not apply the utility calculus to economics. He began his *Principles* with the quotation of Smith's distinction between value in use and value in exchange and ended the volume with the statement: "Value in use cannot be measured by any known standard; it is differently estimated by different persons"[21] I should be content to notice that he left the theory of utility as highly developed as he found it—as much cannot be said for the theory of value—were it not for a remarkable interpretation of Marshall's:

> Again, in a profound, though very incomplete discussion of the difference between "Value and Riches" he seems to be feeling his way towards the distinction between marginal and total utility. For by Riches he means total utility, and he seems to be always on the point of stating that value corre-

---

20 See Bonar's Preface to *Letters of Ricardo to Malthus* (Oxford: Clarendon, 1887).

21 *Principles of Political Economy and Taxation* (Gonner, ed.; London: Bell, 1932), p. 420.

sponds to the increment of riches which results from that part of the commodity which it is only just worth the while of purchasers to buy; and that when the supply runs short, whether temporarily in consequence of a passing accident, or permanently in consequence of an increase in cost of production, there is a rise in that marginal increment of riches which is measured by value, at the same time that there is a diminution in the aggregate riches, the total utility, derived from the commodity. Throughout the whole discussion he is trying to say, though (being ignorant of the terse language of the differential calculus) he did not get hold of the right words in which to say it neatly, that marginal utility is raised and total utility is lessened by any check to supply.[22]

In the chapter (xx) referred to, Ricardo defines riches as "necessaries, conveniences, and amusements," and value, as usual, is measured by the amount of labor necessary to produce a commodity. The chapter is essentially an exercise in the paradoxes of this definition of value; for example, if the productivity of labor doubles, riches double, but value changes only if the number of laborers changes. We may properly identify "necessaries, conveniences, and amusements" with total utility; but what of marginal utility? Ricardo says that, if a person receives two sacks of corn where formerly he received one, "he gets, indeed double the quantity of riches—double the quantity of utility—double the quantity of what Adam Smith calls value in use."[23] Hence he did not believe that marginal utility diminishes as quantity increases. He continued:

---

22 *Principles of Economics* (8th ed.; London: Macmillan, 1920), p. 814.

23 *Principles*, p. 265.

> When I give 2,000 times more cloth for a pound
> of gold than I give for a pound of iron, does it
> prove that I attach 2,000 times more utility to gold
> than I do to iron? certainly not; it proves only as
> admitted by M. Say, that the cost of production of
> gold is 2,000 times greater than the cost of produc-
> tion of iron . . . if utility were the measure of value,
> it is probable I should give more for the iron.[24]

The writer of this passage cannot be said to have been close
to the notion of marginal utility. I cannot find a single sentence that gives support to Marshall's interpretation, and I
think that it should be added to the list of examples of his
peculiar documentation and interpretation of predecessors.

Ricardo's influence was such that James Mill, the logical
person to apply Bentham's system to economics, was content to
present a rigid simplification of Ricardo's *Principles;*[25] and his
son—whose formative work in economics, we must remember,
came chiefly in the 1820's—did little more with utility.[26] Only
the French utilitarian, J. B. Say, attempted to give utility a
substantial place in economic theory, and he was prevented
from doing so effectively by his inability to arrive at a notion
of marginal analysis. In order to support the thesis that prices
are proportional to utilities, he was driven to invent the metaphysical distinction between natural and social wealth:

> One pays 2,000 times as much for a pound of gold
> as for a pound of iron. Here is how, on my theory,
> this phenomenon is explained. I assume with you
> that a pound of iron has the same utility as a pound

---

24 *Ibid.*, pp. 267–68.

25 In his *Elements of Political Economy* (3d ed., 1827).

26 *Principles of Political Economy* (Ashley, ed.; New York: Longmans,
Green, 1929), pp. 442–44, 804.

of gold, although it is worth only one-two-thousandth as much. I say that there are in the iron 1,999 degrees of utility that nature has given us without charge, and 1 degree that we create by work, at an expense that we will assume only if a consumer is willing to reimburse us; hence the pound of iron has 2,000 degrees of utility. The gold also has 2,000 degrees of utility (on your assumption), which however can be obtained only on exacting terms, that is to say, . . . by expenses of 2,000. The 1,999 degrees of utility for which we do not pay when we consume iron are part of our natural wealth. . . . The single degree of utility which must be paid for is part of our social wealth.[27]

II. THE UNSUCCESSFUL DISCOVERERS

The principle that equal increments of utility-producing means (such as income or bread) yield diminishing increments of utility is a commonplace. The first statement in print of a commonplace is adventitious; it is of no importance in the development of economics, and it confers no intellectual stature on its author. The statement acquires interest only when it is logically developed or explicitly applied to economic problems, and it acquires importance only when a considerable number of economists are persuaded to incorporate it into their analyses. Interest and importance are of course matters of degree.

Some economists gave clear statements of the principle of diminishing marginal utility but did not apply it to economic problems; they include Lloyd (1833), Senior (1836), Jennings

[27] Letter to Ricardo, July 19, 1821, in *Mélanges et correspondance* (Paris: Chamerot, 1833), pp. 116–17, 287–89; cf. also *Treatise on Political Economy* (Boston: Wells & Lilly, 1824), Book II, chap. i, and *Cours complet d'économie politique* (Paris: Guillaumin, 1840), I, 65–66, 71–72.

(1855), and Hearn (1864).[28] Others applied utility theory to economic events without explicitly developing the principle of diminishing marginal utility: A. Walras (1831) and Longfield (1834), for example.[29] At least two economists—in addition to Bentham—elaborated the principle or applied it to economic problems but failed to persuade other economists of its usefulness.[30] Their theories will be summarized briefly.

DUPUIT (1844)

Jules Dupuit, a distinguished engineer, was led to the marginal utility theory by his attempt to construct a theory of prices that maximize utility.[31] He distinguished total and marginal utility with great clarity and discovered *"une espèce de bénéfice"* that we now call *consumers' surplus*. It was defined as the excess of total utility over marginal utility times the number of units of the commodity, but it was actually taken to be the area under the demand curve minus the expenditures on the

---

28 W. F. Lloyd, "The Notion of Value," reprinted in *Economic History, Economic Journal Supplement*, May, 1927, pp. 170–83; N. W. Senior, *Political Economy* (New York: Farrar & Rinehart, 1939), pp. 11–12; R. Jennings, *Natural Elements of Political Economy* (London: Longman, Brown, Green & Longmans, 1855), pp. 98–99, 119, 233 n.; W. E. Hearn, *Plutology* (London: Macmillan, 1864), p. 17. Lloyd, the third occupant of the Drummond chair in political economy at Oxford, gave much the most elaborate statement of the principle. Instead of applying it to contemporary economic problems, however, he emphasized the fact that marginal utility is not the same thing as exchange value and applied the theory to Robinson Crusoe to show this.

29 A. Walras, *De la nature de la richesse et de l'origine de la valeur* (Paris: Alcan, 1938), esp. chap. xi; M. Longfield, *Lectures on Political Economy* ("London School Reprints" [London, 1931]), pp. 27–28, 45–46, 111 ff.

30 Daniel Bernoulli's much earlier discovery will be treated later.

31 His chief essays (published in 1844 and 1849) are reprinted in *De l'utilité et de sa mesure* (Torino: La Riforma Sociale, 1934).

commodity (i.e., Marshall's measure without his restrictions).[32]

Armed with this concept, he investigated the optimum toll on a bridge. His analysis was as follows. Let NP be the demand (and marginal utility) curve, Op the price (Fig. 1). Then $OrnP$ is the absolute utility consumers obtain from the use of the bridge, and pnP is the relative utility. If the toll is reduced by

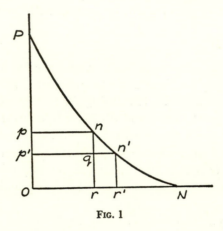

FIG. 1

pp', there is a net gain of consumer utility of qnn' (equal to the area under the demand curve between r and r' minus the expenditure $rr'n'q$).

Dupuit's general conclusion is: "The utility of a means of communication, and in general of any product, is at a maximum when the toll or the price is zero."[33] This is little more

---

[32] Dupuit's instruction for measuring utility reveals the tacit identification of utility and demand curves: "Assume that all the like commodities whose general utility one wishes to determine are subjected to a tax which is increased by small steps. At each increase, a certain quantity of the commodity will no longer be purchased. The utility of this quantity in terms of money will be the quantity multiplied by the tax. By increasing the tax until all purchases cease, and adding the partial products, one will obtain the total utility of the commodity" (*ibid.*, p. 50; also p. 180).

[33] *Ibid.*, p. 161. I have transposed the axes of Dupuit's diagram.

than a tautology, and Dupuit did not draw the further and illegitimate conclusion that the optimum toll rate is zero:

> It will not be our conclusion [that tolls should be small or zero], when we treat of tariffs; but we hope to have demonstrated that [tariff rates] must be studied, combined on rational principles to produce simultaneously the greatest possible utility and a revenue which will repay the expense of maintenance and the interest on the capital investment.[34]

We see that he was not afraid of interpersonal comparisons of utility, and in fact he argued that the effects of price changes on the distribution of income must be ignored because they were merely transfers.[35]

Dupuit could not reach a complete theory of optimum prices because he did not devise a coherent theory of cost.[36]

---

[34] *Ibid.*, p. 51. Elsewhere he says that the ideal toll would be one proportional to the consumers' total utility, but this is impracticable because of *"l'improbité universelle"* (*ibid.*, p. 141); and the effects of alternative methods of financing public works (e.g., the incidence of taxes) must be studied before a practical recommendation can be made (*ibid.*, p. 161). Multiple price systems were also considered (*ibid.*, pp. 64–65, 140 ff.).

[35] *Ibid.*, p. 52.

[36] This is illustrated by the following quotation, in which price fluctuations are treated as exercises of arbitrary power:
"In order that there be an increase or decrease in utility, it is necessary that there be a decrease or increase in [a commodity's] cost of production—there being no change in its quality. When there are only variations in market price [*prix vénal*], the consumer gains what the producer loses, or conversely. Thus, when an article costing 20 francs to produce is sold for 50 francs, as a result of a monopoly or concession, the producer deprives every buyer of 30 francs of utility. If some circumstance forces him to lower his price by 10 francs, his income diminishes by 10 francs per unit and that of each buyer increases by 10 francs. There is a cancellation; no utility is produced" (*ibid.*, pp. 52–53).

One is impressed by the narrowness of his vision; the explicit formulation of the concept of consumer surplus is elegant, but there is no intuition of the difficulties in the concept, nor is there an attempt to construct the larger theoretical framework necessary to solve his problem.

Gossen (1854)

Heinrich Gossen is one of the most tragic figures in the history of economics. He was a profound, original, and untrained thinker who hid his thoughts behind painfully complex arithmetical and algebraic exercises.[37] He displayed every trait of the crank,[38] excepting only one: history has so far believed that he was right. Only a few distinctive features of his work will be commented upon.

First, Gossen's discussion of the laws of satisfaction is concerned only with individual acts of consumption, such as the eating of slices of bread.[39] Correspondingly, in his early diagrams marginal utility is a function of time (duration of the act of consumption), and only after a considerable elaboration of this approach does he take quantity of a (perishable) commodity as proportional to duration of consumption.[40] Yet he

---

[37] Only a person who has labored through the volume can savor the magnificent understatement of Edgeworth: "He may seem somewhat deficient in the quality of mathematical elegance" ("Gossen," *Palgrave's Dictionary of Political Economy* [London: Macmillan, 1923], II, 232).

[38] His *Entwicklung der Gesetze des menschlichen Verkehrs* (3d ed.; Berlin: Prager, 1927), which is not encumbered with chapters, begins with the famous sentences: "On the following pages I submit to public judgment the result of 20 years of meditation. What a Copernicus succeeded in explaining of the relationships of worlds in space, that I believe I have performed for the explanation of the relationships of men on earth."

[39] For a good summary see M. Pantaleoni, *Pure Economics* (London: Macmillan, 1898), pp. 28 ff.

[40] *Entwicklung*, p. 29; his treatment of durable goods is not sound (see pp. 25, 29–30).

does not attempt to work out a theory of the temporal pattern of consumption, and this portion of his theory seems misdirected.

Second, he presents a theory of the marginal disutility of labor that is completely symmetrical with that of the marginal utility of consumer goods. Gossen's curve of the marginal disutility of income is essentially identical with that which Jevons made famous: the early hours of work yield utility, but, as the duration of labor increases, the marginal utility diminishes to zero and then to negative values.[41] He defines the condition of maximum utility as that in which the marginal utility of a unit of product is numerically equal to the marginal disutility of the labor necessary to produce a unit of product.[42]

Third, Gossen was the first writer to formulate explicitly what I shall call the fundamental principle of marginal utility theory:

> A person maximizes his utility when he distributes his available money among the various goods so that he obtains the same amount of satisfaction from the last unit of money (*Geldatom*) spent upon each commodity.[43]

We may translate this statement into semisymbolic form:

$$\frac{MU_1}{p_1} = \frac{MU_2}{p_2} = \frac{MU_3}{p_3} = \cdots ,$$

where MU_i represents the marginal utility of the ith commodity and p_i its price. (We shall adhere to the notation: x_i is the quantity of commodity X_i, p_i is its price, MU_i is its marginal utility, and R is money income.) This equation marked a long step forward in the development of the relationship between utility and demand curves.

---

[41] *Ibid.*, p. 36.   [42] *Ibid.*, p. 45.   [43] *Ibid.*, pp. 93–94.

Finally, Gossen's views on the measurability of utility are vague but tantalizing:

> We can conceive of the magnitudes of various pleasures only by comparing them with one another, as, indeed, we must also do in measuring other objects. We can measure the magnitudes of various areas only by taking a particular area as the unit of measurement, or the weights of different bodies only by taking a particular weight as the unit. Similarly, we must fix on one pleasure as our unit, and hence an indefiniteness remains in the measurement of a pleasure. It is a matter of indifference which pleasure we choose as the unit. Perhaps the consequences will be most convenient if we choose the pleasure from the commodity which we use as money.[44]

He did not notice that there might be no unit of utility comparable with that of area or weight; and it is probably going too far to read into this passage the later position that it is sufficient to deal with the ratios of marginal utilities.

III. THE BEGINNINGS OF THE
MODERN THEORY

The utility theory finally began to win a place in generally accepted economics in the 1870's, under the triple auspices of Jevons, Menger, and Walras. Independently these economists arrived at positions similar in the main and sometimes in detail.[45] I shall compare their treatments of certain basic prob-

---

44 *Ibid.*, p. 123.

45 Marshall was a contemporary discoverer of the theory but did not publish it until later (*Memorials of Alfred Marshall* [London: Macmillan, 1925], p. 22). J. B. Clark was a somewhat later discoverer and never devel-

lems of the theory, and henceforth our organization will be by subject.

A. Criticism of Received Doctrine

Each of these founders of utility theory criticized the Ricardian theory of value, but for each this was an incidental and minor point; they deemed the positive merits of the utility theory a sufficient basis for acceptance. Thus, only after completing the presentation of his utility theory did Jevons point out the deficiencies in Ricardo's labor value theory. These deficiencies were three: (1) Ricardo required a special theory for commodities with fixed supplies, such as rare statues. This proved that labor cost is not essential to value. (2) Large labor costs will not confer high value on a commodity if the future demand is erroneously forecast; "in commerce bygones are for ever bygones."[46] (3) Labor is heterogeneous, and the various types of labor can be compared only through the values of their products.[47] On the other hand, the cost of production theory of value fits in nicely as a special case of the utility theory, for it explains the relative quantities of commodities that will be supplied.[48]

Menger and Walras took fundamentally the same position. The former also gave the first two criticisms listed above and, in addition, made a parallel criticism to the Ricardian rent theory: if the value of land did not depend upon labor cost,

---

oped the theory to a level comparable with the best contemporary European analysis. He became preoccupied with a neglected problem to which he could not find a useful solution: how to apply marginal analysis to variations in the quality of goods (see *The Philosophy of Wealth* [Boston: Ginn & Co., 1892], Preface and p. 76 n.; *Distribution of Wealth* [New York: Macmillan, 1931], chaps. xiv–xvi).

[46] *Theory of Political Economy* (4th ed.; London: Macmillan, 1911), p. 164.

[47] *Ibid.*, p. 166.   [48] *Ibid.*, p. 165.

this demonstrated a serious lack of generality in the classical theory of value.[49] Walras repeated the criticism that the classical theory lacked generality, emphasized the reciprocal effects of prices of products and of productive services on one another, and denied the existence of the class of commodities whose supplies could be infinitely increased, on the overly literal ground that no productive resource was available in infinite quantity.[50]

The task of elaborating and expounding the theory, and of exaggerating its merits and understating the usefulness of the classical theory—the inevitable accompaniments of intellectual innovations—fell largely to disciples, in particular Wieser and Böhm-Bawerk. These men did not improve on the substance of the theory—in fact, it deteriorated in their hands—so we shall pass them by.[51]

B. The Existence and Measurability of Utility

Without exception, the founders accepted the existence of utility as a fact of common experience, congruent with the most casual introspection. Jevons was most explicit:

> The science of Economics, however, is in some degree peculiar, owing to the fact . . . that its ultimate laws are known to us immediately by intui-

---

49 *Grundsätze der Volkswirtschaftslehre* (Vienna: Braumüller, 1871), pp. 69, 120–21, 144–45.

50 *Éléments d'économie politique pure* (1926 ed.; Paris: Pichon & Durand-Auzias), Leçon 38. The first edition (Lausanne: Carbay, 1874) does not differ materially in substance on the subjects discussed here.

51 Wieser's paradox of value (that marginal utility times quantity may decrease when quantity increases) led to deep confusion (see *Natural Value* [New York: Stechert, 1930], Books I and II). Böhm-Bawerk's greatest polemic is *Grundzüge der Theorie des wirtschaftlichen Güterwerts* ("London School Reprints" [London, 1932]).

tion, or, at any rate, they are furnished to us ready
made by other mental or physical sciences.

. . . The theory here given may be described as
the mechanics of utility and self-interest. Over-
sights may have been committed in tracing out its
details, but in its main features this theory must be
the true one. Its method is as sure and demonstra-
tive as that of kinematics or statics, nay, almost as
self-evident as are the elements of Euclid. . . .[52]

I am inclined to interpret the silence of Menger and Walras on
the existence of utility as indicative of an equally complete acceptance.

Menger glossed over the problem of measurability of utility.
He represented marginal utilities by numbers and employed
an equality of marginal utilities in various uses as the criterion
of the optimum allocation of a good.[53] His word for utility—
Bedeutung—was surely intentionally neutral, but probably it
was chosen for its non-ethical flavor.[54] Walras was equally
vague; he simply assumed the existence of a unit of measure of
intensity of utility and thereafter spoke of utility as an absolute magnitude.[55]

Jevons' attack on the problem of measurability was charac-
teristically frank and confused. He denied that utility was
measurable:

There is no unit of labour, or suffering, or enjoy-
ment.
I have granted that we can hardly form the con-

---

[52] *Op. cit.,* pp. 18 and 21. [53] *Op. cit.,* p. 98 n.

[54] On one occasion he states that his numbers represent only relative utilities and that numbers such as 80 and 40 indicate only that the former
(marginal) utility is twice as large as the latter (*ibid.,* p. 163 n.).

[55] *Éléments,* pp. 74, 102, 153.

ception of a unit of pleasure or pain, so that the numerical expression of quantities of feeling seems to
be out of question.[56]

Yet he seemed also to argue that one cannot be sure that utility
is not measurable but only that it could not presently be
measured.[57] He was somewhat more skeptical of the measurability of utility in the first (1871) than in the second (1879) edition; for example, in the second edition he deleted the following passage:

> I confess that it seems to me difficult even to
> imagine how such estimations [of utility] and sum-
> mations can be made with any approach to accu-
> racy. Greatly though I admire the clear and precise
> notions of Bentham, I know not where his numeri-
> cal data are to be found.[58]

With gallant inconsistency, he proceeded to devise a way to
measure utility. It employed the familiar measuring rod of
money:

> It is from the quantitative effects of the feelings
> that we must estimate their comparative amounts.
>   I never attempt to estimate the whole pleasure
> gained by purchasing a commodity; the theory
> merely expressed that, when a man has purchased
> enough, he would derive equal pleasure from the
> possession of a small quantity more as he would
> from the money price of it.[59]

This position is elaborated ingeniously: We can construct a
demand curve by observation (or possibly experiment), and

---

56 *Op. cit.*, pp. 7 and 12.   57 *Ibid.*, pp. 7–9.

58 *Theory of Political Economy* (1st ed.; London: Macmillan, 1871), p. 12.

59 *Theory* (4th ed.), pp. 11 and 13.

then we can pass to the marginal utility curve by means of the equation,

$$MU_r p_i = MU_i,$$

where MU_r is the marginal utility of income.[60]

> For the first approximation we may assume that the general utility of a person's income is not affected by the changes of price of the commodity. . . .
>
> The method of determining the function of utility explained above will hardly apply, however, to the main elements of expenditure. The price of bread, for instance, cannot be properly brought under the equation in question, because, when the price of bread rises much, the resources of poor persons are strained, money becomes scarcer with them, and $[MU_r]$, the [marginal] utility of money, rises.[61]

This procedure is so similar to Marshall's that we may defer comment until we discuss the latter's more elaborate version.

Unlike Walras and Menger, Jevons considered the question of the interpersonal comparison of utilities. He expressly argued that this was impossible[62] but made several such comparisons, as we shall notice later. Menger avoided the subject and did not engage in such comparisons; and Walras made only incidental interpersonal comparisons.[63]

C. UTILITY MAXIMIZATION AND THE DEMAND CURVE

Menger simply ignored the relationship between utility and demand. He was content to set some demand prices (he worked

---

60 *Ibid.*, pp. 146 ff. (Our notation.)

61 *Ibid.*, pp. 147 and 148.   62 *Ibid.*, p. 14.

63 See *Études d'économie politique appliquée* (Lausanne: Rouge, 1898), pp. 295 ff.; *Études d'économie sociale* (Lausanne: Rouge, 1896), pp. 209 ff.

always with discontinuous schedules) which somehow represented marginal utilities[64] and proceeded to an elementary discussion of pricing under bilateral monopoly (the indeterminacy of which was recognized), duopoly (the complications of which were not recognized—a competitive solution was given), and competition (in which the absence of a theory of production had predictable effects).[65]

Jevons' attempt to construct a bridge between utility and demand was seriously hampered, I suspect, by his inability to translate any but simple thoughts into mathematics. His fundamental equation for the maximization of utility in exchanges was presented as a *fait accompli:*

$$\frac{MU_1}{MU_2} = \frac{p_1}{p_2}.$$

This equation was satisfactory for an individual confronted by fixed prices, but how to apply it to competitive markets?

Jevons devised two concepts to reach the market analysis: the trading body and the law of indifference. A trading body was the large group of buyers or sellers of a commodity in a competitive market.[66] The law of indifference was that there be only one price in a market.[67]

---

64 "The value that a good has for an economizing individual is equal to the significance of that want-satisfaction" (*op. cit.*, p. 120; also chap. v).

65 *Ibid.*, pp. 177 ff., 208–9.

66 The requirement of competition was indirect: one characteristic of a perfect market was that "there must be no conspiracies for absorbing and holding supplies to produce unnatural ratios of exchange" (*Theory* [4th ed.], p. 86). It is evident that the trading body could not properly be used to explain prices, because its composition depended upon prices.

67 Jevons (*ibid.*, p. 95) stated the law of indifference as

$$\frac{dx_2}{dx_1} = \frac{x_2}{x_1}.$$

This notation is ambiguous (see Marshall, *Memorials*, p. 98; F. Y. Edgeworth, *Mathematical Psychics* [London: Paul, 1881], pp. 110 ff.).

He proceeded in the following peculiar manner. Let the equation of exchange be applied to each trading body; for each group of competitive individuals the equation will determine the relationship between the quantity offered and the quantity demanded.[68] Hence we have two equations to determine the two unknowns: the quantities of x_1 and x_2 exchanged. Quite aside from the ambiguous concept of a trading body, this procedure was illicit on his own view that utilities of different individuals are not comparable.[69]

Walras succeeded in establishing the correct relationship between utility and demand. He first derived the equations of maximum satisfaction for an individual: if there are m commodities, and a unit of commodity x_1 is the *numéraire* in terms of which the prices of other commodities are expressed (so $p_1 = 1$), we have $(m - 1)$ equations:[70]

$$MU_1 = \frac{MU_2}{p_2} = \frac{MU_3}{p_3} = \dots .$$

Finally, the budget equation states the equality of values of the initial stocks of commodities $(x^0{}_i)$ and the stocks held after exchange:

$$x_1 + x_2 p_2 + x_3 p_3 + \dots = x_1^0 + x_2^0 p_2 + x_3^0 p_3 + \dots .$$

---

[68] Jevons seems to have introduced the trading bodies to get quickly to market prices, not because of an intuition that bilateral monopoly was indeterminate; at least he overlooked the difficulties in duopoly (*Theory* [4th ed.], p. 117).

[69] "The reader will find, again, that there is never, in any single instance, an attempt made to compare the amount of feeling in one mind with that in another" (*ibid.*, p. 14).

[70] *Éléments*, Leçon 8. Let total utility $= f(x_1) + g(x_2) + h(x_3) + \dots .$ In one of these utility functions, substitute the budget limitation,

$$x_1 + x_2 p_2 + x_3 p_3 + \dots = x_1^0 + x_2^0 p_2 + x_3^0 p_3 + \dots ,$$

where $x^0{}_1, x^0{}_2, x_3, \dots ,$ are the initial stocks. Then maximize total utility to obtain the equations in the text.

We thus have m equations to determine the m quantities of the commodities demanded or supplied by the individual. We may solve the equations for the quantities demanded or supplied as functions of the prices:

$$x_2 = x_2(p_2, p_3, \ldots)$$

$$x_3 = x_3(p_2, p_3, \ldots)$$

$$\ldots \ldots \ldots \ldots \ldots$$

$$x_1 = (x_1^0 + x_2^0 p_2 + x_3^0 p_3 + \ldots) - (x_2 p_2 + x_3 p_3 + \ldots).$$

The $x_1, x_2, x_3, \ldots$, are the quantities held (demanded), and $(x_1^0 - x_1)$, $(x_2^0 - x_2)$, $(x_3^0 - x_3)$, $\ldots$, the quantities supplied.[71]

To determine the market prices, we simply add the demands of all n individuals in the market for each commodity

$$X_2 = \sum^{n} x_2 = \sum^{n} x_2(p_2, p_3, \ldots)$$

$$X_3 = \sum^{n} x_3 = \sum^{n} x_3(p_2, p_3, \ldots)$$

$$\ldots \ldots \ldots \ldots \ldots \ldots \ldots \ldots \ldots \ldots \ldots$$

and equate the quantities demanded to the quantities available (X_i^0):

$$X_2^0 = X_2 :$$

$$X_3^0 = X_3 ,$$

$$\ldots \ldots \ldots$$

There are $(m - 1)$ such equations with which to determine the $(m - 1)$ prices of $x_2, x_3, \ldots$, in terms of x_1. It may appear that we have forgotten the budget equation, but it is not an inde-

---

71 This summary differs in notation and detail, but not in substance, from Walras' exposition (*ibid.*, pp. 123 ff.). The chief difference of detail is that Walras writes the utility as $f(x_i^0 + x_i)$, where I write it as $f(x_i)$, so his x_i can be negative.

pendent relationship because it can be deduced from the other equations. If we multiply the last set of equations by the respective prices of the commodities and add, we obtain

$$p_2(X_2^0 - X_2) + p_3(X_3^0 - X_3) + \ldots = 0 \; .$$

But if we add the individual budget equations we obtain

$$\sum_{}^{n} x_1 - X_1^0 = p_2(X_2^0 - X_2) + p_3(X_3^0 - X_3) + \ldots = 0 \; .$$

Hence if the quantity demanded equals the quantity available in $(m-1)$ markets, the equality must also hold in the mth market. This is equivalent to saying that if we know the amounts of $(m-1)$ commodities that have been exchanged for each other and an mth commodity, and the rates of exchange, we necessarily know the amount of the mth commodity exchanged.

The (Walrasian) demand function is thus the relationship between the quantity of a commodity and all prices, when the individual's (or individuals') money income and tastes (utility functions) are held constant. We shall adhere to this meaning of the demand function or "curve" (the two-dimensional illustration of course requiring that all prices except that of the commodity are held constant), and the relationship between quantity and money income (all prices and tastes being held constant) will be designated as the income curve.

D. The Applications of the Theory

Jevons gave only one application of his utility theory: a demonstration that both parties to an exchange gain satisfaction. The demonstration, as he gave it, was inconsistent with his denial of the possibility of comparing utilities of individuals, for it rested on the marginal utility curves of nations.[72]

---

[72] *Theory* (4th ed.), pp. 142 ff. In the Preface to the second edition he proposed broader applications much closer to those of Menger and Walras but never worked out this position.

Menger was even less specific but surely vastly more persuasive in his applications of the theory: he made it the basis of economic theory. The theory was given many everyday illustrations (mostly hypothetical, to be sure): it explained exchange, the wages of textile workers during the Civil War cotton shortage, the shifts of goods between free and economic, etc. More important, the theory of production became simply an instance of the theory of marginal utility: productive services were distinguished from consumption services only in being goods of higher order. Menger's version had no predictive value, nor did he conjecture any new economic relationships. Indeed at least two of the founders of marginal utility theory— Jevons was the exception—knew much less about economic life than a dozen predecessors such as Smith and Babbage. Yet the theory served to systematize a variety of known facts of everyday observation and seemed to confer an air of generality and structural elegance upon price theory.

Walras also did a good deal of this reorientation of economic theory in terms of utility, whereby the value of productive services was determined by the values of products. But he also attempted a specific and natural application of the theory to demand-curve analysis.

This application was the derivation of the law that price reductions will increase the quantity demanded; price increases will decrease the quantity demanded.[73] Walras treated this as intuitively obvious, but it was a strict implication of his theory. Consider the equations of maximum satisfaction:

$$\frac{MU_1}{p_1} = \frac{MU_2}{p_2} = \frac{MU_3}{p_3} = \dots .$$

Assume p_2 falls by δp_2, and assume that the individual is deprived of his nominal increase in real income, $x_2 \delta p_2$. At the new price, $p_2 - \delta p_2$, the individual obtains a larger marginal utility per dollar from X_2 than from other commodities, hence

---

[73] *Éléments,* pp. 131, 133.

he will substitute X_2 for other commodities. Restore now the increment of income $x_2\delta p_2$, and it will be used to purchase more of every commodity, including x_2. The individual necessarily buys more X_2 at a lower price, and therefore all individuals buy more of X_2 at a lower price: the demand curve for each product must have a negative slope.[74]

A second application of utility theory was made in the theorem on the distribution of stocks: a redistribution of initial stocks of goods among the individuals in a market, such that each individual's holdings have the same market value before and after the redistribution, will not affect prices.[75] It is the amount of income, not its composition in terms of goods, that influences consumer behavior. The most interesting point with respect to this obvious theorem is that Walras stopped here on the threshold of the analysis of the effects of income upon consumption. One may conjecture that his penchant for analyzing what are essentially barter problems in his theory of exchange played a large role in this failure to analyze income effects.[76]

The theory of utility also led Walras to his theory of multiple equilibria.[77] This theory deals with the exchange of one

---

[74] The validity of this argument depends on the assumption that the marginal utility of a commodity is a (diminishing) function only of the quantity of that commodity (see Sec. IV).

[75] *Ibid.*, pp. 145–49.

[76] Perhaps mention should also be made of the applications of utility theory to labor. Jevons' theory of disutility was labored and at times confused (see my *Production and Distribution Theories* [New York: Macmillan, 1941], chap. ii). Walras' treatment was more elegant—he introduced the marginal utility of leisure in complete symmetry to the theory of consumption—but not much more instructive (*Éléments*, p. 209). Menger denied that labor was usually painful (*op. cit.*, p. 149 n.).

[77] Marshall's theory of multiple equilibria is independent of utility analysis; it refers only to the long run, whereas Walras' theory is strictly short run. See Marshall, *Pure Theory of Domestic Values* ("London School Reprints" [London, 1930]).

commodity for another in a competitive market, when both commodities have utility to the individual.[78] The possessors of X_1 have a fixed stock—how much will they offer at various prices of X_1 (in terms of X_2)? When p_1 is zero (no X_2 is given in exchange for a unit of X_1), they will naturally supply no X_1; the supply curve begins at (or above) the origin. At higher p_1, they will offer more X_1 to obtain more X_2, but beyond a certain price, L, further increases in the price of X_1 will lead them to

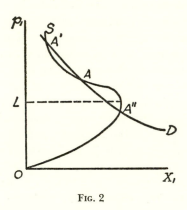

FIG. 2

reduce the quantity of X_1 offered because they become relatively sated with X_2. Walras illustrates this with Figure 2, where D is the demand curve and S the supply curve. A' and A'' are points of stable equilibrium, because at higher prices the quantity supplied exceeds the quantity demanded and at lower prices the quantity demanded exceeds the quantity supplied. Point A, however, is an unstable equilibrium because at higher prices the quantity demanded exceeds the quantity supplied so the price rises even more, and conversely at lower prices. We shall not follow the history of multiple equilibria, in which economists have usually taken an apprehensive pride.

---

[78] *Éléments*, pp. 68–70; Wicksell restates the theory, *Lectures on Political Economy* (London: Macmillan, 1934), I, 55 ff.

In the area of welfare economics, Walras' most important application was the theorem on maximum satisfaction:

> Production in a market governed by free competition is an operation by which the [productive] services may be combined in products of appropriate kind and quantity to give the greatest possible satisfaction of needs within the limits of the double condition that each service and each product have only one price in the market, at which supply and demand are equal, and that the prices of the products are equal to their costs of production.[79]

This theorem, which is not true unless qualified in several respects, gave rise to an extensive literature which lies outside our scope.[80]

IV. THE FORM OF THE UTILITY FUNCTION

The three founders of the utility theory treated the utility of a commodity as a function only of the quantity of the commodity. If x_1, x_2, x_3, . . . , are the commodities, the individual's

---

[79] *Éléments*, p. 231; Jevons also stated the theorem (*Theory* [4th ed.], p. 141).

[80] Among the important writings during our period are: A. Marshall, *Principles of Economics* (1st ed.; London: Macmillan, 1890), Book V, chap. vii; V. Pareto, "Il Massimo di utilità dato dalla libera concorrenza," *Giornale degli economisti*, Series 2, No. 9 (July, 1894), pp. 48–66; E. Barone, "The Ministry of Production in the Collectivist State," reprinted in F. A. Hayek, *Collectivist Economic Planning* (London: Routledge, 1938); K. Wicksell, *Lectures on Political Economy* (London: Macmillan, 1934), I, 72 ff.; L. Bortkewitch, "Die Grenznutzentheorie als Grundlage einer ultra-liberalen Wirtschaftspolitik," *Jahrbuch für Gesetzgebung, Verwaltung und Volkswirtschaft*, XXII (1898), 1177–1216; and A. C. Pigou, *Wealth and Welfare* (London: Macmillan, 1912).

total utility was written (explicitly by Jevons and Walras, implicitly by Menger), as

$$f(x_1) + g(x_2) + h(x_3) + \dots .$$

They further assumed that each commodity yielded diminishing marginal utility. This form of utility function has the implication that the demand curve for each commodity has a negative slope, as I have already remarked. It has also the implication that an increase in income will lead to increased purchases of every commodity. This is easily shown with the fundamental equations,

$$MU_r = \frac{MU_1}{p_1} = \frac{MU_2}{p_2} = \frac{MU_3}{p_3} = \dots .$$

If income increases, the marginal utility of every commodity (and of income) must decrease, but the marginal utility of a commodity can be reduced only by increasing its quantity. This implication was not noticed.

Edgeworth destroyed this pleasant simplicity and specificity when he wrote the total utility function as $\varphi\ (x_1, x_2, x_3, \dots .)$. He appears to have made this change partly because it was mathematically more general, partly because it was congruent with introspection.[81] The change had important implications for the measurability of utility that I shall discuss in Section V.

With the additive utility function, diminishing marginal utility was a sufficient condition for convexity of the indifference curves;[82] with the generalized utility function, diminishing marginal utility was neither necessary nor sufficient for convex

---

[81] *Mathematical Psychics,* pp. 20, 34, 104, 108.

[82] Diminishing marginal utility for each commodity was not necessary, however: the indifference curves could be convex to the origin if every commodity except one yielded diminishing marginal utility, and the marginal utility of this exception commodity did not increase too rapidly. This exceptional case was first analyzed by Slutsky (see Sec. VII).

indifference curves.[83] Nevertheless, Edgeworth unnecessarily continued to assume diminishing marginal utility, but he also postulated the convexity of the indifference curves.[84]

Even with convexity, the generalized utility function no longer has the corollary that all income curves have positive slopes (or, therefore, that all demand curves have negative slopes). After a price reduction, δp_2, we may again segregate the effect of a change in relative prices by temporarily reducing the individual's income by $x_2 \delta p_2$. When we restore this increment of real income, we cannot be sure that each commodity will be consumed in larger quantity. Suppose an increase in X_1 reduces the marginal utility of X_2. Then when a portion of the increment of real income $x_2 \delta p_2$ is spent on X_1, MU_2 may di-

---

[83] In the two-commodity case

$$\frac{d x_2}{d x_1} = -\frac{\varphi_1}{\varphi_2}$$

is the slope of an indifference curve, and the condition for convexity is

$$\frac{d^2 x_2}{d x_1^2} = -\frac{\varphi_2^2 \varphi_{11} - 2 \varphi_1 \varphi_2 \varphi_{12} + \varphi_1^2 \varphi_{22}}{\varphi_2^3} > 0 \, ,$$

where the subscripts to φ denote partial differentiation with respect to the indicated variables. It is clear that diminishing marginal utility (φ_{11} and φ_{22} negative) is not necessary for convexity, since φ_{12} can be positive and large, and it is not sufficient, since φ_{12} can be negative and large. In the additive case ($\varphi_{12} = 0$), at most one marginal utility can be increasing, as was pointed out in the previous footnote.

[84] *Mathematical Psychics*, p. 36. He wrote the utility function as $\varphi(x_1, -x_2)$, in my notation, for reasons which will be pointed out below. He postulated that $\varphi_{12} < 0$, where $-X_2$ is work done by the person and X_1 is remuneration received. This is equivalent to assuming that an increase in remuneration increases the marginal utility of leisure, and would be represented by $\varphi_{12} > 0$ if we write the function as $\varphi(x_1, x_2)$, as is now customary. With diminishing marginal utility this condition leads to convexity (see previous note).

minish so much that the amount of X_2 must be reduced below its original quantity to fulfil the maximum satisfaction conditions.[85]

The only further generalization of the utility function (aside from questions of measurability) was the inclusion of the quantities consumed by other people in the utility function of the individual. Thus one's pleasure from diamonds is reduced if many other people have them (or if none do!), and one's pleasure from a given income is reduced if others' incomes rise. This line of thought is very old,[86] but it was first introduced

---

[85] The conditions for maximum satisfaction are

$$\frac{\varphi_1}{\varphi_2} = \frac{p_1}{p_2},$$

$$x_1 p_1 + x_2 p_2 = R \, .$$

Differentiate these equations with respect to R (holding prices constant) and solve to obtain

$$\frac{\partial x_2}{\partial R} = \frac{p_2 \varphi_{11} - p_1 \varphi_{12}}{p_2^2 \varphi_{11} - 2 p_1 p_2 \varphi_{12} + p_1^2 \varphi_{22}} \, .$$

The denominator of the right side is negative if the indifference curves are convex to the origin. The numerator, however, can be positive with $\varphi_{12} < 0$, so the whole expression may be negative (X_2 may be "inferior"). With the additive function, $\varphi_{12} = 0$ (and of course they assumed $\varphi_{ii} < 0$), so the expression must be positive (X_2 [and X_1] must be "normal"). Similarly, differentiate the equations with respect to p_2 holding p_1 and R constant) and solve to obtain

$$\frac{\partial x_2}{\partial p_2} = \frac{p_1 \varphi_1 + x_2 p_1 \varphi_{12} - x_2 p_2 \varphi_{11}}{p_2^2 \varphi_{11} - 2 p_1 p_2 \varphi_{12} + p_1^2 \varphi_{22}} \, .$$

Again the denominator is negative, and the numerator may be negative if φ_{12} is negative, so the whole expression may be positive. With the additive utility function and diminishing marginal utility, the expression must be negative.

[86] E.g., A. Smith, *Theory of Moral Sentiments* (Boston: Wells & Lilly, 1817), Part III, chap. iii; Part IV, chap. i; N. F. Canard, *Principes d'économie politique* (Paris: Buisson, 1801), chap. v; Senior, *op. cit.*, p. 12.

explicitly into utility analysis in 1892. Fisher casually suggested it:

> Again we could treat [utility] as a function of the quantities of each commodity produced or consumed by *all persons* in the market. This becomes important when we consider a man in relation to the members of his family or consider articles of fashion as diamonds, also when we account for that (never thoroughly studied) interdependence, the division of labor.[87]

Henry Cunynghame made the same suggestion more emphatically in the same year:

> Almost the whole value of strawberries in March, to those who like this tasteless mode of ostentation, is the fact that others cannot get them. As my landlady once remarked, "Surely, sir, you would not like anything so common and cheap as a fresh herring?" The demand for diamonds, rubies, and sapphires is another example of this.[88]

Pigou took up this argument, used it to show that consumer surpluses of various individuals cannot be added, but decided that these interrelationships of individuals' utilities were stable (and hence did not vitiate the consumer surplus apparatus)

---

[87] *Mathematical Investigations in the Theory of Value and Prices* (New Haven: Yale University Press, 1937—reprint of 1892 ed.), p. 102. Fisher independently reached the generalized utility function of Edgeworth (*ibid.*, Preface).

[88] "Some Improvements in Simple Geometrical Methods of Treating Exchange Value, Monopoly, and Rent," *Economic Journal,* II (1892), 37.

when the price changes were small.[89] It was only proper that Marshall's leading pupil should postulate the constancy of the marginal utility of prestige.

Pigou's article elicited the first statistical investigation designed to test a utility theory (and apparently the only such investigation during the period). Edgeworth, a Fellow of All Souls, collected statistics from "a certain Oxford College" to determine "whether the size of the party has any influence upon the depth of the potations"—that is, upon the per capita consumption of wine. The data were presented in relative form lest they "should excite the envy of some and the contempt of others"; the conclusion was that the effect of the size of party was inappreciable.[90]

A few subsequent attempts have been made to revive this extension of the utility function to include the effect on one person's utility of other people's consumption, but the main tradition has ignored the extension. This neglect seems to have stemmed partly from a belief in the unimportance of the effect and partly from the obstacles it would put in the way of drawing specific inferences from utility analysis.

There remain three subordinate topics that may conveniently be discussed here. They are (*a*) the graphical exposition of the theory of the generalized utility function; (*b*) the attitude of contemporary economists toward Edgeworth's generalization; and (*c*) the Bernoulli hypothesis on the shape of the utility function.

---

[89] "Some Remarks on Utility," *Economic Journal,* XIII (1903), 60 ff. He wrote the utility function of the individual as

$$U = \phi\,[\,x,\ y,\ z, w,\ K\,(\,a\,b\,)\,]\,,$$

where x, y, z, and w were quantities consumed by the individual, a_i was the quantity of x possessed by some other individual i, whose social distance was b_i, and K was a symbol "akin to, though not identical with, the ordinary Σ" (*ibid.*, p. 61).

[90] *Papers Relating to Political Economy* (London: Macmillan, 1925), II, 323–24 n.

A. INDIFFERENCE CURVES

With the introduction of the interrelationship of utilities of commodities, it was no longer possible to portray total utility graphically in two dimensions. Edgeworth devised indifference curves, or contour lines, to permit of a graphical analysis of utility in this case. In itself this was merely an expositional advance, but it merits summarization because of its great popularity in modern times and because it later invited attention to questions relating to the measurability of utility.

We restrict ourselves to the case of two commodities, as Edgeworth and almost everyone since has done in graphical analysis.[91] We define the indifference curve as the combinations of X_1 and X_2 yielding equal satisfaction, i.e., $\varphi(x_1,x_2) =$ constant. Edgeworth chose an asymmetrical graphical illustration of these curves that had a definite advantage for his purpose of analyzing bilateral monopoly. He let the abscissa represent the quantity of X_1 obtained by the individual, and the ordinate represent the quantity of X_2 given up.

It is evident that such indifference curves have a positive slope (if both commodities are desirable), for the individual will require more X_1 to offset (in utility) the loss of more X_2. In fact, the slope of the indifference curve with respect to the X_1 axis will be

$$\frac{dx_2}{dx_1} = \frac{MU_1}{MU_2}. \quad {}^{92}$$

In addition, Edgeworth postulated that the indifference curves are concave to the X_1 axis.

---

91 The three commodity indifference surfaces are of course the limit of literal graphical exposition, and even they have been deemed unappetizingly complex.

92 For $dx_1 MU_1$ will be the gain of utility from an increment dx_1, and $dx_2 MU_2$ will be the loss of utility from a decrement dx_2, and these must be equal if the movement is along an indifference curve.

Edgeworth's pioneer demonstration of the indeterminacy of bilateral monopoly will illustrate the advantage of this formulation.[93] A trader possessing X_2 but no X_1 would be at the origin; his indifference curves are those labeled I in Figure 3. The second trader, who possesses X_1 but no X_2, will have the corresponding indifference curves (II), for he will be giving up X_1 and acquiring X_2 in exchange. The points where the two sets of indifference curves are tangent form a curve, CC, which

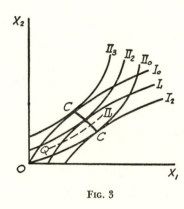

Fig. 3

Edgeworth christened the contract curve. The ends of the contract curve are determined by the condition that no trader be worse off after trading than before, i.e., by the indifference curves, I_0 and II_0. The final contract between the traders must take place on this contract curve, because if it occurred elsewhere, it would be to the gain of one party, and not to the loss of the other, to move to the curve. Thus point Q was not a tenable point of final contract because individual II can move from II_1 to the higher indifference curve II_2, while I remains on the same indifference curve, I_1. Any point on the contract curve is a position of possible equilibrium, and the precise position reached will be governed by "higgling dodges and de-

93 *Mathematical Psychics,* pp. 20 ff.

signing obstinacy, and other incalculable and often disreputable accidents."[94]

Although this mode of exposition is convenient in the analysis of trade in two commodities between two individuals, it has no special advantage in the competitive case, and asymmetrical axes are awkward in algebraic analysis. Fisher introduced the now conventional graphical statement, in which the amounts held (or obtained) of the commodities appear on all axes.[95]

B. Contemporary Practice

Despite the intuitive appeal of Edgeworth's generalized utility function, economists adhered to the additive utility function with considerable tenacity. In the nonmathematical writings, such as those of Böhm-Bawerk, Wieser, and J. B. Clark, the additive function was used almost exclusively. Barone defended it as an approximation.[96] Wicksell used it exclusively in his *Über Wert* (1894), although conceding the greater realism of the generalized function,[97] and found some place for it in his later *Lectures*.[98] Wicksteed used only the additive function in his *Alphabet* (1888)[99] and also in the elementary exposition of the theory in his *Common Sense* (1910) but not in the "advanced" statement.[100] Finally, Marshall and Pareto were so influential as to require more extended discussion.

---

94 *Ibid.*, p. 46.　　　95 *Op. cit.*, Part II.

96 *Le Opere economiche* (Bologna: Zanichelli, 1936), I, esp. pp. 22–23.

97 *Über Wert, Kapital und Rente* (Jena: Fischer, 1894), esp. p. 43.

98 *Lectures on Political Economy*, I, 46–47, 55 ff.; however, the generalized function is preferred (*ibid.*, pp. 41–42, 48–49, 79 ff.).

99 *Alphabet of Economic Science* (London: Macmillan, 1888).

100 *Common Sense of Political Economy* (London: Routledge, 1934), Vol. I, chap. ii; Vol. II, chap. ii; the generalized function is used in Vol. II, chap. iii, esp. p. 479.

Marshall also started with the Jevons-Walras assumption, to which he had probably arrived independently. This assumption was not explicit in the first edition of the *Principles* (1890), but one can cite evidence of its presence.

First, in his mathematical characterization of the utility function Marshall ignores any interdependence of utilities.[101] Second, he asserts the law of negatively sloping demand curves in all generality: "There is then one law and only one law which is common to all demand schedules, viz. that the greater the amount to be sold the smaller will be the price at which it will find purchasers."[102] This is a corollary of diminishing marginal utility only if the utility function is additive. Third, he was prepared to measure the utility of all commodities as the sum of the individual utilities: "We may regard the aggregate of the money measures of the total utility of wealth as a fair measure of that part of happiness which is dependent on wealth."[103]

In the second edition (1891) the assumption became reasonably explicit:

> Prof. Edgeworth's plan of representing U and V as general functions of x and y has great attractions to the mathematician; but it seems less adapted to express the everyday facts of economic life than that of regarding, as Jevons did, the marginal utilities of apples as functions of x simply.[104]

---

101 *Principles of Economics* (London: Macmillan, 1890), Mathematical Notes II, III, VII, [I, II, VI]. References in brackets will be used for corresponding passages in the eighth edition.

102 *Ibid.*, pp. 159–60 [99].

103 *Ibid.*, pp. 179–80, also Mathematical Note VII. His Mathematical Note III [II] also implies an additive function if his p, "the price which [a person] is just willing to pay for an amount [x] of the commodity . . ." is interpreted as our $x_1 p_1$ and the price to the person is treated as constant. See Sec. VII.

104 *Loc. cit.*, p. 756 [845]. See also the deduction of diminishing marginal utility from negatively sloping demand curves (*ibid.*, p. 159 [101 n.]).

The facts both of everyday life and of contemporary theory soon led Marshall to make serious qualifications of his theory but never to qualify this statement.

Even in the first edition Marshall had inconsistently recognized the existence of "rival" products, which were defined as products able to satisfy the same desires.[105] Fisher's discussion of competing and completing goods seems to have been the stimulus to Marshall to give more weight to interrelationships of utilities in the third edition of the *Principles* (1895).[106] Once persuaded, Marshall modified his theory on two points. The first was that he slightly modified his assertion of the universality of negatively sloping demand curves and in fact introduced the Giffen paradox as an exception.[107] The second alteration was in his treatment of consumers' surplus: "When the total utilities of two commodities which contribute to the same purpose are calculated on this plan, we cannot say that the total utility of the two together is equal to the sum of the total utilities of each separately."[108] No important changes were made thereafter.

These alterations were only patchwork repairs; Marshall did not rework his theory of utility. He retained to the last a theory constructed on the assumption of an additive utility function.

Pareto also conceded the validity of the Edgeworth generali-

---

[105] See Sec. VI.

[106] Reference is there made to Fisher's "brilliant" book, precisely on this point (*Principles* [3d ed.; London: Macmillan, 1895], p. 460 n. [390 n.]). For Fisher's discussion see Sec. VI below.

[107] *Loc. cit.*, p. 208 [132]. See my "Notes on the History of the Giffen Paradox," *Journal of Political Economy,* LV (1947), 152–56.

[108] He added the less than candid footnote: "Some ambiguous phrases in earlier editions appear to have suggested to some readers the opposite opinion" (*loc. cit.*, p. 207 and n. [131 and n.]).

zation but continued to use chiefly the additive function in his early work.[109] Indeed, he offered the remarkable argument:

> One sees now that instead of being able to use the indicated properties of the final degree of utility to demonstrate what laws demand and supply must obey, it is necessary to follow the opposite path, and use the knowledge of such laws one may obtain from experience to derive the properties of the final degree of utility. One cannot rigorously demonstrate the law of demand, but rather, from the directly observable fact that demand diminishes with the increase of price we deduce the consequence that the final degrees of utility may each be considered—as far as this phenomenon is concerned—as approximately dependent only on the quantity of the commodity to which it is related.[110]

In the *Manuel,* however, he showed that the additive utility function leads to conclusions which are contradicted by experience,[111] but defended it as an approximation which was permissible for large categories of expenditure and for small changes in the quantities of substitutes or complements.[112] There is no reason to believe that this is true.

C. THE BERNOULLI HYPOTHESIS

The precise shape of the utility function received little attention in the main tradition of utility theory. Occasionally it

---

109 "Considerazioni sui principii fondamentali dell'economia politica pura," *Giornale degli economisti,* Series 2, Vol. V (August, 1892); *Cours d'économie politique* (Lausanne: Rouge, 1897), II, 332 ff.

110 "Considerazioni . . . ," *op. cit.,* VII (1893), 307.

111 Below, Sec. VII.

112 *Manuel d'économie politique* (2d ed.; Paris: Giard, 1927), pp. 253 ff., 274.

was stated that the marginal utility of a necessity falls rapidly as its quantity increases and the like; and there were some mystical references to the infinite utility of subsistence. These were *ad hoc* remarks, however, and were not explicitly developed parts of the formal theory. Only one hypothesis about the marginal utility function ever achieved prominence: it was the Bernoulli hypothesis, which ultimately merged with the Weber-Fechner law, and to this literature we now turn.

In 1713 Nicholas Bernoulli proposed to a French mathematician, Montmort, five problems in probability theory,[113] one of which was equivalent to the following:

> Peter tosses a coin in the air repeatedly until it falls heads up. If this occurs on the first throw, he pays Paul \$1.00; if this occurs first on the second throw, he pays Paul \$2.00; on the third throw, \$4.00; on the fourth throw, \$8.00; and on the nth throw, $\$2.00^{n-1}$. What is the maximum amount Paul should pay for this game?

Montmort replied, perhaps too easily, "Les deux derniers de vos cinq. Problêmes n'ont aucune difficulté,"[114] for this was to become known as the St. Petersburg paradox.

Twenty-five years later Daniel Bernoulli introduced the paradox to fame.[115] Its paradoxical nature is easily explained: The probability of a head on the first throw is ½, so the expected winning from the first throw is ½ times \$1.00, or \$0.50. The probability of a first head on the second throw is ¼ (½ of

---

113 P. R. de Montmort, *Essay d'analyse sur les jeux de hazard* (2d ed.; Paris: Quillau, 1713), p. 402.

114 *Ibid.*, p. 407.

115 In *Specimen theoriae novae de mensura sortis;* references are to the German translation, *Versuch einer neuen Theorie der Wertbestimmung von Glücksfällen* (Leipzig: Duncker & Humblot, 1896).

tails on the first throw times $\frac{1}{2}$ of heads on the second), so the expected winning is $\frac{1}{4}$ times \$2.00, or \$0.50. The probability of a first head on the nth throw is $(\frac{1}{2})^n$, so the expected winnings are $(\frac{1}{2})^n$ times \$2.00^{n-1}, or \$0.50. Since these probabilities are exclusive, we add them to obtain the expected winnings from the game, which are \$0.50 times the infinite possible number of throws. Thus the expected winnings of Paul are infinity—an excessive price for Paul to pay for the game, as even the mathematicians saw.

Bernoulli's solution was to take into account the diminishing marginal utility of money. In the later words of Laplace, he distinguished the mathematical from the moral expectation of a chance event upon which a sum of money depended: the moral expectation was defined as the sum of the products of the various advantages accruing from various sums of money times their respective probabilities.[116] To Bernoulli, "it appears in the highest degree probable" that each equal increment of gain yields an advantage which is inversely proportional to the individual's wealth,[117] i.e.,

$$dU = k \frac{dx}{x},$$

where dU is the increment of utility resulting from an increment dx of wealth and k is a constant. It follows that total utility is a logarithmic function of wealth,

$$U = k \log \frac{x}{c},$$

where c is the amount of wealth necessary for existence.[118]

---

116 *Ibid.*, p. 27.

117 *Ibid.*, pp. 27–28. Marshall properly remarked on the difficulties raised by the use of wealth instead of income (*Principles* [8th ed.], p. 842).

118 On integrating the differential expression, we obtain

$$U = k \log x + \text{constant},$$

and the constant is determined by the condition that, when wealth is at the subsistence level c, $U = 0$.

Bernoulli applied this formula to gambling, obtaining the now traditional result that mathematically fair bets are disadvantageous to both parties because the utility of the sum that may be gained is less than the utility of the sum that may be lost.[119] By a converse application, he calculated the maximum amount one should pay for insurance of specified risks.[120] Finally, he solved the paradox: a person with $1,000 should pay $6; etc.[121]

We should notice one further point in this beautiful memoir:

> If [the initial wealth] appears to be infinitely large relative to the greatest possible gain, the arc [of the total utility curve from initial wealth to initial wealth plus the gain] may be considered an infinitely short straight line, and in this case the usual rule [for calculating mathematical expectations] is again applicable. This case is closely approximated in all games in which relatively small sums are at stake.[122]

---

[119] *Op. cit.*, pp. 39–40.

[120] *Ibid.*, pp. 42–44.

[121] The moral expectation of the individual with initial wealth a is

$$U = \tfrac{1}{2}k \log \frac{a+1}{c} + 1k \log \frac{a+2}{c} + \tfrac{1}{8}k \log \frac{a+4}{c} + \ldots$$

$$= k \log \left(\frac{a+1}{c}\right)^{1/2} \left(\frac{a+2}{c}\right)^{1/4} \left(\frac{a+4}{c}\right)^{1/8} \ldots$$

$$= k \log \frac{v}{c},$$

where v is the sum of money whose utility equals the moral expectation. Hence

$$v = (a+1)^{1/2}(a+2)^{1/4}(a+4)^{1/8} \ldots$$

and $(v - a)$ is the sum of money whose utility equals the expected gain of utility from playing the game.

[122] *Op. cit.*, p. 33.

Thus Bernoulli suggested the assumption of a constant marginal utility of wealth for small variations of wealth.

We cannot follow the immense literature of the paradox in mathematics, but a few views may be noticed.[123] Some mathematicians—the foremost was Laplace[124]—accepted Bernoulli's solution. Some, like Poisson, solved the problem by taking into account Peter's inability to pay if he had a sufficiently long run of tails, so Paul should pay an amount for the game determined by Peter's fortune.[125] Perhaps the most amusing solution was one by Buffon, which was based on the "lemma" that all probabilities smaller than .0001 are equal to zero (because this was the probability of dying during the day for a man of fifty-six, which was commonly treated as negligible).[126] Cournot, here as in demand theory, refused to look at utility and resorted to the market evaluation of the game.[127]

Perhaps the most surprising characteristic of this literature to the economist is the mathematicians' chief requisite of a solution: that a finite value be found for the value of the game. This is the only merit one can attach to the "limited-

---

[123] For the eighteenth century see I. Todhunter, *A History of the Mathematical Theory of Probability* (London: Macmillan, 1865).

[124] *Théorie analytique des probabilités* (3d ed.; Paris: Gauthier-Villars, 1886), pp. xix–xx, chap. x.

[125] S. D. Poisson, *Recherches sur la probabilité des jugements* (Paris: Bachelier, 1837), pp. 74–76. Thus if $F = 2^k$ is Peter's fortune, Paul's expected winnings are

$$\tfrac{1}{2} \cdot 1 + \tfrac{1}{4} \cdot 2 + \ldots + \frac{1}{2^k} \cdot 2^{k-1} + 2^k \left(\frac{1}{2^{k+1}} + \frac{1}{2^{k+2}} + \ldots \right) = \frac{k}{2} + 1 \,.$$

[126] Todhunter, *op. cit.* At the present time the critical probability is .00005.

[127] *Exposition de la théorie des chances* (Paris: L. Hachette, 1843), pp. 108–9, 334. He reformulated the problem: the state (chosen to avoid Poisson's solution) issues tickets: No. 1 pays $1.00 if the first throw is heads; No. 2 pays $2.00 if the first heads comes on the second throw; etc. He argued that no one would buy the high-numbered tickets.

fortune" solution of Poisson and others, and even its spurious plausibility depends upon the particular formulation of the problem.[128] Bernoulli was right in seeking the explanation in utility (or, alternatively, as Cournot did, in market appraisals), and he was wrong only in making a special assumption with respect to the shape of the utility curve for which there was no evidence and which he submitted to no tests.[129]

In 1860 this line of thought was joined by the independent series of researches that culminated in the Weber-Fechner law. E. H. Weber had proposed the hypothesis: the just noticeable increment to any stimulus is proportional to the stimulus (R — *Reiz*), or

$$\frac{dR}{R} = k .$$

Fechner made this constant of just noticeable differences the unit of sensation (S), to obtain

$$dS = C \frac{dR}{R} ,$$

or, integrating, $S = C \log R/R_0$, where R_0 is the threshold of sensation. Fechner performed a vast number of experiments on weight, temperature, tonal, and other types of discriminations which the formula fitted fairly well, and in the process he de-

---

128 J. Bertrand was surely right in this respect: "If one plays with centimes instead of francs, with grains of sand instead of centimes, with molecules of hydrogen instead of grains of sand, the fear of insolvency may be reduced without limit" (*Calcul des probabilités* [Paris: Gauthier-Villars, 1889], p. 64). Alternatively, one may alter the game, increasing the probability of longer runs and decreasing the rewards correspondingly.

129 The arbitrariness is illustrated by the fact that the Genevese mathematician, Cramer, had suggested that the utility of income be taken as proportional to the square root of income, in a letter to Nicholas Bernoulli, from which Daniel Bernoulli quotes an extract (*op. cit.*, pp. 55 ff.). It should be noted that, unless the utility of income has an upper bound, it is possible to devise some variant of the St. Petersburg paradox which will have an infinite moral expectation.

vised several methods of measurement (such as the constant method, in which Weber's *k* is determined by the proportion of [e.g.] "greater" to total responses in weight comparisons).[130] This was construed—by Fechner also—as proof of Bernoulli's hypothesis, with stimulus identified with income, sensation with pleasure.[131]

We need not follow the detailed evolution of psychologists' treatment of the Fechner law. For decades it was a lively topic of discussion,[132] but for a generation or more it has been declining in importance. Many exceptions have been found to Fechner's formula.[133] The concept of sensation has been severely restricted in meaning, and the form of response of a subject was found to affect his sensitivity.[134] At present Fechner's *Elemente* is important chiefly for the basic methods of measurement he invented and improved.

Many economists in this later period noticed the Bernoulli or Weber-Fechner "laws." The majority simply referred to the hypothesis, favorably or otherwise, and made no real use of

---

[130] *Elemente der Psychophysik* (reprint; 2 vols.; Leipzig: Breitkopf & Härtel, 1889). See also E. G. Boring, *A History of Experimental Psychology* (New York: Appleton-Century, 1929), chap. xiii.

[131] *Psychophysik,* I, 236 ff.

[132] For a summary see E. B. Titchener, *Experimental Psychology* (New York: Macmillan, 1905), II, xiii–clxx.

[133] J. P. Guilford, *Psychometric Methods* (New York: McGraw-Hill Book Co., 1936), chaps. iv and v.

[134] H. M. Johnson, "Did Fechner Measure 'Introspectional' Sensations?" *Psychological Review,* XXXVI (1929), 257–84. Johnson reports a subject whose sensitivity was 18 per cent greater when distinguishing weights by voice than when distinguishing them by pushing the heavier weight toward the experimenter. It would be interesting to know the effect on sensitivity of pushing money.

the theory. In this group we may list Edgeworth,[135] Pareto,[136] and Wicksell,[137] as well as many lesser figures.[138]

Marshall took the Bernoulli hypothesis much more seriously than did any other leading economist. In 1890 he was prepared to apply it directly to whole income classes:

> If however it should appear that the class affected [by a particular event] in the one case is on the average, say, ten times as rich as in the other, then we shall probably not be far wrong in supposing that the increment of happiness measured by a given sum of money in the one case is, so far at least as its direct results go, about one-tenth as great as in the other.[139]

Whatever the reason, this use of the hypothesis disappeared in the second edition, but lesser evidences of Marshall's affection for the Bernoulli theory persisted.[140]

A group of writers on tax justice, mostly Dutch, made con-

---

135 *Mathematical Psychics*, pp. 7, 62; *Papers*, I, 210; II, 107 ff. Edgeworth flirted with the theory at first but later rejected it as arbitrary and accepted the equally arbitrary view that the marginal utility of income falls faster than the Bernoulli hypothesis suggests.

136 "Considerazioni . . . ," *Giornale degli economisti*, Series 2, VI (1893), 1–8. Pareto also deemed it arbitrary and pointed out that strictly it pertained to consumption, not to possessions.

137 "Zur Verteidigung der Grenznutzenlehre," *Zeitschrift für die gesamte Staatswissenschaft*, LVI (1900), 580. Wicksell thought the Weber-Fechner work might eventually permit interpersonal comparisons of utility.

138 E.g., O. Effertz, *Les Antagonismes économiques* (Paris: Giard & Bière, 1906), pp. 30–32; he encountered the theory first at a beer party where a professor of physiology made a "humorous and detailed application to the consumption of beer" (F. A. Lange, *Die Arbeiterfrage* [5th ed.; Winterthur: Ziegler, 1894], pp. 113 ff., 143 ff.; F. A. Fetter, *Economic Principles* [New York: Century, 1915], pp. 40–41).

139 *Principles* (1st ed., 1890), pp. 152–53; also p. 180.

140 *Principles* (8th ed., 1920), pp. 135, 717, 842–43.

siderable use of the theory in discussions of the ideal rate of income-tax progression.[141] The enthusiasm for the Bernoulli hypothesis diminished when it was discovered that it led to proportional taxation under the equal sacrifice doctrine (each taxpayer to sacrifice an equal amount of utility).[142] Although the doctrine of proportional sacrifice (each taxpayer to sacrifice an equal proportion of his utility) leads to progressive taxation with the Bernoulli utility function,[143] the minimum sacrifice doctrine (which insured progression if the marginal utility of income diminished) soon triumphed.

Two Italian writers used the logarithmic law in quantitative work: Gini, in the analysis of demand;[144] del Vecchio, in the

---

[141] For references and summaries see E. Sax, "Die Progressivsteuer," *Zeitschrift für Volkswirtschaft, Sozialpolitik und Verwaltung*, I (1892), 43 ff.

[142] If $U = k \log R$, a tax of T involves a sacrifice of

$$k \log \frac{R}{R-T}.$$

On the equal sacrifice doctrine,

$$k \log \frac{R}{R-T} = \text{constant} = c,$$

$$\frac{R}{R-T} = e^{c/k},$$

so

$$\frac{T}{R} = e^{-c/k}(e^{c/k} - 1) = \text{constant}.$$

[143] Using the notation of the previous footnote, the doctrine requires that

$$\frac{k \log \dfrac{R}{R-T}}{k \log R} = \text{constant} = m$$

or

$$\frac{R}{R-T} = R^m,$$

whence

$$\frac{T}{R} = 1 - R^{-m}.$$

[144] "Prezzi e consumi," *Giornale degli economisti*, Series 3, XL (1910), 99–114, 235–49.

analysis of budgetary data.[145] These studies belong in the history of demand theory, however; and we shall not discuss them here.

Max Weber's famous essay on the Weber-Fechner law is commonly, and perhaps properly, interpreted as a final demonstration that economists can ignore this law. Weber had three main points. First, the law does not hold in all cases ("Tiffany-Vasen, Klosettpapier, Schlackwurst, Klassiker-Ausgaben, Prostituierten . . ."). Second, the law refers to psychical reactions to external stimuli, whereas economics deals with observable behavior in response to subjective needs. Third, economics can get along with the empirical fact that man has limited means to satisfy competing ends and can allocate these means rationally to maximize the fulfilment of the ends.[146] This pungently written essay is hardly conclusive, however, on whether economists should adopt the law. This turns on whether it yields fruitful hypotheses concerning economic behavior. Since it does not,[147] it should not be used.

V. THE MEASURABILITY OF UTILITY

The first careful examination of the measurability of the utility function and its relevance to demand theory was made by Fisher.[148] He solved the measurability problem quite satis-

---

145 "Relazioni fra entrata e consumo," *Giornale degli economisti*, Series 3, XLIV (1912), 111–42, 228–54, 389–439.

146 "Die Grenznutzlehre und das 'psychophysisches Grundgesetz' " (1908), reprinted in *Gesammelte Aufsätze zur Wissenschaftslehre* (Tübingen: Mohr, 1922). The fundamental argument is in the third paragraph (pp. 361–68).

147 As applied to commodities, it puts unrealistic limitations on the income elasticities; as applied to income, it implies that there will be no gambling.

148 Walras had already pointed out that only the ratios of the marginal utilities enter into demand analysis:

"What are v_a, v_b, v_c, . . . [the exchange values]? They are absolutely nothing but the indeterminate and arbitrary terms which have meaning

factorily for the case in which the marginal utilities of the various quantities are independent of one another.[149] His procedure was as follows:

Select arbitrarily a quantity of any commodity, say, 100 loaves of bread. Let the marginal utility of this quantity of commodity be the unit of utility (or util). Grant the ability of the individual to order the utilities of specified amounts of two goods, i.e., to indicate a preference (if one exists) or indifference between the two quantities. Then it is possible to construct the utility schedule of (say) milk. Start with no milk, and find the increment of milk ($\triangle m_1$) equivalent to the hundredth loaf of bread, i.e., the minimum amount of milk the individual would accept in exchange for the hundredth loaf of bread. Find a second increment ($\triangle m_2$), given the possession of $\triangle m_1$, equivalent to the hundredth loaf, etc. We obtain thus a schedule (or function) such as that given in Table 1. This function gives the amounts of milk necessary to obtain equal increments of utility; by interpolation we determine the amounts of utility obtained from equal increments of milk (Table 2).

---

only in their proportionate relationship to one another. . . . Thus value in exchange is essentially relative, being always based upon marginal utility, which alone is absolute" (*Éléments*, pp. 139–40). He dropped the discussion at this point.

[G. B. Antonelli, an Italian engineer, anticipated some of the most important work in his *Sulla teoria matematica della economia politica* (Pisa, 1886), which has been reprinted in the *Giornale degli economisti e annali di economia*, X (N.S., 1951), 233–63, with expository articles by G. Demaria and G. Ricci. In this remarkable memoir, Antonelli investigates the possibility that, if an individual is observed to consume various combinations at various prices, there exists a (utility) function which is maximized for these quantities. He demonstrates that such a function can always be found by integration when there are only two commodities and states the (integrability) conditions under which the function exists when there are three or more commodities. The sufficient conditions for a maximum are stated but not exploited to derive conditions on the demand functions. The complete lack of contemporary notice or effect is the only excuse for the brevity of these remarks.—Note added, 1964.]

149 *Op. cit.*, pp. 11 ff.

This initial choice of a unit is arbitrary, but this is not objectionable:

> Any unit in mathematics is valuable only as a divisor for a second quantity and constant only in the sense that the quotient is constant, that is independent of a third quantity. If we should awaken tomorrow with every line in the universe doubled, we should never detect the change, if indeed such can be called a change, nor would it disturb our sciences or formulae.[150]

TABLE 1

SYMBOL	INCREMENT OF MILK		
	Quantity (Cubic Inches)	Utility of Increment of Milk	Total Utility of Milk
Δm_1.............	3	1	1
Δm_2.............	4	1	2
Δm_3.............	5	1	3
Δm_4.............	6	1	4
Δm_5.............	7	1	5

TABLE 2

Milk (Cubic Inches)	Total Utility of Milk	Marginal Utility of Milk*
3.............	1.0000	....
6.............	1.7667	0.7667
9.............	2.4333	.6667
12.............	3.0000	.5667
15.............	3.4667	0.4667

* Per 3 cubic inches.

[150] *Ibid.*, p. 18.

Suppose now that the marginal utility of milk depends not only upon the quantity of milk but also upon the quantities of bread and beer—more generally, suppose the generalized utility function of Edgeworth holds. We could proceed as before in finding the quantities of milk, Δm_1, Δm_2, . . . , whose utilities equaled that of the hundredth loaf of bread. Let us now shift to the marginal utility of (say) 60 bottles of beer as our unit and proceed in identical fashion to find $\Delta m'_1$, $\Delta m'_2$, . . . , and thus measure the utility of milk in terms of beer. We shall find the new increments of milk, $\Delta m'_1$, $\Delta m'_2$, . . . , are not proportional to the old,[151] because the marginal utilities of beer and of bread will vary differently as the quantity of milk increases. Hence the total utility curve of milk will take on an entirely new shape, and not merely differ by a proportionality factor, when we change the commodity in terms of which it is measured. Thus we can no longer use this procedure to measure utility.[152]

Fisher concludes his brilliant dissertation with the argument that the total utility function cannot in general be deduced from the indifference curves and that, for purposes of explaining consumers' reactions to prices and income changes, there is no occasion to introduce total utility:

> Thus if we seek only the causation of the *objective facts of prices and commodity distribution* four attributes of utility as a quantity are entirely unessential, (1) that one man's utility can be compared to another's, (2) that for the same individual the marginal utilities at one consumption-combination can be compared with those at another, or at one time with another, (3) even if they could, total utility and gain might not be integratable, (4) even

---

151 That is, $\Delta m_1 : \Delta m_2 : \Delta m_3 :$ . . . will not equal $\Delta m'_1 : \Delta m'_2 : \Delta m'_3 :$ . . . .

152 Fisher, *op. cit.*, p. 67.

if they were, there would be no need of determining
the constants of integration.[153]

Fisher's statement of the difficulty of constructing total utility
functions from differential equations of the indifference curves
was extremely concise,[154] and we shall elaborate it in connection with Pareto. We may note in passing that thirty-five years
later Fisher qualified much of this argument. He was now
willing to assume independence of utilities (at least for broad
categories such as food and housing) and comparability of utilities of different persons—in order, apparently, to achieve concrete results applicable to income taxation.[155]

Pareto was the great proponent of doubts on the existence
of unique utility functions and of the relevance of such functions to economic behavior. Apparently independently of
Fisher, Pareto noticed the problem of the existence of a utility
function as early as 1892.[156] Soon thereafter most of his basic
mathematical theory was developed.[157] The import of the

---

[153] *Ibid.*, p. 89.

[154] *Ibid.*, pp. 74–75, 88–89.

[155] See "A Statistical Method of Measuring 'Marginal Utility' and Testing the Justice of a Progressive Income Tax," in *Economic Essays Contributed in Honor of John Bates Clark* (New York: Macmillan, 1927), pp.
157 ff.

[156] "Considerazioni . . . ," *Giornale degli economisti*, Series 2, IV (1892),
415. He refers casually to the fact that when the differential equation of
the indifference curve is of the form

$$Q(x, y)dx + R(x, y)dy,$$

"it may happen that $P[R]$ and Q are not partial derivatives of the same
function and then the function will not exist." This was not quite correct:
in the two-commodity case there always exists an integrating factor.

[157] "Considerazioni . . . ," *Giornale degli economisti*, Series 2, VII (1893).
He introduces the index functions (p. 297), recognizes that it is always possible to integrate the differential equations when the marginal utilities are
independent, and presents the integrability condition for the three-com-

theory was realized only slowly, however: in the *Cours* (1896 and 1897) he was still willing to accept the interpersonal comparison of utilities for welfare purposes.[158] In the *Manuel* (1909), however, measurable utility had fallen into the background—of his theory, if not of his exposition. For Pareto, two questions on measurability were at issue.

The first, and to Pareto the major, problem is this: We can deduce the slopes of indifference curves at (in principle) all possible combinations of goods from budgetary data, because the slopes of the price lines equal the ratios of the marginal utilities (slopes of indifference curves). Thus we obtain empirically the differential equation of the indifference curves. Can we integrate it to obtain the equation of the indifference curves?

Before we look at the mathematics, we may present the problem verbally. Will the choices that an individual makes between combinations of goods differing by infinitesimal

---

modity case (p. 300). Let the differential equation of the indifference surface be

$$dx_1 + Rdx_2 + Sdx_3 = 0 .$$

Then Pareto gives the integrability condition:

$$\frac{\partial R}{\partial x_3} = \frac{\partial S}{\partial x_2} .$$

He should have given,

$$\frac{\partial R}{\partial x_3} - \frac{\partial S}{\partial x_2} = S \frac{\partial R}{\partial x_1} - R \frac{\partial S}{\partial x_1} .$$

He also corrected the statement in the last footnote: "If there are only two economic goods, equation (52) is always integrable" (p. 299 n.). Subsequently he forgot this again (*Manuale di economia politica* [Milan: Piccola Biblioteca Scientifica, 1919—first published in 1906], pp. 499 ff.). He was gently reminded of it by V. Volterra, "L'Economia matematica," *Giornale degli economisti,* Series 2, XXXII (1906), 296–301.

158 *Cours d'économie politique* (Lausanne: Rouge, 1897), II, 47–48. The comparisons were limited to types or classes of people to avoid personal idiosyncrasies. The measurability problem was referred to only incidentally (*ibid.,* I, 10 n.).

amounts be consistent with the choices he makes between combinations differing by finite amounts? For example, the individual starts with the combination $100X_1$, $100X_2$, $100X_3$. By infinitesimal steps we obtain an infinite number of combinations, each equivalent to the preceding, reaching ultimately the combination $90X_1$, $85X_2$, $120X_3$. Will the individual consider this last combination equivalent to the first? The intuitive answer usually is: Yes, he is consistent in his preferences. The mathematical answer is equivalent: If the preference system displays a proper continuity, the equation is integrable. If we postulate indifference surfaces, there is no problem: then by hypothesis the infinitesimal comparisons are consistent with discrete comparisons. Economists have usually been willing to admit that the individual can well display this type of consistency. Pareto at times did likewise.[159]

Mathematically, the issue is: Does the line integral of

$$f(x_1, x_2, x_3, \ldots)dx_1 + g(x_1, x_2, x_3, \ldots)dx_2$$
$$+ h(x_1, x_2, x_3, \ldots)dx_3 + \ldots = 0$$

exist independently of the path between the beginning and end points? Pareto's first two answers are Fisher's: (1) Yes, if f is a function only of x_1, g only of x_2. . . .[160] (2) Yes, if there exists an integrating factor, that is, if the integrability conditions are fulfilled.[161] He adds: (3) If the integrability conditions are not fulfilled, the integral depends on the order of

---

[159] *Manuel*, pp. 169 n., 264.

[160] *Ibid.*, pp. 545–46, 555; "Économie mathématique," *Encyclopédie des sciences mathématiques* (Paris: Gauthier-Villars, 1911), I, iv, 614.

[161] *Manuel*, pp. 545 ff.; "Économie mathématique," *op. cit.*, pp. 598 ff. The equations are

$$f\left(\frac{\partial h}{\partial x_2} - \frac{\partial g}{\partial x_3}\right) + g\left(\frac{\partial f}{\partial x_3} - \frac{\partial h}{\partial x_1}\right) + h\left(\frac{\partial g}{\partial x_1} - \frac{\partial f}{\partial x_2}\right) = 0,$$

and similarly for all triplets of goods.

integration, and if this is known the equation can be integrated.[162]

Pareto displayed a peculiar literalness of mind when he tried to translate this third case into economic terms. He identified the order of integration with the order of consumption of the goods.[163] This was absurd for precisely the same reason that dinner-table demonstrations of diminishing marginal utility are objectionable; they do not bear on the problems economics is interested in. Acts of consumption are of little concern; the purpose of the theory of consumption is to explain the pattern of consumption, not its episodes. Economics is usually interested only in the time rates of purchase and consumption of goods, and it is not interested in whether the soup precedes the nuts, or whether the consumer drinks three cups of coffee at breakfast or one after each meal, or pours them down the sink. The correct translation of the integrability problem was in terms of the consistency of consumer preferences, not of the temporal sequence of consumption.[164] Pareto indicated elsewhere that economics is interested in repetitive patterns of behavior, and we may view this discussion as a minor aberration.[165]

Given the indifference curves, we come to the second issue: Can we deduce a unique total utility surface? In general, "No." There are in general an infinite number of total utility surfaces whose contours constitute these indifference curves. If we construct one utility surface, we can get another by squaring the amounts of utility, another by taking the logarithm of utility, etc. So far as observable behavior is concerned, one

---

[162] *Manuel,* pp. 553 ff.

[163] *Ibid.,* pp. 251, 270, 539 ff.

[164] Pareto might equally well have debated how one consumer can consume all goods at once, since the equality of marginal utilities divided by prices is a set of simultaneous equations.

[165] *Manuel,* p. 262.

utility surface will do as well as another. We shall return to this, Pareto's basic answer.

He gave also an introspective reply. We can construct a unique total utility function if the consumer can tell us the magnitude of the utility gained by moving from one indifference curve (I_1) to a second (I_2) relative to the utility gained by a move from I_2 to I_3. If he can tell us that the move from I_1 to I_2 gains (say) three times as much utility as the move from I_2 to I_3, then utility is "measurable." That is, if we have one utility surface, we may no longer submit it to transformations such as squaring the amount of utility—then we should have increased the utility of the move from I_1 to I_2 to *nine* times the utility of the move from I_2 to I_3. We can still take the utility function (U) and write it as ($aU + b$), but this merely says that the origin and unit of measurement are arbitrary for utility just as they are for length and other measurements.[166] But Pareto believed the consumer could not rank utility differences.

He did not adhere to these views with consistency. The *Manuel* is strewn with passages that are meaningful only if utility is measurable. Two examples will suffice: First, Pareto's definitions of complementary and competing goods were dependent on the measurability of utility.[167] Second, the marginal utility of income was discussed at length.[168]

Yet much of the foregoing discussion is a digression from the viewpoint of Pareto's mature theory of utility. This digression reflects the heavy hand of the past, and it is justified (rather weakly) chiefly on expository grounds.[169] Fundamentally, Pareto argued that the differential equation of the indifference surface is given by observation and that this is all that is necessary to derive the demand functions:

---

[166] *Ibid.*, pp. 264–65.

[167] See below, Sec. VI.

[168] *Manuel,* pp. 579 ff.

[169] *Ibid.*, p. 160.

The entire theory . . . rests only on a fact of experience, that is to say, on the determination of the quantities of goods which constitute combinations which are equivalent for the individual. The theory of economic science thus acquires the rigor of rational mechanics; it deduces its results from experience, without the intervention of any metaphysical entity.

[Edgeworth] assumes the existence of utility (ophelimity) and from it he deduces the indifference curves; I instead consider as empirically given the curves of indifference, and I deduce from them all that is necessary for the theory of equilibrium, without having recourse to ophelimity.[170]

Observations on demand consistent with any utility function ϕ will also be consistent with an arbitrary utility index-function $F(\phi)$ so long as the order of preference among the combinations is preserved $[F'(\phi) > 0]$.[171]

Two mathematicians consolidated this position, that all notions of measurable utility could be eliminated from economics. W. E. Johnson demonstrated that the variation of quantity purchased with price and income was independent of the measurability of utility:

This impossibility of measurement does not affect any economic problem. Neither does economics need to know the marginal (rate of) utility of a commodity. What is needed is a representation of the ratio of one marginal utility to another. In fact, this ratio is precisely represented by the *slope* of any point of the utility-curve [indifference curve].[172]

---

[170] *Ibid.*, pp. 160, 169 n.; see also pp. 539–44.   [171] *Ibid.*, p. 542.

[172] "The Pure Theory of Utility Curves," *Economic Journal*, XXIII (1913), 490. Of course the first sentence is too strong. See M. Friedman and L. J.

Johnson thereafter dealt only with ratios of marginal utilities.

Two years later E. E. Slutsky published his magnificent essay on the equilibrium of the consumer.[173] To put economics on a firm basis, "we must make it completely independent of psychological assumptions and philosophical hypotheses."[174] His utility function was accordingly an objective scale of preferences. Slutsky did not deny the interrelations of "economic" utility and "psychological" utility but sought to deduce empirical tests of any psychological hypotheses. If introspection suggests that the marginal utilities of commodities are inde-

---

Savage, "The Utility Analysis of Choices Involving Risk," *Journal of Political Economy*, LVI (1948), 279–304.

[173] "Sulla teoria del bilancio del consumatore," *Giornale degli economisti*, Series 3, LI (1915), 1–26.

E. E. Slutsky was born in 1880 in Novom, Yiaroslavskoi Gubernii, and died in Moscow on March 10, 1948. As a student of mathematics at the University of Kiev in 1901, "because of his participation in an illegal meeting he was drafted as a soldier, and only a large wave of protests by students in the big cities of the country forced the government to return him to the University in the same year. At the beginning of the next year, 1902, E. E. was dismissed from the University without the right to study in any institution of higher education. Only after 1905 was he able to return to the University of Kiev, but this time he entered the law school.

"This choice was dictated by E. E.'s desire to prepare himself for scientific work in the field of mathematical economics, an interest which he had developed from a thorough study of works of Ricardo, Marx, and Lenin. He finished at the law school in 1911, and received a gold medal for his final paper. However, because of his reputation for being 'unreliable' he was not asked to continue his academic career at the University." Thereafter he worked intensively in probability and mathematical statistics, teaching at the Institute of Commerce at Kiev from 1912 to 1926, when he went to Moscow "to work in a number of scientific research institutions of the capital."

This information is from N. Smirnov's obituary notice, *Izvestiya Akademiia Nauk SSSR* ("Mathematical Series"), XII (1948), 417–20, a translation of which was kindly made for me by Dr. Avram Kisselgoff.

[174] *Op. cit.*, p. 1.

pendent, we can test the hypothesis by the equation it implies.[175] Slutsky assumes that the increment of utility obtained
by moving from one combination to another is independent
of the path of movement and offers an empirical test of its
validity.[176] Conversely, he shows that a full knowledge of demand and expenditure functions is not sufficient in general to
determine whether marginal utility diminishes.[177] The beauty
and power of the essay are unique.

With Slutsky's development, introspection no longer plays
a significant role in utility theory. There is postulated a function which the consumer seeks to maximize, and the function
is given the characteristics necessary to permit a maximum.
This is perhaps subjective in origin: the notion of maximizing
behavior was probably derived from introspection, although
it need not be. Slutsky posits such a function merely because
it contains implications that observation can contradict, and
hence yields hypotheses on observable behavior. We shall return later to the question whether this is an efficient method
of obtaining hypotheses.

We have been marching with the vanguard; we retrace our
steps now and examine the views of the other leading economists of the period on measurability.

A. Contemporary Practice

None of the other leading economists of this period rejected
the measurability of utility; we may cite Wicksteed,[178] Wick-

---

175 *Ibid.*, p. 25.

176 *Ibid.*, pp. 3, 15–16. That is, the integrability condition is fulfilled.

177 *Ibid.*, pp. 19–23.

178 *Common Sense of Political Economy*, I, 148 ff.; II, 470, 473, 661.

sell,[179] Barone,[180] Edgeworth,[181] and Pigou.[182] It is true that by the end of the period the leading economists were realizing that measurability of utility was not essential to the derivation of demand curves, but they were loath to abandon the assumption. In part this reluctance was based on the desire to employ utility theory in welfare analysis; in part it was psychological theorizing. Yet with the passage of time, caution increased, as Marshall's evolution will illustrate.

Marshall was at first unqualified in his acceptance of the measurability of utility:

> Thus then the desirability or utility of a thing to a person is commonly measured by the money price that he will pay for it. If at any time he is willing to pay a shilling, but no more, to obtain one gratification; and sixpence, but no more, to obtain another; then the utility of the first to him is measured by a shilling, that of the second by sixpence; and the utility of the first is exactly double that of the second.
>
> The only measurement with which science can directly deal is that afforded by what a person is willing to sacrifice (whether money, or some other commodity, or his own labour) in order to obtain the aggregate of pleasures anticipated from the possession of the thing itself.[183]

---

179 *Lectures,* I, 29 ff., 221; he apparently did not fully understand the Pareto analysis (see his review of the *Manuel, Zeitschrift für Volkswirtschaft, Sozialpolitik, und Verwaltung,* XXII [1913], 136 ff.).

180 *Principi di economia politica* (Rome: Bertero, 1908), pp. 12–13, 22–24.

181 *Papers,* II, 473 n., 475.

182 *Wealth and Welfare* (London: Macmillan, 1912), *passim.*

183 *Principles* (1st ed.), pp. 151, 154 n.

Moreover, he fully accepted the intergroup comparisons of utility:

> Nevertheless, if we take averages sufficiently broad to cause the personal peculiarities of individuals to counterbalance one another, the money which people of equal incomes will give to obtain a pleasure or avoid a pain is an *extremely accurate* measure of the pleasure or the pain.[184]

Indeed, as we have already noticed, he believed that one can even compare the utilities of groups with different incomes, by using Bernoulli's hypothesis.

We need not trace in detail the growth of Marshall's caution and reticence in this area. He became unwilling to attribute precision to interpersonal comparisons.[185] The discussion of consumer surplus becomes increasingly defensive. Probably because of the growing criticism of hedonism, many terminological changes are made: "benefit" for "pleasure"; "satisfaction" for "utility"; etc. Bentham's dimensions of pleasure were approved at first;[186] they lose their sponsor and place in the text.[187] The distinction between desires and realized satisfactions becomes prominent.[188] Yet Marshall seems never to have been seriously skeptical of the measurability of utility, and the changes in his exposition were not accompanied by any change in the fundamentals of his theory.

---

184 *Ibid.*, p. 152. (My italics.) See also *ibid.*, p. 179.

185 The Bernoulli hypothesis is no longer applied to social classes. The "extremely accurate" comparison of groups with equal incomes becomes "there is not in general any very great difference between the amounts of the happiness in the two cases [two events with equal money measures]" (*Principles* [8th ed.], p. 131).

186 *Principles* (1st ed.), p. 153.

187 *Principles* (8th ed.), p. 122 n.

188 *Ibid.*, p. 92.

VI. COMPLEMENTARITY

Jevons had noticed the case of "equivalent" (substitute) commodities and implicitly defined them by the constancy of the ratio of their marginal utilities.[189] In this he was inconsistent, for he treated the marginal utility of X_1 as dependent only on the quantity of X_1 in his general theory, whereas if X_1 and X_2 are "equivalent," the marginal utility of X_1 depends also on the quantity of X_2. One cannot define the usual relationships among the utilities of commodities with an additive utility function, so the utility theory of complementarity had to wait for Edgeworth's generalization of the utility function. In fact, it had to wait a little longer, for Edgeworth glossed over this problem in the *Mathematical Psychics*.

The first formal definition of the relationship between utilities of commodities was given by the remarkable Viennese bankers, Auspitz and Lieben:

The mixed differential quotient,

$$\frac{\partial^2 \phi}{\partial x_a \partial x_b},$$

indicates what influence (if any) an algebraic increase in x_b—a larger purchase or a smaller sale of B—has on the utility of the last unit of A purchased or not sold. If we consider the simplest case, in which only A and B are consumed,

$$\frac{\partial^2 \phi}{\partial x_a \partial x_b} \gtreqless 0,$$

according as B complements the satisfaction derived from A, has no influence on it, or competes with A.[190]

---

189 *Theory of Political Economy*, p. 134.

190 *Untersuchungen über die Theorie des Preises* (Leipzig: Duncker & Humblot, 1889), p. 482; see also pp. 154 ff., 170 ff.

Fisher repeated this definition and illustrated certain limiting cases by indifference curves. He defined two commodities to be perfect substitutes if the ratio of the marginal utilities of the amounts "actually consumed" was absolutely constant; they were perfect complements if the quantities consumed were in a constant ratio.[191] Edgeworth gave the same criterion in 1897.[192]

Let us illustrate the use of this criterion with a numerical example. We may construct a table of total utilities as a function of the quantities of X_1 and X_2 and from it calculate the marginal utilities of X_1 (Table 3). Our example has been so

TABLE 3

		Total Utility Quantity of X_1		Marginal Utility of X_1
		1	2	
Quantity of X_2	1.........	3.0	5.4	2.4
	2.........	5.4	9.0	3.6

chosen that the marginal utility of a given quantity of X_1 increases when the quantity of X_2 increases, hence X_1 and X_2 are complements.

Now let us construct a new table, in which total utility is equal to the logarithm of the total utility in Table 3. This is the kind of transformation we may make if utility is not measurable; it does not preserve the relative differences be-

---

191 *Mathematical Investigation,* pp. 65–66, 69, 70–71. The definitions of these limiting cases are independent of the existence of a unique utility function.

192 He was so punctilious in acknowledging predecessors that his tone suggests independence of discovery. See "The Pure Theory of Monopoly," reprinted in *Papers,* I, 117 n. His criterion differed in one detail—ϕ was the utility function in terms of money and hence involved the marginal utility of money (the complicating effects of which were not discussed). This was not inadvertent; he desired symmetry with the definition of complementarity of products in production (*ibid.,* I, 127; II, 123). The Auspitz and Lieben definition was given later (*ibid.,* II, 464).

tween utilities, but it preserves their order. We now find (Table 4) that by the same criterion, X_1 and X_2 are substitutes. We have shown that the criterion is ambiguous if utility is not uniquely measurable.[193]

Perhaps Fisher was so casual on this point because he saw the dependence of the definition on the measurability of utility, and Edgeworth was unconcerned because he believed utility was measurable. But Pareto was inconsistent; he made extensive use of this definition at the same time that he was rejecting the measurability of utility.[194]

TABLE 4

		Total Utility Quantity of X_1		Marginal Utility of X_1
		1	2	
Quantity of X_2	1...........	0.4771	0.7324	0.2553
	2...........	0.7324	0.9542	0.2218

Marshall displayed greater inconsistency than Pareto, for he implicitly followed the Auspitz-Lieben definition even though he employed an additive utility function which did not permit of complementarity. Thus he speaks of "rival commodities, that is, of commodities which can be used as substitutes for it."[195]

---

[193] Equivalently, let φ be a utility function, $F[\varphi]$ a transformation of it such that $F' > 0$. Then

$$U = F[\varphi(x_1, x_2)] ,$$
$$U_1 = F'\varphi_1 ,$$
$$U_{12} = F'\varphi_{12} + F''\varphi_1\varphi_2 ,$$

so F'' must be zero—the transformation must be linear—if the sense of the definition is to be preserved.

[194] *Manuel,* chap. iv, pp. 576 ff.

[195] *Principles* (1st ed.), p. 160; see also pp. 438 and 178 n., with its accompanying Mathematical Note VI referring to "several commodities which will satisfy the same imperative want. . . ."

In the third edition this definition in terms of utility becomes reasonably explicit.[196] I suspect that Marshall was led into the inconsistency by his preoccupation with the role of rival and competing goods in production. That Pareto and Marshall adhered to the criterion is weighty testimony for its intuitive appeal.

W. E. Johnson supplied a definition of complementarity in terms of utility that was independent of the measurability of utility.[197] His criterion turned on the behavior of the slope of the indifference curve when one quantity was increased. That is to say, X_1 and X_2 are complements if the more of X_1 the individual possesses, the larger the increment of X_1 he will give up to obtain a unit of X_2.[198] For the fairly broad classes of commodities usually dealt with in budget studies, all commodities are probably complements on the Johnson definition. Slutsky offered no definition of complementarity.[199]

It is difficult to see the purpose in Johnson's definition of complements, or, for that matter, in more recent versions such as that of Hicks and Allen. They cannot be applied introspectively to classify commodities (as the Auspitz-Lieben defi-

---

[196] "The loss that people would suffer from being deprived both of tea and coffee would be greater than the sum of their losses from being deprived of either alone: and therefore the total utility of tea and coffee is greater than the sum of the total utility of tea calculated on the supposition the people can have recourse to coffee, and that of coffee calculated on a like supposition as to tea" (*loc. cit.*, p. 207 n. [131–32 n.]).

[197] *Op. cit.*, p. 495. See also Henry Schultz, *The Theory and Measurement of Demand* (Chicago: University of Chicago Press, 1938), pp. 608–14.

[198] The commodities are complements if both of the following inequalities hold:

$$\frac{\partial \left(\dfrac{\varphi_1}{\varphi_2}\right)}{\partial x_1} < 0, \qquad \frac{\partial \left(-\dfrac{\varphi_1}{\varphi_2}\right)}{\partial x_2} < 0.$$

They are substitutes if one of the inequalities is reversed; the stability condition (convex indifference curves) inhibits the reversal of both inequalities.

[199] His compensated variation of price is intimately related to the later definition of Hicks and Allen.

nition could be), so they offer no avenue to the utilization of introspection. Hence no assumption concerning their magnitude or frequency is introduced into the utility function—except for the condition that their frequency and magnitude be consistent with the assumption of stability.[200] As a result, such criteria can be applied concretely only if one has full knowledge of the demand functions. If one has this knowledge, they offer no important advantage over simple criteria such as the cross-elasticity of demand; if one does not have this knowledge, the simple criteria are still often applicable. The chief reason for presenting criteria in terms of utility, I suspect, is that, when familiar names are given to unknown possibilities, an illusion of definiteness of results is frequently conferred.

VII. THE DERIVATION OF DEMAND FUNCTIONS

Walras' derivation of the demand curves from utility functions was complete and correct for the generalized utility function of Edgeworth as well as for the additive utility function. But Walras passed from utility to demand intuitively and failed to demonstrate that any limitations on demand curves followed from the assumption of diminishing marginal utility.

Pareto was the first to make this logical extension of utility theory. Working with the simple additive utility function, he showed in 1892 that diminishing marginal utility rigorously implies that the demand curves have negative slopes.[201] A year later he partially solved the problem when the marginal

---

200 Thus, in the two-commodity case, both commodities cannot be substitutes on Johnson's definition; however, neither need be.

201 "Considerazioni . . . ," *Giornale degli economisti,* Series 2, V (1892), 119 ff. His demonstration is equivalent to ours (above, Sec. III). He also suggested the analysis of the problem of the simultaneous variation of all prices—which can be made equivalent to an income variation—but did not solve the problem explicitly (*ibid.,* p. 125). As we have noticed (Sec. IV), under the less stringent assumption of a convex utility function, one commodity can have a positively sloping demand curve.

utilities of the commodities are interdependent.[202] He could no longer deduce any meaningful limitation on the slope of the demand curve, and dropped the analysis. In the *Cours* he went further and argued that the demand curve for wheat may have a positive slope.[203]

A corresponding derivation of the effect of a change in income on the consumption of a commodity was presented in the *Manuel,* but Pareto gave no explicit mathematical proof and the analysis has generally been overlooked:

> If we assume that the ophelimity of a commodity depends only on the quantity of that commodity that the individual consumes or has at his disposal, the theoretical conclusion is that, for such commodities, consumption increases when income increases; or, at the limit, that the consumption is constant when income exceeds a certain level. Consequently, if a peasant subsists only on corn, and if he becomes rich, he will eat more corn, or at least as much as when he was poor. He who has only one pair of sabots a year because they are too expensive, may when he becomes rich use a hundred pairs, but he will always use one pair. All this is in manifest contradiction to the facts: our hypothesis must therefore be rejected. . . .[204]

Despite this admirable test of the hypothesis of independent utilities, Pareto continued to find some use for the additive utility function.

Pareto also made a number of minor applications of utility

---

202 "Considerazioni . . . ," *Giornale degli economisti,* Series 2, VII (1893), 304–6. This is equivalent to our illustration (Sec. IV).

203 *Cours,* II, 338. The discussion was hypothetical, employing the same argument that Marshall used for the Giffen case.

204 *Manuel,* pp. 273–74.

theory to demand analysis. He showed that the demand and supply curves cannot be linear when there are three or more commodities and that the demand curve of a commodity cannot have constant elasticity when there are three or more commodities. Both demonstrations rested on the independence of the marginal utilities of the commodities.[205] We shall notice later his analysis of the constancy of the marginal utility of money.

Fisher had shown graphically in 1892 that if the utility function is not additive, an increase in income may lead to decreased consumption of a commodity.[206] The compatibility of negatively sloping income curves with convex indifference curves was first shown mathematically by W. E. Johnson.[207] Johnson also demonstrated that a rise in price may lead to an increase in the quantity of the commodity purchased.[208] Moreover, Johnson was first to carry through the explicit analysis of utility with the use only of the ratios of marginal utilities. His exposition was concise and peculiar, however, and was slow to receive attention.[209]

The complete and explicit analysis of the general case was given in lucid form by Slutsky.[210] We may illustrate his general

---

[205] "Économie mathématique," *Encyclopédie*, I, iv, 616 ff.

[206] *Mathematical Investigations*, pp. 73–74.

[207] *Op. cit.*, p. 505. [208] *Ibid.*, p. 504.

[209] A good discussion was given by Edgeworth, *Papers*, II, 451 ff.

[210] It is summarized by Schultz, *op. cit.*, chaps. i, xix; R. G. D. Allen, "Professor Slutsky's Theory of Consumers' Choice," *Review of Economic Studies*, February, 1936. Slutsky takes the equation,

$$d^2\varphi = \varphi_{11}dx_1^2 + \varphi_{22}dx_2^2 + \ldots + 2\varphi_{12}dx_1dx_2 + \ldots$$

and by a linear transformation puts it in the canonical form,

$$d^2\varphi = A_1da^2 + A_2db^2 + A_3dc^2 + \ldots.$$

He carries through two analyses, one for all $A_i < 0$, called the normal case, and a second for one $A_i > 0$, called the abnormal case. If two or more A_i are positive, $d^2\varphi$ will not be negative along the budget constraint (*op. cit.*, pp. 4–5).

logic with a numerical example. Let the individual consumer buy

> 100 units of X_1 at $1.00, a cost of $100,
> 60 units of X_2 at $0.75, a cost of $ 45,

exactly equaling his income of $145. Let now the price of X_1 rise to $1.10. Then the apparent deficiency of income, in Slutsky's language, is 100 times $0.10 = $10, for this is the amount that must be added to the individual's income to permit him to purchase the former quantities. If, simultaneously with the rise in the price of X_1, we give the individual $10, Slutsky calls it a compensated variation of price. Although the individual experiencing a compensated rise in the price of X_1 can still buy the same quantities, he will always substitute X_2 for X_1, because X_2 is now relatively cheaper: Slutsky demonstrated that this is a consequence of the convexity of the indifference curves.[211] The individual will move to perhaps

> 86.36 units of X_1 at $1.10, a cost of $95,
> 80.00 units of X_2 at $0.75, a cost of $60.

The changes in quantities

> 86.36 — 100 = —13.64 units of X_1,
> 80.00 — 60 = — 20.00 units of X_2,

were called the residual variabilities. If now we withdraw the $10 of income used to compensate for the variation in price, the individual may move to, say,

> 80 units of X_1 at $1.10, a cost of $88,
> 76 units of X_2 at $0.75, a cost of $57.

In our example the individual reduces the quantities of both goods when income falls; Slutsky calls such goods relatively

---

211 More precisely, he demonstrated that it is a consequence of the stability of the maximum the consumer has achieved (Slutsky, *op. cit.*, p. 14, Eq. 52).

indispensable. Had X_1 been relatively dispensable, the decline in income of $10 would have led to a rise in the quantity purchased, conceivably sufficient to offset the residual variation. We have thus the laws of demand:

1. The demand for a relatively indispensable good is necessarily normal, that is to say, it diminishes when its price increases and rises when the price diminishes.
2. The demand for a relatively dispensable good may in certain cases be abnormal, that is to say, it increases with the increase of price and diminishes with its decrease.[212]

In addition, he deduced integrability equations connecting the effects of the price of X_1 on X_2 and the price of X_2 on X_1:

$$\frac{\partial x_1}{\partial p_2} + x_2 \frac{\partial x_1}{\partial R} = \frac{\partial x_2}{\partial p_1} + x_1 \frac{\partial x_2}{\partial R}. \quad [213]$$

And so we have fulfilled the historian's wish: the best has come last.

MARSHALL

Marshall constructed a demand curve superior to Walras' for empirical use but related it to utility by an exposition less than masterly. This demand curve was of the form

$$x_i = f(p_i, R, I),$$

where I is an index number of all prices. Marshall assumed, of course, that tastes are fixed.[214] The constancy of the "purchasing power of money" (the reciprocal of our I) is an assump-

---

212 *Ibid.*, p. 14.   213 *Ibid.*, p. 15.

214 *Principles* (1st ed.), p. 155 [94]: "If we take a man as he is, without allowing time for any change in his character. . . ."

tion governing the entire *Principles,* and it is specifically re-affirmed in the discussion of demand.[215] The role of money income is clearly recognized.[216]

I interpret I in Marshall's equation as an index number representing the average price of all commodities excluding X_i. Then his demand curve differs from the Walrasian demand curve in that he holds constant the average of other prices rather than each individual price. Changes in I may be measured by an index number embracing all commodities (including X_i), as in effect Marshall proposes, but only at the cost of inconsistency: when all prices except p_i are constant, I will vary with p_i. Unless the expenditure on X_i is large relative to income, and unless its price varies greatly, however, the quantitative error will be small.[217] We could eliminate this inconsistency (and certain ambiguities too) in Marshall's treatment by interpreting I as the average of all prices, so real income is held constant along the demand curve.[218] But then we should encounter new inconsistencies.[219]

---

215 "Throughout the earlier stages of our work it will be best . . . to assume that there is no change in the general purchasing power of money" (*ibid.,* p. 9 [62]).

216 In addition to a reference discussed below (*ibid.,* p. 155 [95]), we may cite Book III, chap. iii [iv], with its discussion of rich and poor buyers and the "disturbing cause." "Next come the changes in the general prosperity and in the total purchasing power at the disposal of the community at large" (*ibid.,* p. 170 [109]).

217 It is sufficient, Marshall says, to "ascertain with tolerable accuracy the broader changes in the purchasing power of money" (*ibid.,* p. 170 [109]); elsewhere he proposes to do this with an index number of wholesale prices (*Memorials,* pp. 207–10).

218 See M. Friedman, "The Marshallian Demand Curve," *Journal of Political Economy,* LVII (1949), 463–95.

219 Examples are the Giffen paradox and the statement that, in cases of multiple equilibria, consumers prefer to buy the quantity at the largest intersection of the supply and demand curves (*Principles* [1st ed.], p. 451 n. [472 n.]).

Marshall insists that the prices of rival goods be held constant.[220] This proviso is troublesome to reconcile with his utility theory but not to explain. The reconciliation is troublesome because rival goods are defined in terms of utility and cannot exist with an additive utility function.[221] (We can of course eliminate this difficulty by generalizing the utility function or shifting to a definition of rival products in terms of demand cross-elasticities.) The purpose of the proviso is obvious, however; when p_i rises, consumers will shift to close rivals, and their prices will tend to rise even if the price level is stable, so the effect of changes only in p_i on purchases of X_i will be obscured.[222]

This Marshallian demand curve can be derived by the conventional Walrasian technique simply by grouping together all commodities except the one under consideration and identifying their price with the price level.[223] But then what is the role of that famous assumption, the constancy of the marginal utility of money (income)? The answer is that this additional assumption is quite indispensable to his textual instruction on how "to translate this Law of Diminishing Utility into terms of price."[224] Marshall moves directly and immediately from marginal utility to demand price by the (implicit) equation,

$$MU_i = \text{constant} \times p_i,$$

and adds, "so far we have taken no account of changes in the

----

220 "One condition which it is especially important to watch is the price of rival commodities . . ." (*ibid.*, p. 160 [100]). Complements' prices were added in the second edition (*loc. cit.*, p. 158 [100 n.]).

221 See Sec. VII.

222 Marshall also assumes in effect that the anticipated future price equals the present price (*Principles* [1st ed.], p. 161).

223 No explicit derivation was given along these lines, but one can be read into Mathematical Note III [II].

224 The phrase, but not the thought, dates from the second edition (*loc. cit.*, p. 151 [94]).

marginal utility to [the buyer] of money, or general purchasing power."[225] The assumption of constancy of the marginal utility of money is essential to his exposition of the relationship between utility and demand curves, and essential also to the substance of the apparatus of consumers' surplus. But it is not essential to the Marshallian demand curve if expositional simplicity is sacrificed.

Precisely what does Marshall mean by the constancy of the marginal utility of income? He tells us (in Book V!):

> There is a latent assumption which is in accordance with the actual conditions of most markets; but which ought to be distinctly recognized in order to prevent its creeping into those cases in which it is not justifiable. We tacitly assumed that the sum which purchasers were willing to pay, and which sellers were willing to take for the seven hundredth bushel would not be affected by the question whether the earlier bargains had been made at a high or a low rate. We allowed for the diminution in the marginal utility of corn to the buyers as the amount bought increased. But we did not allow for any appreciable change in the marginal utility of money; we assumed that it would be practically the same whether the early payments had been at a high or a low rate.
>
> This assumption is justifiable with regard to most of the market dealings with which we are practically concerned. When a person buys anything for his own consumption, he generally spends on it a

---

225 *Principles* (1st ed.), p. 155 [95]. In the first edition this was the only explicit statement of the assumption in the book on demand; but see also Mathematical Note VI with its cross-reference to pp. 392–93 [334–35]. After the quoted sentence, Marshall discusses the effect of income on the marginal utility of money but is eloquently silent on the effect of price changes.

small part of his total resources; while when he buys it for the purposes of trade, he looks to re-selling it, and therefore his potential resources are not diminished. In either case the marginal utility of money to him is not appreciably changed. But though this is the case as a rule, there are exceptions to the rule.[226]

It seems beyond doubt that Marshall treated the marginal utility of money as approximately, and not rigorously, constant, and fairly clear that it is constant with respect to variations in the price of a commodity whose total cost is not too large a part of the budget.

The large volume of writing on Marshall's assumption adds an ironical overtone to our phrase "expositional simplicity." Some of the studies have been concerned with the implications of strict constancy.[227] Pareto and Barone gave such interpretations in our period.[228] The approximate constancy of the marginal utility of income has also been discussed.[229] Pareto skirted such an interpretation;[230] it can be elaborated to show

---

226 *Ibid.*, pp. 392–93 (334–35); see also (p. 132).

227 See M. Friedman, "Professor Pigou's Method for Measuring Elasticities of Demand from Budgetary Data," *Quarterly Journal of Economics*, L (1935), 151–63; P. A. Samuelson, "Constancy of the Marginal Utility of Income," in Oscar Lange *et al.* (eds.), *Studies in Mathematical Economics and Econometrics* (Chicago: University of Chicago Press, 1942), pp. 75–91.

228 In 1892 Pareto argued that the assumption implied that each demand curve has unitary elasticity; "Considerazioni . . . ," *Giornale degli economisti*, Series 2, IV (1892), 493. In 1894 Barone made a more elaborate analysis and reached a similar conclusion; *Le Opere*, I, 48. A few months later he offered a second interpretation: when p_i varies, money income varies by an amount equal to the change in expenditure on X_i (*ibid.*, pp. 59 ff.).

229 N. Georgescu-Roegen, "Marginal Utility of Money and Elasticities of Demand," *Quarterly Journal of Economics*, L (1936), 533–39.

230 *Manuel*, pp. 582 ff.; "Économie mathématique," *op. cit.*, p. 631.

that approximate constancy has no implications beyond those
already implicit in the additive utility function.[231] The assumption looms large in economic literature but marks a
fruitless digression from the viewpoint of the progress of utility
theory.

A. The Abandonment of Utility

Demand functions, as we have already noticed, had been
treated as empirical data in the classical economics and in the
work of economists such as Cournot.[232] Gustav Cassel was the
first of the modern theorists to return to this approach. His
theory was developed in 1899 and never changed thereafter in
essentials.[233] He attacked the utility theory along two lines.

His first and constructive thesis was that one can employ
demand functions directly, without a utility substructure:

> The individual has a value scale in terms of
> money, with which he can not only classify his
> needs but also express numerically their intensities.
> . . . If I adopt the fiction that the needs of indi-
> viduals A and B are of the same intensity, if both

---

231 Let X_1 be the commodity, X_2 all other commodities. I interpret Marshall to mean that the rate of change of the marginal utility of X_2 is small
relative to the rate of change of the marginal utility of X_1, or—introducing
prices to eliminate the units in which commodities are measured—that

$$\frac{\varphi_{22} p_1^2}{\varphi_{11} p_2^2}$$

is approximately zero.

232 A. A. Cournot, *Mathematical Principles of the Theory of Wealth* (New
York: Macmillan, 1929), esp. chap. iv.

233 "Grundriss einer elementaren Preislehre," *Zeitschrift für die gesamte
Staatswissenschaft,* LV (1899), 395 ff.; cf. *The Theory of Social Economy*
(New York: Harcourt, Brace, 1932), esp. pp. 80 ff., where the tone is much
more gentle and conciliatory.

value a given need at one mark, then I have ex-
tracted from the psychological assumptions everything that is relevant to the economic side of the
matter.[234]

> The subjective element which we seek to isolate
> is the relationship between valuation and external
> factors [income and prices]. In order to discover
> this relationship, we must allow the external fac-
> tors to vary; then the value the individual at-
> tributes to the good in question will also vary. This
> value is therefore a function of the external factors,
> and in this functional relationship we have the
> complete and pure expression of the subjective ele-
> ment, that is, of the nature of the individual so far
> as it affects the formation of prices.[235]

But Cassel made no studies of the properties of the demand
functions.

No doubt it was psychologically inevitable that Cassel had
also a second thesis: that the utility theory was full of error.
This theory, he charged, required a unit of utility that no one
could define;[236] it required unrealistic divisibility of commodities and continuity of utility functons;[237] it required, or at least
always led to, meaningless interpersonal comparisons of utility;[238] the assumption of constancy of the marginal utility of
money is meaningless or objectionable;[239] etc.

Wicksell quickly replied for the utility theorists and with

---

234 "Grundriss . . . ," pp. 398–99.

235 *Ibid.*, p. 436.

236 *Ibid.*, pp. 398 ff.

237 "The fact is, that every person who is even moderately well off buys
the greater part of the articles he uses for much less than the value they
have for him" (*ibid.*, p. 417).

238 *Ibid.*, p. 402.   239 *Ibid.*, pp. 428–29.

sufficient vigor to estrange Cassel for life.[240] He properly pointed out the weaknesses in Cassel's criticisms of the marginal utility theory: that it did not require measurability of utility or interpersonal comparisons except for welfare analyses; that Cassel's discontinuity objections were unrealistic and in any event did not affect the substance of the theory; etc. Wicksell also properly pointed out the considerable use of utility language in Cassel's positive theory and his implicit use of utility to reach welfare conclusions. And, finally, Wicksell criticized Cassel for his rough treatment of predecessors on the rare occasion when he recognized them at all—a charge that was exaggerated but not unfounded.[241]

But Wicksell did not meet the substantive claim of Cassel that it was possible to start directly with demand functions and that the utility theory added no information on the nature of these functions. He seemed content at this point merely to argue that the utility theory incorporated reliable psychological information into economics.[242]

Barone employed the same empirical approach to demand in his famous article on collectivist planning:

> There is no need to have recourse to the concepts of *utility,* of the *final degree of utility,* and the like; and neither is it necessary to have recourse to Pareto's concept of the *Indifference Curve.* . . .
> . . . the *tastes* of the various individuals. On these last we will make no presupposition, no preliminary inquiry, limiting ourselves simply to assuming

---

240 "Zur Verteidigung der Grenznutzenlehre," *Zeitschrift für die gesamte Staatswissenschaft,* LVI (1900), 577–91; amplified in some respects in "Professor Cassel's System of Economics," reprinted in *Lectures,* I, 219 ff. Cassel replied in an appendix to "Die Produktionskostentheorie Ricardos," *Zeitschrift für die gesamte Staatswissenschaft,* LVII (1901), 93–100.

241 Cassel was not the equal of Pareto in this respect (see especially the latter's "Économie mathématique").

242 "Zur Verteidigung . . . ," p. 580.

the fact that at every given series of prices of products and productive services, every single individual portions out the income from his services between consumption and saving in a certain manner (into the motives of which we will not inquire) by which, at a given series of prices, the individual makes certain demands and certain offers. These quantities demanded and offered vary when the series of prices vary.

Thus we disengage ourselves from every metaphysical or subtle conception of utility and of the functions of indifference, and rely solely on the authenticity of a fact.[243]

Yet Barone is not an important figure in the movement to abandon utility. He employed this approach only in the one article,[244] and there perhaps chiefly to bring out the analogies between competitive and collectivist economies. What is more important, he did not discuss the crucial problem: Can one say more about the demand functions if they are derived from utility functions?

One final theorist of the period consistently ignored utility in his work on demand—Henry L. Moore. It was Moore's program to join economic theory with the then recent developments of statistical theory to quantify the important economic functions. In this lifelong task he has found no assistance in utility theory and paused only briefly to criticize it:

In the closing quarter of the last century great hopes were entertained by economists with regard to the capacity of economics to be made an "exact

---

243 "The Ministry of Production in the Collectivist State" (1908), translated in F. A. Hayek, *Collectivist Economic Planning* (London: Routledge, 1938), pp. 246, 247.

244 Conventional utility analysis is used in his *Principi di economia politica*, Part I.

science." According to the view of the foremost theorists, the development of the doctrines of utility
and value had laid the foundation of scientific economics in exact concepts, and it would soon be possible to erect upon the new foundation a firm structure of interrelated parts which, in definiteness and
cogency, would be suggestive of the severe beauty
of the mathematico-physical sciences. But this expectation has not been realized. . . .

The explanation is to be found in the prejudiced
point of view from which economics regarded the
possibilities of the science and in the radically
wrong method which they pursued. . . . Economics
was to be a "calculus of pleasure and pain," "a
mechanics of utility," a "social mechanics," a *"physique social."* . . . They seemed to identify the method of physical sciences with experimentation, and
since, as they held, scientific experimentation is impossible in social life, a special method had to be
devised. The invention was a disguised form of the
classical *caeteris paribus,* the method of the static
state.[245]

This is not the place to quarrel with certain aspects of
Moore's methodological views, nor is it the place to discuss the
deficiencies in his statistical work on demand, nor is it the
place to give him his due as a major figure in the history of
demand theory. It is a suitable place, however, to conclude our
history of the theory of utility.

VIII. A THEORY OF ECONOMIC THEORIES

We have before us a fairly complete account of the major
developments in one branch of economic analysis. I wish now

---

245 *Economic Cycles: Their Law and Cause* (New York: Macmillan, 1914),
pp. 84–86.

to review this history with a view to isolating the characteristics of successful (and hence of unsuccessful) theories, where success is measured in terms of acceptance by leading economists. (It would require a different history to answer the interesting question: To what extent, and with what time interval, do the rank and file of economists follow the leaders?) The bases on which economists choose between theories may be summarized under the three headings of generality, manageability, and congruence with reality.

A. THE CRITERION OF GENERALITY

The successful theory was always more general than the theory it supplanted. The marginal utility theory was more general than the classical theory of value (with its special cases of producible and non-producible goods); the generalized utility function was more general than the additive utility function; the non-measurable utility function was more general than the measurable utility function. On the other hand, the Bernoulli hypothesis was rejected as arbitrary (i.e., particularizing). There was no important instance in which a more specific theory supplanted a more general theory, unless it was Marshall's assumption of the constant marginal utility of money, and this assumption had little vogue outside Cambridge circles.

What does generality mean here? Occasionally it is simply an application of Occam's razor, of using a weaker assumption that is sufficient to reach the conclusion in which one is interested. The nonmeasurable utility function was the leading instance of this kind of generality, although I shall argue below that perhaps logical elegance was not the major reason for abandoning measurability. Very seldom has Occam's razor beautified the face of economic theory.

More often, generality meant the encompassing of a wider range of phenomena. The marginal utility theory enabled economists to analyze the values of non-producible goods and

the short-run values of producible goods. The generalized utility function allowed the analysis of interrelationships of the
marginal utilities of commodities, which previously had been
outside the domain of utility theory.

Yet we must note that generality is often only verbal, or at
least ambiguous. The Walrasian theory was more general than
the Ricardian theory in that the former applied to both producible and non-producible goods, but it was less general in
that it took the supply of labor as given. Cassel's empirical demand curves seemed more general in that they were valid even
if every element of utility theory was banished;[246] but the
utility theorist Wicksell could reply that the utility theory was
more general because it permitted welfare judgments. Unless
one theory encompasses all the variables of the others, their
order of generality will vary with the question in hand.

Generality, whether formal-logical or substantive, is a loose
criterion by which to choose among theories. It is always easy
and usually sterile to introduce a new variable into a system,
which then becomes more general. Yet a more general theory
is obviously preferable to a more specific theory if other things
are equal, because it permits of a wider range of prediction.
We turn now to the other things.

B. The Criterion of Manageability

The second criterion employed in choosing between theories
has been manageability. Economists long delayed in accepting
the generalized utility function because of the complications in
its mathematical analysis, although no one (except Marshall)
questioned its realism. They refused to include in the individual's utility function the consumption of other individuals,

---

246 Actually he put sufficient conditions on his demand functions to make
them logically equivalent to those derived from indifference curves (see
H. Wold, "A Synthesis of Pure Demand Analysis," *Skandinavisk Aktuarie-
tidskrift*, XXVII [1944], 77 ff.).

although this extension was clearly unimportant only in the social life of Oxford. The non-integrable differential equation of the indifference curves was similarly unpopular. In these cases manageability was the prime consideration: economists tacitly agreed that it is better to have a poor, useful theory than a rich, useless one.

Of course, this is true, although the choice is not really this simple as a rule. Manageability should mean the ability to bring the theory to bear on specific economic problems, not ease of manipulation. The economist has no right to expect of the universe he explores that its laws are discoverable by the indolent and the unlearned. The faithful adherence for so long to the additive utility function strikes one as showing at least a lack of enterprise. I think it showed also a lack of imagination: no economic problem has only one avenue of approach; and the non- and semi-mathematical utility theorists could have pursued inquiries suggested by theories beyond their powers of mathematical manipulation.[247] The investigator in his science is not wholly dissimilar to the child in his nursery, and every parent has marveled at how often unreasoning obstinacy has solved a problem.

C. The Criterion of Congruence with Reality

The criteria of generality and manageability are formal; the empirical element entered through the criterion of congruence with reality. It was required of a new theory that it systematize and "explain" a portion of the empirical knowledge of the times. It must perform tasks such as accounting for the fact that often goods sold for less than their costs of production (which the marginal utility theory did) or for liking bread

---

[247] E.g., the generalized utility function suggested studies of the interrelations of prices in demand; the effect of other people's consumption on one's utility suggested the use of relative income status rather than absolute income in demand analysis; etc.

more when there was butter on it (which the generalized utility function did).

The reality with which theories were required to agree was one of casual observation and general knowledge. It was composed of the facts and beliefs that the men of a time mostly share and partly dispute and of the observations of men who earned and spent incomes and watched others do so. Of course the type and amount of such information varied widely among economists. Some, like Marshall, had a deep knowledge of their economies; others, like Edgeworth and Pareto, were more worldly scholars; still others, like Walras and the young Fisher, kept the world at a distance.

This casual knowledge was loose and relatively timeless with respect to utility theory; these economists knew little more about utility and not a great deal more about demand than their ancestors. In this respect utility theory is not wholly representative of economic theory; in population theory, for example, casual knowledge changed radically with the times and exercised a decisive influence on the comparative acceptabilities of various population theories. The one changing element in the general knowledge was the growing skepticism of hedonism in academic circles. Economists were surely (if improperly) more susceptible to the proposal to abandon the measurability of utility when the psychologists chided them:

> Important as is the influence of pleasures and pains upon our movements, they are far from being our only stimuli. . . . Who smiles for the pleasure of smiling, or frowns for the pleasure of the frown? Who blushes to avoid the discomfort of not blushing?[248]

---

248 William James, *Psychology* (New York: Holt, 1893), p. 445. William McDougall was more emphatic and pointed (as well as absurd and illogical): "Political economy suffered hardly less from the crude nature of the psychological assumptions from which it professed to deduce the explanations

The sieve of casual knowledge was broad in its gauge. It could reject the notion (of Cassel) that consumers do not equate marginal utilities divided by prices because they do not know the prices, or the notion (of the abstemious Fisher) that the marginal utility of liquor increases with quantity. But it could not reject even the imaginary Giffen paradox. Casual knowledge is better calculated to detect new error than to enlarge old truth.

This third criterion of congruence with reality should have been sharpened—sharpened into the insistence that theories be examined for their implications for observable behavior, and these specific implications compared with observable behavior. The implication of the diminishing marginal utility of money, that people will not gamble, should have been used to test this assumption, not to reproach the individuals whose behavior the theory sought to describe.

Not only were such specific implications not sought and tested, but there was a tendency, when there appeared to be the threat of an empirical test, to reformulate the theory to make the test ineffective. Thus, when it was suggested that there might be increasing marginal utility from good music, as one acquired a taste for it, this was interpreted as a change in the utility function.[249] Yet if in the time periods relevant to economic analysis this phenomenon is important, it is a significant problem—the defenders had no right to rush to the dinner table. When it was suggested that the marginal utility of the last yard of carpet necessary to cover a floor was greater than

---

of its facts and its prescriptions for economic legislation. It would be a libel, not altogether devoid of truth, to say that the classical political economy was a tissue of false conclusions drawn from false psychological assumptions. And certainly the recent progress in economic science has largely consisted in, or resulted from, the recognition of the need for a less inadequate psychology" (*An Introduction to Social Psychology* [3d ed.; London: Methuen, 1910], pp. 10–11).

[249] Marshall, *Principles* (8th ed.), p. 94; Wicksteed, *Common Sense*, I, 85.

that of fewer yards, the theory was modified to make the covering of the entire floor the unit of utility analysis.[250] They did not anxiously seek the challenge of the facts.

In this respect Pareto was the great and honorable exception. Despite much backsliding and digression, he displayed a constant and powerful instinct to derive the refutable empirical implications of economic hypotheses. He was the first person to derive the implications of the additive utility function with respect to demand and income curves. It was left for Slutsky to carry out this task for the generalized utility function, but Pareto—and he alone of the economists—constantly pressed in this direction.

But exception he was. The ruling attitude was much more that which Wieser formulated:

> Any layman in economics knows the whole substance of the theory of value from his own experience, and is a layman only in so far as he does not grasp the matter theoretically,—i.e., independently, and for and by itself,—but only practically,—that is to say, in some given situation, and in connection with its working out in that situation. If this be true, how else shall be better proved our scientific statements than by appealing to the recollection which every one must have of his own economic actions and behavior?[251]

That this criterion was inadequate was demonstrated by the slowness with which utility theory progressed. The additive utility function was popularized in the 1870's; it was 1909 before the implication of positively sloping income curves was derived. The generalized utility function was proposed in

---

250 Marshall, *Principles* (8th ed.), p. 94; Wicksteed, *Common Sense*, I, 83; Pareto, *Manuel*, p. 266.

251 *Op. cit.*, p. 5.

1881; it was 1915 before its implications were derived. The chief of these implications is that, if consumers do not buy less of a commodity when their incomes rise, they will surely buy less when the price of the commodity rises. This was the chief product—so far as hypotheses on economic behavior go—of the long labors of a very large number of able economists. These very able economists, and their predecessors, however, had known all along that demand curves have negative slopes, quite independently of their utility theorizing.

Had specific tests been made of the implications of theories, the unfruitfulness of the ruling utility theory as a source of hypotheses in demand would soon have become apparent. Had these economists sought to establish true economic theories of economic behavior—that is, to isolate uniformities of economic events that permitted prediction of the effects of given conditions—they would not long have been content with the knowledge that demand curves have negative slopes. They would have desired knowledge on the relative elasticities of demand of rich and poor, the effects of occupation and urbanization on demand, the role of income changes, the difference between short- and long-run reactions to price changes, and a whole host of problems which we are just beginning to study. They would have given us an economic theory which was richer and more precise.

These remarks shall have been completely misunderstood if they are read as a complaint against our predecessors' accomplishments. It would be purposeless as well as ungracious to deprecate their work. They improved economics substantially, and, until we are sure we have done as much, we should find gratitude more fitting than complaint. But we should be able to profit not only from their contributions to economics but also from their experiences in making these contributions. That such able economists were delayed and distracted by the lack of a criterion of refutable implications of theories should be a finding as useful to us as any of the fine theoretical advances they made.

6

The Ricardian Theory of Value and Distribution

January 22, 1821

To David Ricardo

MY DEAR SIR:

I hope you will have the goodness to state to me your opinion on this point [the effect of changes in wages on values of goods], for it is one on which of all others I most wish to have sound opinions.

Yours most faithfully,

J. R. McCULLOCH

English economics was in a state of ferment at the beginning of the nineteenth century; Adam Smith had founded no cult. The period teemed with able economists; yet David Ricardo, within a decade of his debut, was the acknowledged leader of the young science of economics. Within this decade, indeed, his chief work was done; and it was sufficient to make him the most influential economist of his century. This was an extraordinary achievement of an extraordinary man.

Reprinted from *The Journal of Political Economy*, Vol. LX (June, 1952).

I propose to set forth in this essay my understanding of Ricardo's basic contributions to the theory of value and distribution. In order to provide a sketch of the setting in which Ricardo wrote, I shall first trace the development of two main strands of his theory, the theories of population and rent.[1]

I. THE THEORY OF POPULATION

If we put aside Smith's principles of the workings of competitive markets, the first pillar of the Ricardian system to be erected was the theory of population. Although this theory has an extensive pre-Malthusian history and gave rise to an enormous early nineteenth-century literature, we shall begin with a sketch of the immediate setting in which Malthus presented the theory and shall trace its development in Malthus' and Ricardo's hands.

William Godwin, an exponent of an intellectual naturalism which did not quite extend to anarchism, achieved considerable fame in the closing years of the eighteenth century. He proposed the abolition of property, almost all government and law, marriage, the division of labor, and diverse other social institutions—but by peaceful means. It was inseparable from his thought that such "reforms" were meritorious only in the measure that they were freely embraced by all men; for example:

> If, in any society, wealth be estimated at its true
> value, and accumulation and monopoly be regarded
> as the seals of mischief, injustice, and dishonour,
> instead of being treated as titles to attention and
> deference, in that society the accommodations of

[1] A draft of this paper was completed before the magnificent edition of Ricardo's works edited by Sraffa and Dobb began to appear. I have decided to leave for another occasion the discussion of the new information which this edition contains.

human life will tend to their level, and the inequality of conditions will be destroyed. A revolution of opinions is the only means of attaining this inestimable benefit. Every attempt to effect this purpose by means of regulation, will probably be found ill conceived and abortive. Be this as it will, every attempt to correct the distribution of wealth by individual violence, is certainly to be regarded as hostile to the first principles of public security.[2]

Godwin accordingly not only opposed violence and revolution but explicitly stated that "the equality for which we are pleading, is an equality which would succeed to a state of great intellectual improvement."[3]

The rationale of this philosophy is that social systems mold the characters of their members and that most or all of the vices of man are therefore attributable to social institutions: "What is born into the world is an unfinished sketch, without character or distinctive feature impressed upon it."[4] The gradual elimination of institutions such as property, together with the irresistible triumph of truth, would eliminate unsocial ambitions, avarice, sloth, and other imperfections of man. Godwin's vision was noble and his arguments candid and often ingenious. If he was inexcusably neglectful of the influence of men on institutions, he was right in stressing the influence of institutions on men.

In the penultimate chapter of *Political Justice,* we should note, Godwin discussed Robert Wallace's earlier rejection of equality because of "the principle of population." Godwin disputed this pessimistic view on two scores. The first was a brief allusion to the efficacy of moral restraint: "It is impossible where the price of labour is greatly reduced, and an

---

2 *Enquiry concerning Political Justice* (3d ed.; London, 1798), II, 441.

3 *Ibid.,* p. 480.   4 *Ibid.,* I, 37.

added population threatens a still further reduction, that men should not be considerably under the influence of fear, respecting an early marriage, and a numerous family."[5] The second was that the problem was of no immediate concern: three-quarters of the globe was uncultivated, men wasted most of their productive efforts (under existing institutions) on meretricious objects, and "myriads of centuries" would pass before overpopulation was a real problem.[6]

By a different route Condorcet reached a similar view of the good society—which, however, allowed a much larger place to the sciences.[7] He believed also in the perfectibility of man and the inevitability of progress, less on moral grounds than because a historical survey emphasized to him the cumulative character of knowledge and liberty. He, too, noticed the population problem in a regime of equality:

> It may, however, be demanded, whether, amidst this improvement in industry and happiness, where the wants and faculties of men will continually become better proportioned, each successive generation possesses more various stores, and of consequence in each generation the number of individuals be greatly increased; it may, I say, be demanded, whether these principles of improvement and increase may not, by their continual operation, ultimately lead to degeneracy and destruction? Whether the number of inhabitants in the universe at length exceeding the means of existence, there will not result a continual decay of happiness and population, and a progress towards barbarism, or at least a sort of oscillation between good and evil?[8]

---

5 *Ibid.*, II, 517.   6 *Ibid.*, p. 518.

7 *Outlines of a Historical View of the Progress of the Human Mind* (London: J. Johnson, 1795); the original French edition appeared in 1793.

8 *Ibid.*, pp. 344–45.

This problem, however, lay far in the future because of the prospective great advances of technology, and, should it ever threaten to become real, Condorcet alluded to the possible development of contraceptives:

> . . . prior to this period [of overpopulation] the progress of reason will walk in hand with that of the sciences; that the absurd prejudices of superstition will have ceased to infuse into morality a harshness that corrupts and degrades, instead of purifying and exalting it; that men will then know, that the duties they may be under relative to propagation will consist not in the question of giving *existence* to a greater number of beings, but *happiness;* will have for their object, the general welfare of the human species; of the society in which they live; of the family to which they are attached; and not the puerile idea of encumbering the earth with useless and wretched mortals.[9]

Among the admirers of Godwin and Condorcet, as we know, there was a Daniel Malthus, and his advocacy of their doctrines led his son, Thomas Robert, to devise the counterarguments soon published as *An Essay on the Principle of Population* (1798). The *Essay* sought to demonstrate the impossibility of all such schemes for the major improvement of mankind because they violated natural (biological) laws. We may summarize the argument briefly in Malthus' own words. Two postulates are stated to be sufficient for this vast demonstration:

> First, That food is necessary to the existence of man.
> Secondly, That the passion between the sexes is

---

[9] *Ibid.*, pp. 346–47.

necessary, and will remain nearly in its present state.[10]

Actually, several further assumptions are required, and they are implied in the basic statement of the theory:

> Assuming then, my postulata as granted, I say, that the power of population is indefinitely greater than the power in the earth to produce subsistence for man.
>
> Population, when unchecked, increases in a geometrical ratio. Subsistence increases only in an arithmetical ratio. A slight acquaintance with numbers will show the immensity of the first power in comparison of the second.
>
> By that law of our nature which makes food necessary to the life of man, the effects of these two unequal powers must be kept equal.
>
> This implies a strong and constantly operating check on population from the difficulty of subsistence. This difficulty must fall somewhere; and must necessarily be severely felt by a large portion of mankind.[11]

Thus the argument moves rapidly; by page 37, Malthus feels "at a loss to conjecture what part of it can be denied."

The ratios are supported with a parsimony of evidence. Only one example was necessary to show the power of population to grow at a geometrical rate—it doubled every twenty-five years in the United States.[12] The law of growth of subsistence is supported by assertions of incredulity:

---

10 *Essay* ("Reprints of the Royal Economic Society" [London, 1926]), p. 11.

11 *Ibid.*, pp. 13–14.

12 *Ibid.*, p. 20. This fact came from Richard Price's *Observations on Reversionary Payments* (4th ed.; London, 1783), I, 282, where it is restricted to

Let us now take any spot of earth, this Island for instance, and see in what ratio the subsistence it affords can be supposed to increase. We will begin with it under its present state of cultivation.

If I allow that by the best possible policy, by breaking up more land, and by great encouragements to agriculture, the produce of this Island may be doubled in the first twenty-five years, I think it will be allowing as much as any person can well demand.

In the next twenty-five years, it is impossible to suppose that the produce could be quadrupled. It would be contrary to all our knowledge of the qualities of land. The very utmost that we can conceive, is, that the increase in the second twenty-five years might equal the present produce. Let us then take this for our rule, though certainly far beyond the truth; ... The most enthusiastic speculator cannot suppose a greater increase than this. In a few centuries it would make every acre of land in the Island like a garden.

Yet this ratio of increase is evidently arithmetical.[13]

The contradiction between the ratios is solved by the checks to population, all of which may be classified under two heads. The basic, inevitable check is misery, operating through all the channels that malnutrition may find. A second, highly probable, check is vice, under which Malthus includes not only sexual promiscuity but at times also war. Still another check—postponement of marriage because of prudence—is mentioned, but it is given little attention, because in Malthus' opinion it

the "northern colonies." It represents the estimate of a Dr. Styles, and the role of immigration is not discussed by Price or by Malthus.

[13] *Essay,* pp. 21–22.

is almost always accompanied by vice.[14] Condorcet's suggestion of contraception is dismissed with a reprimand.[15]

Let us now probe more deeply. Are the two ratios to be taken literally? One cannot be too sure of Malthus' intention; certainly he used these ratios frequently enough to the end of his life. But one can say that they were often taken literally and that to them the *Essay* owed its powerful impact. It would have been enough for Malthus' position if he had merely asserted that the rate of growth of population, unless repressed by the checks, *far* exceeded the rate of growth of subsistence. Yet, from the viewpoint of persuasion, the ratios probably had to be of different mathematical forms. Although an annual increase of population by 2 per cent would as surely overwhelm an annual increase of 1 per cent in the means of subsistence—the former doubles in thirty-five years, the latter in seventy years—it would have reduced the argument to the question of the facts of growth, and here no man's voice was loud.

No explicit trace of the law of diminishing returns was present; yet Malthus' ratios implicitly assumed sharply diminishing returns, for his numbers define the production function,

$$L = 2^{P-1},$$

where L is labor (proportional to population) and P is produce. With this production function, indeed, if workers received a wage equal to their marginal product, the aggregate wage bill would be independent of the size of the labor force, and population simply could not grow![16]

---

14 *Ibid.*, pp. 28–29, 62–70.

15 "He alludes, either to a promiscuous concubinage, which would prevent breeding, or to something else as unnatural. To remove the difficulty in this way, will, surely, in the opinion of most men, be, to destroy that virtue, and purity of manners, which the advocates of equality, and of the perfectibility of man, profess to be the end and object of their views" (*ibid.*, p. 154).

16 For

$$L \frac{dP}{dL} = \frac{1}{\log 2}.$$

Finally, was the level of subsistence of the masses some biological minimum or was it culturally determined? Malthus is
reasonably clear that usually it is a cultural minimum, well
above the biological minimum. For he admits of "some variation for the prevalence of luxury, or of frugal habits," and
agrees with Adam Smith that the population would increase
greatly if Englishmen were to adopt a potato diet.[17] We should
notice that this cultural minimum impairs some of the arguments against perfectibility, for men can presumably be taught
to insist upon a high minimum. It does not affect the law as an
economic generalization, however, if the minimum is fairly
stable.

Godwin replied to Malthus (and to other less temperate
critics) with courtesy and cogency.[18] The principle of population was greeted as a major contribution to political economy
and to the understanding of society. But, Godwin properly
argued, this principle denied all possibility of large progress
and had no special relevance to Godwin's proposals.[19] Nevertheless, it did bear also on Godwin's hopes; and against it he
had two defenses. First, infanticide, abortion, and similar
practices, though "painful and repulsive," are preferable to
Malthus' checks of misery and vice: "If the alternative were
complete, I had rather such a child should perish in the first
hour of its existence, than that a man should spend seventy
years of life in a state of misery and vice."[20] Second, men of the
more enlightened classes already postpone marriage to avoid
the poverty resulting from a great family, and in Godwin's
society this prudence will be characteristic of the entire popu-

---

[17] *Essay,* pp. 55, 130–37.

[18] *Thoughts Occasioned by the Perusal of Dr. Parr's Spital Sermon* (London, 1801).

[19] "The reasonings of the *Essay on Population* did not bear with any
particular stress upon my hypothesis . . ." (*ibid.,* p. 55).

[20] *Ibid.,* p. 65.

lation.[21] Surely Godwin was right, judged not only by the historical fact that this was the one objection to his system that the nineteenth century removed but also by contemporary evidence of widespread postponement of marriage, which indicated that this sort of behavior was not beyond mortal man.

Malthus capitulated, while still claiming victory, when in the second edition of the *Essay* (1803) he gave special prominence to a new preventive check (in addition to vice) to population—moral restraint:

> The preventive check, is peculiar to man, and arises from that distinctive superiority in his reasoning faculties, which enables him to calculate distant consequences. . . . These considerations are calculated to prevent, and certainly do prevent, a great number of persons in all civilized nations from pursuing the dictate of nature in an early attachment to one woman.
>
> If this restraint does not produce vice, as in many instances is the case, and very generally so among the middle and higher classes of men, it is undoubtedly the least evil that can arise from the principle of population.[22]

Given the possible—although in Malthus' opinion the improbable—efficacy of the moral restraint, Godwin had carried this

---

21 *Ibid.*, pp. 72–73.

22 *Parallel Chapters from the First and Second Editions of an Essay on Population*, ed. W. J. Ashley (New York: Macmillan and Company, 1895), pp. 87, 88. Moral restraint is formally defined as the preventive check "which is not followed by irregular gratifications" (*ibid.*, p. 90). It is apparent that only on strained meanings will misery, vice, and moral restraint embrace all checks to population, as Malthus repeatedly claims. He is forced to discuss emigration as a short-lived palliative and alludes to contraceptives as a form of vice.

issue; and, with the steady decline of his popularity and influence, he was also losing the argument for perfectibility. Henceforth, however, population received more attention, and Godwin's schemes less. Yet this origin left a permanent imprint on the formulation of Malthus' doctrine, and it explains in part why he was content to leave the economics of population at a very preliminary stage.

Aside from the addition of the check by moral restraint, only one substantially new factor was introduced in the later editions of the *Essay,* and this was diminishing returns:

> When acre has been added to acre till all the fertile land is occupied, the yearly increase of food must depend upon the melioration of the land already in possession. This is a stream, which, from the nature of all soils, instead of increasing, must be gradually diminishing.
>
> The improvements of the barren parts [of a nation] would be a work of time and labour; and it must be evident to those who have the slightest acquaintance with agricultural subjects, that in proportion as cultivation extended, the additions that could yearly be made to the former average produce, must be gradually and regularly diminishing.[23]

This concept of diminishing returns—if anything so muddy can be called a concept—was not elaborated or given much emphasis, and Malthus was quite willing to deny diminishing returns when a particular point might be served.[24]

---

23 *Ibid.,* pp. 82, 84.

24 For example, he asserts that in England diminishing returns did not hold in the twenty years before 1814 (*Essay* [8th ed.; London, 1878], pp. 360–61). Here Malthus was arguing for import duties on corn.

Indeed, one is impressed by Malthus' lack of interest in the economics of population. The concept of a subsistence level is not analyzed, nor are the factors which determine its height and changes isolated. The time necessary for population to respond to changes in the means of subsistence is left vague: Is it two years,[25] or is it the generations during which social customs respecting marriage are slowly modified?

Most important of all, there is no analysis of the factors which govern the rate of growth of output and hence (on his theory) of population. Some elements of such a theory are implicit in Malthus' defense of the mixed agricultural-commercial (industrial) economy.[26] Malthus was a forerunner of the current writers on the "industrialization of backward areas"; his variation, however, was the equally desirable "agriculturalization of industrial areas."

Malthus assumed that the welfare of the masses of population depended chiefly on the supply of bread; so agriculture was the basic industry. The chief role of manufactures—and this only in a society with an unequal ("feudal") distribution of property—was to entice the landlords to cultivate the land intensively to procure luxuries. In his own words:

> Agriculture is not only, as Hume states, that species of industry, which is chiefly requisite to the subsistence of multitudes, but it is in fact the *sole* species by which multitudes can exist; and all the numerous arts and manufactures of the modern world, by which such numbers appear to be supported, have no tendency whatever to increase population, except so far as they tend to increase the quantity

---

25 *Ibid.*, p. 373.

26 *Ibid.*, Book III, chaps. viii–x. His proagricultural bias diminished but did not disappear with time (see J. Bonar, *Malthus and His Work* [London, 1924], pp. 245 ff.).

and facilitate the distribution of the products of agriculture.[27]

This would suggest that a nation ought to be agricultural; and Malthus skirts this view but rejects it because—a characteristic irrelevance—some agricultural nations have poor governments or a poor distribution of ownership of property and because manufactures provide a market for labor that undermines feudalism.[28]

Yet he rejects the commercial nation even more completely. Foreign competition will eventually eliminate large profits from manufacturing, and so also will domestic competition. (Malthus seems to have had the peculiar notion that the competitive rate of return in manufactures must soon fall to low levels, with the accumulation of capital, but that in agriculture it remains high.) The industrial nation may suffer if its agricultural customers suffer from indolence or misgovernment, and more certainly it must decline when eventually the agricultural nations develop their own manufactures. The mixed economy somehow avoids all these objections and reaps all the advantages of both systems.

Here, as elsewhere, Malthus purveyed a strange mixture of occasional insights and drab fallacies. His belief in the essentially developmental role of a nation's specialization clashed with his belief that a balanced economy represented an optimum and stable policy. He was able to dismiss the prosperity flowing from trade and industry only by shrinking generations into hours, and England would never have risen to its pinnacle if it had followed his advice.

The *Essay* became much longer and vastly duller, when

---

27 *Essay* (8th ed.), p. 112.

28 Another advantage claimed for manufactures is that wages are in proportion to corn prices, so the non-food component of the standard of living of the masses will be larger with cheap manufactures. This is simply inconsistent with the principle of population.

Malthus added long accounts of population in ancient, primitive, and modern agricultural and industrial states. These descriptive accounts did not demonstrate the principle of population, as he claimed; rather, they demonstrated that death comes in many forms and that births are influenced by social customs. Malthus simply had no canons of evidence. He recited —and embroidered—travelers' accounts of primitive societies, seizing like a gossip columnist upon every reference to misery and vice and ignoring those to prosperity or virtue. He found the principle of population confirmed in the prosperity of England during the twenty years before 1811 and also by the depression after the Napoleonic Wars.[29]

What evidence could have been used to test the theory? If the subsistence level has any stability, and hence any significance, Malthus' theory was wrong if the standard of living of the masses rose for any considerable period of time. He did not investigate this possibility (but see below) and ignored the opinions of such authorities as Sir Frederick Eden that it had been rising for a century.[30] His theory was also contradicted if population grew at a constant geometrical rate in an "old" country, for then the means of subsistence were also growing at this rate, since population never precedes food.[31] Despite the rapid increase of population in almost all western European nations at the time, which he duly noted, he persisted in considering this as only a confirmation of his fecundity hypothesis.[32]

Malthus kept his *Political Economy* in a separate compart-

---

[29] *Essay* (8th ed.), p. 425.

[30] *The State of the Poor* (London, 1797), I, 560 ff.

[31] *Essay* (8th ed.), p. 384 n.

[32] In the first edition of the *Essay*, Malthus conjectured that the population of England was almost stable: "It is difficult, however, to conceive that the population of England has been declining since the revolution; although every testimony concurs to prove that its increase, if it has increased, has been very slow" (p. 314).

ment from his *Essay.* Though there were many uses of, and many deferential references to, the principle of population in the *Political Economy,* in the discussion of wages the principle was substantially ignored. For example:

> This great increase of command over the first necessary of life [from 1720 to 1750] did not, however, produce a proportionate increase of population. It found the people of this country living under a good government, and enjoying all the advantages of civil and political liberty in an unusual degree. The lower classes of people had been in the habit of being respected, both by the laws and the higher orders of their fellow citizens, and had learned in consequence to respect themselves. The result was, that their increased corn wages, instead of occasioning an increase of population exclusively, were so expended as to occasion a decided elevation in the standard of their comforts and conveniences.[33]

In a historical survey of wages, he finds them rising from the mid-fourteenth to the sixteenth century, then falling for a century—hardly a clear example of a strong tendency of wages to approach a subsistence level.[34] Indeed, Malthus goes so far as to investigate the factors (liberty and education) which lead workers to increase their standard of comfort rather than their numbers when income rises. Like a successful general, Malthus occupied all the positions.

------

[33] *Principles of Political Economy* (2d ed.; "London School Reprints," 1936), p. 228.

[34] *Ibid.,* Book I, chap. iv. The investigation was tenuous in the extreme, however; only the prices of corn and labor were compared, on his customary assumption that grain was the basic element of the standard of living of the workers. If it ever had this role, it had probably lost it by the seventeenth century.

Ricardo accepted the simple version of the first edition of the *Essay,* in which wages were always equal to some fixed ("subsistence") level in the long run:

> . . . No point is better established, than that the supply of labourers will always ultimately be in proportion to the means of supporting them.
>
> . . . So great are the delights of domestic society, that in practice it is invariably found that an increase of population follows the amended condition of the labourer.[35]

This was Ricardo's general assumption; but, when he came to analyze wages, the Malthusian theory was virtually ignored:

> Notwithstanding the tendency of wages to conform to their natural rate, their market rate may, in an improving society, for an indefinite period, be constantly above it; for no sooner may the impulse, which an increased capital gives to a new demand for labour be obeyed, than another increase of capital may produce the same effect; and thus, if the increase of capital be gradual and constant, the demand for labour may give a continued stimulus to an increase of people.
>
> It is not to be understood that the natural price of labor, estimated even in food and necessaries, is absolutely fixed and constant. It varies at different times in the same country, and very materially differs in different countries.[36]

Even the arithmetic rate of growth of subsistence is questioned:

---

[35] *Principles of Political Economy and Taxation,* ed. P. Sraffa and M. Dobb (Cambridge, England: Cambridge University Press, 1951), pp. 292, 407; also pp. 219, 398.

[36] *Ibid.,* pp. 94–95, 96.

> It has been calculated, that under favourable cir-
> cumstances population may be doubled in twenty-
> five years; but under the same favourable circum-
> stances, the whole capital of a country might pos-
> sibly be doubled in a shorter period.[37]

One can disregard the last passage, as pertaining only to new countries, but the indefinitely prolonged excess of the market over the natural wage rate and the possibility of a steady upward movement of the natural rate must simply be recorded as correct views which Ricardo did not know how to incorporate into his theoretical system.

The later history of the Malthusian theory is beyond our province, but we should notice that it was not popular among the best economists. Longfield rejected the theory,[38] and Senior proposed, in an ironical letter to Malthus, an alternative "nomenclature": "I should still say, that, in the absence of disturbing causes, food has a tendency to increase faster than population, because, in fact, it has generally done so. . . ."[39] Had not John Stuart Mill lent to it his great authority, it would have been declining rapidly in importance by mid-century.

The "principle of population" had the dubious honor of receiving from history one of the most emphatic refutations any prominent economic theory has ever received. It is now fashionable to defend Malthus by saying that his theory applies to other places and times than those to which he and his readers applied it. This may be true, but it is tantamount to scientific nihilism to deduce from it any defense of Malthus. It is an odd theory that may not some day and somewhere find a role; for every answer one can find a correct question.

---

37 *Ibid.*, p. 98.

38 *Lectures on Political Economy* ("London School Reprints" [London, 1931]), Appendix.

39 *Two Lectures on Population* (London, 1829), p. 58.

And yet Malthus deserves commendation for two important services that rise above the quality of his work. The first is that he gave population an important role in economic theory. The very failure of his theory was a large cause for the near-abandonment of population studies by later economists, and this seriously reduces his contribution to economics but does not eliminate it. The second service was the recognition that it is possible to deal fruitfully with population in terms of conventional economic theory. The identification of cost of subsistence with cost of production was illegitimate, but the explanation of birth-rate differentials through differentials in costs may well prove to be an important avenue through which economists may make contributions to the study of population.

II. THE THEORY OF RENT

England began its era of continuous importation of wheat —sporadic importation began a generation earlier—in the same year that it embarked upon the Napoleonic Wars, 1793. In June of this year, wheat was 51s. a quarter. It rose to 80s. in 1796, and after a drop rose again to 128s. in 1801, fell again up to 1804, and then began to rise and finally reached 152s. in August, 1812. Thereafter it fell sharply but irregularly, until it had fallen to 41s. by 1822.[40] The law of 1804 provided for export bounties if the price fell below 54s. and high import duties (30s.) when the price was less than 60s., but low duties (7½d.) when the price was above 66s. The wartime inflation had wholly outmoded this act, and moves for new protection began in 1813, as prices began to fall; and in 1814 both Lords and Commons appointed committees to report on the question. Their reports were the apparent stimulus to the publication of the pamphlets of West and Malthus. (At least West's pamphlet, however, was no stimulus to Lords and Commons; in

---

[40] See C. R. Fay, *The Corn Laws and Social England* (Cambridge, England: Cambridge University Press, 1932); and Thomas Tooke, *A History of Prices* (London, 1838), II, 390.

1815 they enacted a prohibition on importation when the price fell below 80*s*. and free importation at higher levels.)

The hearings before these committees emphasized the relationship between the high corn prices and the more intensive and extensive cultivation of the soil in the years up to 1812. Indeed, even the questions before the Lords' committee were sufficiently emphatic on the relationship:

> If the prices continue as low as at present, even if you were to pay no rent for such a farm as yours is, could you continue to raise grain and cultivate it in the same expensive manner you have recently cultivated it? (Reply: "Certainly not; . . . I must certainly discharge one third of my hands.")
>
> Supposing that wheat was to fall to 3*l*. 10*s*. permanently upon an average, . . . could the farmer continue to cultivate that species of land which you have mentioned as being poor cold land? (Reply: "I think not; that would be the lowest price; he could scarcely get any profit upon that.")[41]

Although there were ample clues for the development of the classical rent theory, it would be unjust to treat the inventors of the theory as mere codifiers of generally accepted and realized truth. These hearings had their full share of irrelevancies and inconsistencies—as hearings usually do—and the outlines of the theory in the facts of the time are undoubtedly much clearer to modern than to contemporary eyes.[42]

---

41 *Reports Respecting Grain, and the Corn Laws* ("Sessional Papers, 1814–15"), V, 18, 30.

42 Thus Arthur Young listed the rise of population, taxes, and foreign trade (as a measure of wealth) as the sufficient explanations for the rising price of corn, and he attributed the rise of rents chiefly to investments of landlords (*Report from the Select Committee on Petitions Relating to the Corn Laws of This Kingdom* ["Sessional Papers, 1813–14"], III, 82, 86).

Had Sir Edward West been less successful in the law, he might have been a leading economist of the era. His pamphlet displays a mind that was inventive and logically bent, and he had a rare talent for marshaling evidence to bear on a theory.[43] He immediately sets forth "a principle in political economy":

> The principle is simply this, that in the progress of the improvement of cultivation the raising of rude produce becomes progressively more expensive, or, in other words, the ratio of the net produce of land to its gross produce is continually diminishing. . . .
>
> Each equal additional quantity of work bestowed on agriculture, yields an actually diminished return, and of course if each equal additional quantity of work yields an actually diminished return, the whole of the work bestowed on agriculture in the progress of improvement, yields an actually diminished proportionate return. Whereas it is obvious that an equal quantity of work will always fabricate the same quantity of manufactures.[44]

The "progress of improvement" must be interpreted to mean the growth of output; West, like Malthus and Ricardo, gave little thought to technological improvements. The mistaken identification of diminishing average and diminishing marginal products also continued throughout the Ricardian literature. West found diminishing returns to be due to the necessity for resort to inferior lands,[45] but more fundamentally it was due

---

[43] *The Application of Capital to Land* (1815), reprinted with an Introduction by J. H. Hollander (Baltimore, 1903).

[44] *Ibid.*, pp. 9, 12. The mistaken equivalence of the first two parts of the first sentence will be noticed later.

[45] "Consider the case of a new colony; the first occupiers have their choice of the land, and of course cultivate the richest spots in the country: the

to the diminishing returns from more intensive cultivation. This was proved by what was essentially an inference from the fact that simultaneous cultivation of different grades of soil existed in stable equilibrium:

> And the very fact that in the progress of society new land is brought into cultivation, proves that additional work cannot be bestowed with the same advantage as before on the old land. For 100 acres of the rich land will, of course, yield a larger return to the work of 10 men, than 100 acres of inferior land will do, and if this same rich land would continue to yield the same proportionate return to the work of 20 and 30 and 100 as it did to that of 10 labourers, the inferior land would never be cultivated at all.[46]

West contributed two additional lines of demonstration of the law, and both were ingenious, although unconvincing. The first is summarized in his own words:

> The division of labour and application of machinery render labour more and more productive in manufactures, in the progress of improvement; the same causes *tend* also to make labour more and more productive in agriculture in the progress of improvement. But another cause, namely, the necessity of having recourse to land inferior to that already in tillage, or of cultivating the same land more expensively, *tends* to make labour in agricul-

---

next comers must take the second in quality, which will return less to their labour, and so each successive additional set of cultivators must necessarily produce less than their predecessors" (*ibid.*, p. 13).

46 *Ibid.*, p. 14.

ture less productive in the progress of improvement. And the latter cause more than counteracts
the effects of machinery and the division of labour
in agriculture; because, otherwise agricultural labour would either become more productive, or remain equally productive, in the progress of improvement.

In either of which cases, since labour in manufactures becomes more productive, *all* labour would
become more productive, and the profits of stock,
which are the net reproduction, would, of course,
rise in the progress of improvement. But the profits
of stock are known to fall in the progress of improvement, and, therefore, neither of the two first
suppositions is the fact, and labour in agriculture
must, in the progress of improvement, become actually less productive. It is then shewn that this
effect cannot be produced by a rise in the real wages
of labour.[47]

Unfortunately, the last sentence claims too much: he was not
able to show that the fall in the rate of profits could not be
due to a rise of wages.[48] This elegantly contrived analysis is

---

[47] *Ibid.*, pp. 23–24.

[48] West used three lines of argument to show this. First, he asserted that
the rate of population increase diminishes in the progress of improvement,
so that, on Malthusian grounds, real wages must be diminishing (*ibid.*, p.
20). He was factually wrong on population growth, and it seems inconsistent to employ Malthus' theory, which assumes constant real wages, to
disprove the existence of rising real wages. Second, he argued that high
wages are always accompanied by a high rate of profits. In substance he held
a wage-fund doctrine and believed that high profit rates would lead to a
high rate of increases of the wages fund (the degree of parsimony being
given) and thus to a more rapid rise of wage rates (*ibid.*, pp. 22–23). Third,
he argued that wages and profits are both high in America, so that high
wages are not the cause of low profits (*ibid.*, pp. 21–22). But at most this
shows that profits depend upon other variables as well as on wage rates.

very similar to Ricardo's theory, except that the fall of profits is a historical generalization rather than (as with Ricardo) an analytical theorem.

The second proof was that, as a matter of historical fact, rent was a declining share of the total product of agriculture, and this was equivalent to diminishing returns—an equivalence so complete that this was an alternative way of stating the law of diminishing returns. But a decline of rent relative to total produce does not rigorously imply either diminishing average product or diminishing marginal product of labor; wage rates may be rising enough to cause the decline in the share of rent.[49] The argument is perverse, in that if rent were a rising share of total product, then one could deduce the existence of diminishing marginal returns.[50] The whole analysis, however, is dependent on a constant state of technology.

From the theory of diminishing returns, West succinctly developed the classical rent theory:

> If in case of any increased demand for corn, capital could be laid out to the same advantage as be-

---

[49] Let P be product, N, the number of laborers, and P' the marginal product of labor. Then the proportion of rent to total product is

$$\frac{P - NP'}{P},$$

and its derivative with respect to N is negative if

$$NPP'' + PP' > N(P')^2$$

or

$$PP'' > P'\left(P' - \frac{P}{N}\right).$$

One cannot deduce from this either a decreasing average product—which requires $(P' - P/N)$ to be negative—or a decreasing marginal product, $P'' < 0$.

[50] In the notation of the previous footnote, then $NPP'' + PP' < N(P')^2$ and, since $-P'(P - NP')$ must be negative if rents are positive, P'' must be negative.

fore, the growing price of the increased quantity would be the same as before, and competition would, of course, soon reduce the actual price to the growing price, and there could be no increase of rent. But on any increased demand for corn, the capital I have shewn which is laid out to meet this increased demand is laid out to less advantage. The growing price, therefore, of the additional quantity wanted is increased, and the actual price of that quantity must also be increased. But the corn that is raised at the least expense will, of course, sell for the same price as that raised at the greatest, and consequently the price of all corn is raised by the increased demand. But the farmer gets only the common profits of stock on his growth, which is afforded even on that corn which is raised at the greatest expense; all the additional profit, there-fore, on that part of the produce which is raised at a less expense, goes to the landlord in the shape of rent.[51]

The theory is deftly used to refute the arguments of Sir Henry Parnell that the prohibition of importation of grain will lower the domestic price, and to estimate the price of wheat under such a prohibition (at least 90s.) and in the absence of all import duties (perhaps 60s.). West also makes an elegant anal-ysis of the effects of the 1688 export bounty on grain. His pamphlet contains a quality of economics that is not exceeded in his generation.

Almost simultaneously Malthus proposed much the same theory, but with much less incisiveness and clarity.[52] He man-

---

[51] *The Application of Capital to Land,* p. 39.

[52] *An Inquiry into the Nature and Progress of Rent,* reprinted with an Introduction by J. H. Hollander (Baltimore, 1903).

aged to invent two errors for each truth, and some of Ricardo's analysis can be viewed as a reaction to Malthus' peculiar approach. Three causes of the high price of raw produce (relative to the cost of production) were found:

> First, and mainly, That quality of the earth, by which it can be made to yield a greater portion of the necessaries of life than is required for the maintenance of the persons employed on the land.
>
> 2dly, That quality peculiar to the necessaries of life of being able to create their own demand, or to raise up a number of demanders in proportion to the quantity of necessaries produced.
>
> And, 3dly, The comparative scarcity of the most fertile land.[53]

The first cause of rent may charitably be read as a clumsy statement that land must be productive.[54] The second cause is formally irrelevant: rent could appear in a society in which the demand for corn was forever constant.[55] Yet the statement contains an important element of truth: rents will be higher, the more rapidly the demand for agricultural produce grows. The third cause is, of course, a sufficient, although not a necessary, condition for the existence of rent.[56]

---

[53] *Ibid.*, p. 15.

[54] Actually, Malthus means it as a requirement that the total produce be in excess of the subsistence level of the worker. This is a condition necessary for the continuous *payment* of rent by tenants to landlords but not for the existence of a surplus over the quantity of labor times its marginal product.

[55] Malthus states the contrary: if population is constant, an abundant produce "might reduce the price of raw produce, like the price of manufactures, to the cost of production" (*Nature and Progress of Rent,* p. 16). The trivial condition under which this is true is excluded by the third cause.

[56] Ricardo wrote to Malthus that "your first and third causes of high price appear to me to be directly at variance with each other. The first

The existence of diminishing returns on superior land was demonstrated by Malthus, as by West, by the resort to inferior land.[57] The determination of rent was also substantively identical with West's theory: rent was the excess of produce over the return on the capital (wage advances) of the farmer (tenant), which equaled the marginal product of labor times the amount of labor. Aside from this one contribution, however, the pamphlet was an undistinguished performance. It had many erroneous dicta, such as that improvements in agriculture always increase rent[58] and that the theory of rent for corn lands differs from the theory for vineyards, because the products of the latter have no influence on population! A tortured defense of a high price of corn and large rents was his chief theme (it was dictated by Malthus' protectionism), and it was argued on such grounds as that it is a sign of wealth for a nation to pay a high price for corn[59] and that laborers are not injured by a high price of corn if wages rise even more than corn prices.[60]

---

is the fertility of land, the third the scarcity of fertile land" (January 24, 1817, *Letters of David Ricardo to Thomas Robert Malthus* [Oxford, 1887], p. 127). The paradox is verbal: fertility in this realm of discourse is an economic property of land and is measured by its price; hence scarcity and fertility represent the same forces.

57 *Nature and Progress of Rent*, p. 27. It may be remarked that no one stated the law correctly with reference to this point. All these writers applied equal quantities of capital and labor to equal areas of land to measure differential rent. This violated the "best technology" assumption: equal quantities of capital-and-labor on different lands would not reveal the full difference in their productivity and might even reverse it. One should apply equal quantities of capital-and-labor to such quantities of each quality of land that the optimum technology is used on each quality of land.

58 *Ibid.*, p. 24.   59 *Ibid.*, p. 39.

60 Even for Malthus the argument is extraordinarily imprecise; consider the relations between these three statements:

"There is nothing so absolutely unavoidable in the progress of society as the fall of wages . . ." (*ibid.*, p. 22).

"We see in consequence, that in spite of continued improvements in agri-

The muddled protectionism of Malthus offered a natural foil to Ricardo, who had no trouble pointing out many inconsistencies in Malthus' argument.[61] Whether from an unrestrained love of paradox or from a general antipathy toward landlords, Ricardo wrote with more malice than reason:

> It follows, then, that the interest of the landlord is always opposed to the interest of every other class in the community.
>
> I shall greatly regret that considerations for any particular class, are allowed to check the progress of the wealth and population of the country. If the interests of the landlord be of sufficient consequence, to determine us not to avail ourselves of all the benefits which would follow from importing corn at a cheap price, they should also influence us in rejecting all improvements in agriculture, and in the implements of husbandry. . . .[62]

In his own formulation of the rent doctrine, Ricardo went beyond West at one point: the analysis of the effects of im-

---

culture, the money price of corn is *caeteris paribus* the highest in the richest countries . . ." (*ibid.*, p. 38).

"With regard to the labouring classes of society, it is a very short-sighted view of the subject, which contemplates, with alarm, the high price of corn as certainly injurious to them. . . . And I do not scruple distinctly to affirm, that under similar [prudential] habits, and a similar demand for labour, the high price of corn, when it has time to produce its natural effects, so far from being a disadvantage to them, is a positive and unquestionable advantage" (*ibid.*, pp. 39–40).

The last view is based, on the belief, already encountered in the *Essay*, that population follows food supply, not real wages.

61 See esp. *Principles,* chap. xxxii.

62 *An Essay on the Influence of a Low Price of Corn on the Profits of Stock* (*Works,* ed. Sraffa and Dobb, IV, 21, 41); also *Principles,* pp. 335–36, 400.

provements on rent.[63] Improvements were classified in two types: those which increase the output from given land and those which reduce the amount of labor necessary to produce a given product from given land.[64] These classes are not mutually exclusive, although Ricardo so implies.

In dealing with the first, or land-saving, improvements, Ricardo assumed (i) that the quantity of corn demanded was independent of its price—his customary assumption—and (ii) that the marginal product curve of labor on land was shifted upward a constant amount by the improvement. It then follows, as he argues from numerical examples, that rent will be reduced.[65] In the second class of improvements (which is surely vacuous under his definition), the effect on rent depends on the changes in the shape of the marginal product of labor curve.

Ricardo was prone to exaggerate the conflict of interests between landlords and other economic classes, and his discussions of improvements in agricultural techniques is an important example of this. Under his usual assumptions his conclusion should have been that improvements always benefit the landlords: the marginal product curve of capital-and-labor is higher relative to the cost of capital-and-labor,[66] and, since the supply of labor is infinitely elastic at a given real wage, rents

---

[63] Ricardo was independently approaching the theory of rent before the pamphlets of West and Malthus appeared (see his letters to Malthus in 1814).

[64] *Principles*, p. 80.

[65] For a geometrical illustration see A. Marshall, *Principles of Economics* (8th ed.; London, 1920), p. 835. In effect, Ricardo defined the production function as $\phi(N)$ where N is the number of laborers, before the improvement, and as $\phi(N) + aN$ after the improvement. With diminishing marginal returns, rent varies with the number of workers; and fewer workers are now needed to produce the same product.

[66] He believed that improvements had little effect on the shape of the marginal product curve (*Principles*, pp. 412–13).

must rise in the long run. It cannot be said that he wholly ignored this implication,[67] but he chose, for a change, to emphasize only the short-run effects, and then only in the adverse case.[68]

The theory of rent as these men used it could be properly applied only to a resource whose commercial supply was rigidly fixed and which could be used for only one purpose—the raising of corn. It is astonishing how easily and implicitly they identified this resource with British agricultural land, although the supply of land was being increased, and hardly without cost, and although this land was improved by investments of infinitely varied durability. Ricardo may be interpreted as attempting to avoid this identification by his definition of rent as the payment for the use of "the original and indestructible powers of the soil."[69] Yet, after this preliminary gesture—which is inadequate—he usually identified rent with the contemporary payments to landlords. The aggregation of all uses of land into "raising corn" is noticed rather than questioned by Malthus.[70]

This *Anschauung* may not have been particularly objectionable with respect to the problems in which Ricardo was interested. Grain formed a very large part of the standard of living of the working classes (perhaps one-third of total expenditures), and the elasticity of supply of land was doubtless relatively small in the moderately short run. But it is illuminating to see what an astonishingly narrow range of problems Ricardo could be interested in if he found this theory adequate. The structure and trend of individual prices, which had called forth some of Smith's best analysis[71] and which became the

---

[67] *Ibid.*, pp. 79–80, 412.

[68] Clearer notice of long-run effects was taken in the third edition, in answer to Malthus' criticisms (*ibid.*, pp. 81 n., 335–36).

[69] *Ibid.*, p. 44; see, however, p. 261 n.

[70] *Nature and Progress of Rent*, p. 17.

[71] *Wealth of Nations*, Book I, chap. xi.

central concern of neoclassical economics, were simply outside his domain.

At the level of technical analysis, the theory of rent marked a large advance over Smith's looser formulations. Yet it is noteworthy that Ricardo did not have that instinct for symmetry and generality which we now associate with the formal theorist. The law of diminishing returns was never applied outside agriculture, and the assumption of fixity of supply was not viewed as a limiting case of the infinite array of possible supply elasticities. Despite his penchant for abstract analysis, Ricardo was not a formalist: he was a theorist who wished to answer definite questions (presented by economic problems), and he made his theory no more general than these questions required.

III. THE RICARDIAN THEORY

In the theories of population and rent, as we have seen, Ricardo was chiefly a borrower, and he did not improve upon either theory in any basic respect. In the synthesis of these theories into a general theory of value and distribution, he struck out on his own. The peculiar combination of doctrines that makes up his system is truly original.

The outlines of his theory were beginning to emerge in his *Essay on the Influence of a Low Price of Corn on the Profits of Stock* (1815). We shall sketch the main elements of this theory before we turn to the *Principles*. The argument rested upon four propositions:

First, in the (domestic) production of corn, there is diminishing returns to composite dose of capital-and-labor. What is the dose of capital-and-labor? Strictly speaking, it is a dose of capital, and this capital consists of fixed capital (buildings, machinery, etc.) and circulating capital (the advances to laborers). The amount of circulating capital is set by the amount of labor (which is in fixed proportion to the fixed capital), and the wage rate.[72]

Second, the return to this dose of capital (and labor) is equal to the marginal product—cost of production equals price.

Third, the return on capital in agriculture fixes the rate of return that must also be obtained in other industries.[73]

Ricardo defended this amazing proposition as follows: Given the population, the demand for food is fixed in amount. Unless population changes, the output of corn will not change, and therefore—in the absence of technological improvements in agriculture—the investment in agriculture is fixed. Competition will not allow two profit rates; hence the profit rate in non-agricultural industries must equal that in agriculture.

This is a violent sequence. If new inventions raise the profit rate in manufactures, how is it restored to the agricultural rate? The internally consistent reply for Ricardo to make would have been: With an absolutely inelastic demand for corn, the attempt of capital to leave agriculture would force up the price of corn and hence the profit rate in agriculture until it equaled the profit rate in manufactures. But this is the reverse of Ricardo's conclusion; he argued, instead, that the profit rate in manufactures would fall back to the agricultural rate, as capital flowed into manufactures.[74]

A somewhat more comprehensible explanation can be inferred from his letters to Malthus. Innovations in non-agricultural industries will have no effect upon the cost of subsistence and hence upon wages (Ricardo temporarily forgot that other things besides food enter the worker's budget). Profits can be high for a short time (say five years), but soon the effects of the innovations will be overcome by the accumulation of capital. The only persistent force working to lower profits is

---

72 *The Works and Correspondence of David Ricardo,* ed. Sraffa and Dobb (Cambridge, England: Cambridge University Press, 1951), IV, 10–11.

73 *Ibid.,* pp. 13 n., 23–24.

74 *Works,* IV, 24.

diminishing returns in agriculture.[75] This proposition was not advanced in the *Principles*.

Fourth, the rent of land will be equal to the total product minus the amount of agricultural capital times its profit rate.

This is not a complete system because, in the absence of more explicit theories of population and capital accumulation, the aggregate output of the economy is not determined. The system does determine the division of product between landlords and others, but not between capitalists and laborers. Ricardo avoided this latter problem (although the subsistence wage theory lurked in the background). He denied, in fact, that the division between wages and profits was determinate:

> As experience demonstrates that capital and population alternately take the lead, and wages in consequence are liberal or scanty, nothing can be positively laid down, respecting profits, as far as wages are concerned.[76]

The *Essay* thus contained two main *elements* of the Ricardian system: the theory of rent and the dominant influence of diminishing returns in agriculture upon the rate of profits. The completed system required two further elements: the subsistence theory of wages and the measure of value. These were presented in the *Principles,* to which we now turn. Neither the organization nor the exposition is very felicitous, and I shall restate the central argument in my own words.

The competitive firm sells its product at a price which, on the average, equals its cost of production.[77] These costs of production are the various outlays of the entrepreneur on productive services; but from the social viewpoint one class of costs is pure transfer payments, which are unnecessary to call

---

[75] *Letters*, pp. 43, 46, 52, 57.   [76] *Works*, IV, 23.

[77] "... We mean always such commodities ... on the production of which competition operates without restraint" (*Principles,* p. 12).

forth the (fixed quantity of) productive services. These transfer payments are the rents paid for the use of land, and they can be eliminated from consideration by discussing costs at the extensive or intensive no-rent margins.

The various outlays of the entrepreneur are bewilderingly numerous, and they must be aggregated into fewer classes if useful generalizations are to be made. Let us classify all expenditures in two classes: fixed capital and circulating capital. Circulating capital is used up in a short time—say, a year or less; fixed capital is the remainder.[78] The chief employment of circulating capital is advances of wages to laborers.[79]

The wages of labor are also diverse, varying with skill, cost of education, and the like. Yet the occupational wage structure is very stable, so we may treat a skilled laborer as (say) three unskilled laborers if the former's wage is three times that of unskilled labor. Thus the expenditure on wages may be taken as proportional to the number of "equivalent unskilled" laborers.[80] (Ricardo should also have specified that the occupational structure of laborers is stable.)

Let us turn now to fixed capital—machines, buildings, and other durable equipment. Here we face a double problem: the machines are of very different durabilities; and the value of machines per worker varies widely among industries. Therefore, a rise in wages relative to interest (profits) will raise the prices of goods made with little fixed capital or with capital of short life, relative to the prices of goods in which more, and more durable, fixed capital is used.[81] But for broad purposes

---

[78] *Ibid.*, p. 31.

[79] "In one trade very little capital may be employed as circulating capital, that is to say in the support of labour . . ." (*ibid.*, p. 32). The other use of circulating capital is presumably to purchase raw materials, whose costs are, in turn, resolvable into rent or payments for fixed or circulating capital.

[80] *Ibid.*, chap. i, sec. 2.

[81] *Ibid.*, secs. 4 and 5. The period of turnover of circulating capital is also recognized as a factor in the effects of wage changes.

this refinement is not important: "The reader . . . should remark, that this cause of the variation of [relative values of] commodities is comparatively slight in its effects."[82] It is unimportant because the relative prices of labor and capital can vary little, whereas the quantities of labor necessary to produce various commodities can undergo large changes. (He should also have specified that the ratio of fixed capital to wage payments cannot undergo large changes.)

As a corollary of this theory of value, there exists no perfect measure of value, i.e., a measure of value independent of the fluctuations of wage and profit rates. The varying proportions of fixed to circulating capital and the varying durability of fixed capital imply that, given a change in the ratio of wage rates to profit rates, the values of goods will change differently, depending on the choice of the commodity used to measure their values.[83] But find a commodity which is produced with an average ratio of labor to capital (and this of average durability), then the ideal measure will be approximated.[84] Assume we have found such a near-ideal measure of value—the amount of labor (and corresponding amount of fixed capital) necessary to produce, say, gold.

Ricardo can now solve his basic problem: the distribution of the total produce among the various productive factors. Let us begin with the situation where 10 men on a given farm produce 180 bushels of corn.[85] This corn sells for $1 in terms of the measure of value, that is, the production of a bushel of corn requires the same quantity of capital and labor as the production of the quantity of gold designated as $1. More-

---

[82] *Ibid.*, p. 29; *Letters to Malthus*, p. 176.

[83] Commodities made with relatively much labor will rise in relative price when wage rates rise relative to profit rates.

[84] *Principles*, pp. 44–45. For a discussion of the measure of value in the first edition, see *ibid.*, pp. xlii ff.

[85] *Ibid.*, pp. 112 ff.

over, let each worker receive a subsistence wage of 5 bushels plus $5 of other necessaries. (We quote these other necessaries in value terms because their production is subject to constant costs.) We may summarize the situation (Table 1).

Now, with the progress of capital and population, resort must be had to Grade II land, on which 10 men (and corresponding capital) produce 170 bushels. The price of wheat

TABLE 1

Value of product = $180 \times \$1 = \$180$
Wage rate = $5 \times \$1 + \$5$ =   10
Wage bill = $10 \times \$10$ = 100
Total profits = $\$180 - \$100$ =   80
Rent   =   0

TABLE 2

	Grade I Land	Grade II Land
Value of product	$180 \times \$1.0588 =$ $190.58	$170 \times \$1.0588 =$ $180.00
Wage bill*	102.94	102.94
Profits.	77.06	77.06
Rent.	10.58	0

* The wage rate is $5 \times \$1.0588 + \$5 = \$10.294.$

must rise to $18/17 = \$1.0588$ per bushel, because the quantity of labor (and capital) per bushel has risen in this proportion relative to the ideal standard. The new situation is as shown in Table 2. (Recall that the rate of profits on marginal land sets the rate obtainable on superior land.) We could continue the arithmetic, but we have already reached the great conclusion: With the growth of population, the rate of wages rises, the rate of profit falls, and aggregate rents rise—all in terms of the measure of value.

Ricardo's basic theorem on distribution—"a rise of wages . . . would invariably lower profits"[86]—is thus strictly depend-

---

[86] *Ibid.,* p. 127.

ent on his measure of value. The product of a given quantity of capital and labor, be it large or small, always has the same value; hence the larger the value of labor (wages), the smaller will be the value of capital (profits). This is not equivalent to the proposition that a rise in wages will lead to a fall in the share of total income received by capitalists, for Ricardo had no theory of the share of total income going as rent.

Ricardo argues, almost parenthetically, that under certain conditions the inverse relationship between wages and profits holds also when they are expressed in terms of ordinary money rather than in an ideal standard. If a country is on the gold standard, its price level cannot vary (much) because of changes in domestic factor prices; gold flows will soon restore its former level. If, further, the productivity of capital and labor do not change, a rise in money wages will lead to a fall of money profits—in no other way can international monetary equilibrium be restored.[87]

One could criticize Ricardo's theory on many grounds. The population was not at a subsistence level, the occupational structure of the labor force and the relative wage structure were not stable, improvements in agricultural technology were neither negligible nor sporadic, technological progress in non-agricultural industries could offset diminishing returns in agriculture, etc. Malthus, however, concentrated his criticisms chiefly on one point: the ratio of circulating to fixed capital varies greatly among industries, and this fact vitiates Ricardo's measure of value. Extreme examples were adduced to demonstrate this: wine (and oak trees) increase in value without any direct labor expenditures (circulating capital); shrimp may be collected on the seashore without any fixed capital.[88]

This was a serious ambiguity, as Ricardo frankly recognized. Suppose corn is produced with much labor and little fixed cap-

---

[87] See *ibid.*, pp. 104–5, 126–27, 213–14; and *Works*, IV, 213–16.

[88] *Letters to Malthus*, pp. 179, 222.

ital, whereas the ideal commodity used to measure value is produced with a lower ratio of labor to fixed capital. Then diminishing returns in agriculture no longer entail a proportional rise in the value of corn (in terms of the ideal commodity), and, in fact, there is no method of determining how much the value of corn will rise. Ricardo would have had to introduce variable proportions between labor and fixed capital in each industry in order to cope with this problem, and this modification would have had radical consequences for his general system.

Ricardo summed up the general historical implications of this theory as follows:

> The natural tendency of profits then is to fall; for, in the progress of society and wealth, the additional quantity of food required is obtained by the sacrifice of more and more labour. This tendency, this gravitation as it were of profits, is happily checked at repeated intervals by the improvements in machinery, connected with the production of necessaries, as well as by discoveries in the science of agriculture which enable us to relinquish a portion of labour before required, and therefore to lower the price of the prime necessary of the labourer. The rise in the price of necessaries and in the wages of labour is however limited; for as soon as wages should be equal . . . to the whole receipts of the farmer, there must be an end to accumulation; for no capital can then yield any profit whatever, and no additional labour can be demanded, and consequently population will have reached its highest point. Long indeed before this period, the very low rate of profits will have arrested all accumulation, and almost the whole produce of the country, after paying the labourers, will be the property of

the owners of land and the receivers of tithes and taxes.[89]

Depending on the relative strengths of technological progress and diminishing returns, the dismal stationary state lies near or far in the future—but in any case, it lies farther in the future with free trade in corn! Ricardo pays little attention to this final, historical equilibrium, so we are entitled to infer that he did not believe that it was near.

Although both Adam Smith and Ricardo had cost theories of value, there were important differences even in the basic principles, of which four may be noted here. First, Smith believed that population changes lagged behind changes in the quantity of capital; therefore, wages were indefinitely above the subsistence level in an advancing society.[90] Second, the tenor of Smith's theory of rent, which was not given a coherent statement, was that aggregate rents are a residual but that the rent of any one use of land is a cost determined by the alternative uses of the land.[91] Ricardo ignored the multiplicity of uses of land. Third, Smith believed that the accumulation of capital led to a fall in the rate of profits,[92] whereas Ricardo—arguing from Say's law—denied that capital accumulation had any effect upon the rate of profits (unless the cost of food increased).[93] Finally, Smith's measure of value (ideally, money wages; as an approximation, corn prices) was designed to answer the same question as modern index numbers: how to eliminate differences in the value of money and thus ascertain the "real" changes. Ricardo's measure, on the other hand, was not a price deflator; it was designed to locate the source of changes in value in order to connect wages and profits to la-

[89] *Principles*, pp. 120–21.

[90] *Wealth of Nations* ("Modern Library" ed. [New York, 1937]), p. 69.

[91] *Ibid.*, Book I, chap. xi, esp. pp. 144–46, 149, 152, 159.

[92] *Ibid.*, pp. 87 ff.   [93] *Principles*, pp. 289–93.

bor's and capital's shares in the national income minus rents.

Modern economics is closer to Smith's position than to Ricardo's on each of these differences, although in the case of rent we use Ricardo's technique to analyze Smith's problem. This is not surprising: Ricardo had neither Smith's genius for isolating fundamental empirical relationships nor his supreme common sense. Yet Ricardo was, in his own terrain of technical analysis, superior to Smith. We may illustrate this superiority by comparing the two men's analyses of the effects of a tax on agricultural profits.

Smith, after describing and criticizing the French *taille,* makes the following analysis:

> When a tax is imposed upon the profits of stock in a particular branch of trade, the traders are all careful to bring no more goods to market than what they can sell at a price sufficient to reimburse them for advancing the tax. Some of them withdraw a part of their stocks from the trade, and the market is more sparingly supplied than before. The price of the goods rises, and the final payment of the tax falls upon the consumer. But when a tax is imposed upon the profits of stock employed in agriculture, it is not the interest of the farmers to withdraw any part of their stock from that employment. Each farmer occupies a certain quantity of land, for which he pays rent. For the proper cultivation of this land a certain quantity of stock is necessary; and by withdrawing any part of this necessary quantity, the farmer is not likely to be more able to pay either the rent or the tax. . . . The farmer, however, must have his reasonable profit as well as every other dealer, otherwise he must give up the trade. After the imposition of a tax of this kind, he can

get this reasonable profit only by paying less rent to the landlord.[94]

Smith does not explain why less land cannot be tilled; he does not explain how the threat of farmers to abandon farming will lower rents; nor does he explain why, if some farmers do leave the industry, the price of the product will not rise at the same time that rents fall.

Ricardo begins in a similar fashion:

> A partial tax on profits will raise the price of the commodity on which it falls: a tax, for example, on the profits of the hatter, would raise the price of hats; for if his profits were taxed, and not those of any other trade, his profits, unless he raised the price of hats, would be below the general rate of profits, and he would quit his employment for another.[95]

The conclusion is generalized:

> If it be agreed, that by taxing the profits of one manufacturer only, the price of his goods would rise, to put him on an equality with all other manufacturers; and that by taxing the profits of two manufacturers, the prices of two descriptions of goods must rise, I do not see how it can be disputed, that by taxing the profits of all manufacturers, the prices of all goods would rise, provided the mine which supplied us with money, were in this country, and continued untaxed.[96]

---

[94] *Wealth of Nations,* p. 807.

[95] *Principles,* p. 205.   [96] *Ibid.,* p. 213.

Prices will rise in varying proportions because of the varying ratios of fixed capital to circulating capital, the varying durability of fixed capital, etc. Now consider the effect upon landlords of a tax on profits (1) in every industry except corn, (2) in every industry, and (3) in the industry growing corn only.[97] In the first case every price except that of corn would rise. The landlord's corn and money rents being unchanged, he would suffer a fall in real income. In the second case corn would also rise in price, and, since its output was constant (on the customary assumption of zero demand elasticity), money rents would rise correspondingly; so the landlord's rent would retain its full purchasing power. In the third case money rents would rise, and real rents would therefore also rise.

Ricardo's analysis is perhaps little more rigorous than Smith's—for example, in the first case it is difficult to believe that profits in agriculture would not fall. Yet Ricardo's analysis is more consistent with his general theoretical system, and it is more subtle and systematic. It is perhaps worth adding, however, that the landlord who accepted Smith's opinion in preference to Ricardo's and opposed a tax on (and especially a tax only on) agricultural profits would be taking better care of his interests.

I shall not go further with the applications that Ricardo makes of his theory to taxation, currency, international trade, and in his polemics with other economists. These applications are not impeccable—for example, the celebrated chapter on machinery rests upon a logical error[98]—but they were made with rare consistency. Much of the appeal of the Ricardian system must have come from these demonstrations of the certainty, almost the routine, with which it seemed to dispose of

---

97 *Ibid.*, pp. 210–13.

98 Ricardo tacitly assumes that workers displaced by a technological advance cannot be employed elsewhere; for a good analysis see K. Wicksell, *Lectures on Political Economy* (London, 1934), I, 133–41.

troublesome problems and opinions. The age of formulas had begun.

IV. CONCLUSION

The legendary figure of Ricardo as a stern logician and a powerful debater is, I think, correct in essentials. I should prefer to say that his logic was severe in its simplifications rather than superlative in its rigor, but the dominant characteristic of the man was undoubtedly his perseverance and consistency in dealing with a few basic ideas.

Economics is the body of substantive generalizations on the workings of economic systems. Ricardo did not enlarge much this body of knowledge: his one addition to Smith's work was the systematic, though only partial, recognition of diminishing returns. Perhaps no other economist has ever fully shared Smith's immense understanding of the forces that govern the structure and development of economies; certainly Ricardo was not distinguished for his ability to discover great inductive generalizations.

Economics is also an engine of analysis, and Ricardo, with his great powers of abstraction and synthesis, was a master-analyst. Population, natural resources, capital accumulation, and the distribution of income—these were woven into a sweeping theoretical system. Measured by the significance of the variables and the manageability of the system, he fashioned what is probably the most impressive of all models in economic analysis.

It is here that Ricardo's service to economics lies. His naked logic and pseudo-logic helped to establish a professional frame of mind which did much to reduce promiscuous fact-gathering and *ad hoc* theorizing and to incite order and precision. This was the basic "Ricardo effect"; and, even with our modern knowledge of the painful extremes to which it can be carried, we must thank him for it.

7

The Early History of Empirical Studies of Consumer Behavior

Until recent times economists have studied consumer behavior chiefly through the theory of utility-maximizing individuals. The alternative approach—the establishment of generalizations on the basis of observed behavior—was also initiated and developed in its early stages chiefly by economists, but not by any economists prominent in the traditional history of our science.

My purpose in examining the early empirical work on consumer behavior is not to appraise the relative fruitfulness of the two approaches. Their scientific roles are, of course, complementary, and the utility theorists as a class have always expressed the greatest enthusiasm for empirical work compatible with abstention from it. Rather, my purpose is to examine the relationship of the empirical work to the theoretical work. The quantitative analysis of the effects of income on

Reprinted from *The Journal of Political Economy*, Vol. XLII (April, 1954).

consumer behavior developed fully seventy years before income became an important variable in the formal theory, while the formal theory of demand was developed forty years before empirical work on demand curves began in earnest. These sequences and lags pose the central problem of this paper.

I. INCOME THEORY

The differences in consumption of poor and rich families excited attention and often compassion, but apparently never quantitative analysis, for many centuries. Finally, in England in the 1790's, two very different investigators made extensive compilations of workingmen's budgets. Both were stimulated to this task by the distress of the working classes at this time.[1]

One investigator was David Davies, a clergyman about whom little is known. He collected budgets first in his own parish and then through correspondents elsewhere, until he amassed 127 budgets, which he reported in detail but did not summarize.[2] His results are presumably not characteristic of agricultural laborers generally, since he was interested only in the poorest families, and he used the data only to solicit sympathy and assistance for them. His chief proposal was the enactment of a minimum-wage law.

Two years later Eden published his monumental study, which contains a history of the poor and of the poor law as well as a wealth of detail on the various counties of England. He collected a few budgets himself, prevailed upon "a few respectable clergymen" for others, and employed an agent for more than a year to collect the remainder. He published budgets of sixty agricultural families and twenty-six non-agricultural families.

---

[1] Thus Eden says he was led to his splendid study by "the difficulties, which the labouring classes experienced, from the high price of grain, and of provisions in general, as well as of cloathing and fuel, during the years 1794 and 1795" (*The State of the Poor* [London, 1797], I, i).

[2] *The Case of Labourers in Husbandry* (Bath, 1795).

Neither Davies nor Eden made any summary of their budgets; they are summarized in Tables 1 and 2.[3] To them and to their successors for half a century,[4] budget data were merely a particular form of historical data, to be summarized much

TABLE 1*

BUDGETS OF FAMILIES OF AGRICULTURAL WORKERS
IN GREAT BRITAIN, 1787–93

	ANNUAL FAMILY INCOME (£)				
	10–20	20–25	25–30	30–45	All
	1. Percentage of Expenditures				
Expenditure category:					
Food......................	70.1	69.5	75.3	81.8	72.2
Rent......................	5.3	5.1	4.9	4.3	5.0
Fuel......................	2.6	3.0	4.2	3.1	3.2
Clothes...................	9.1	11.3	7.7	4.9	9.3
Medical care..............	5.2	4.5	2.3	1.6	3.9
Sundries..................	7.8	6.7	5.7	4.2	6.5
	2. Absolute Data				
No. of families...........	34	58	25	10	127
Average no. of persons in family...	5.2	6.0	5.8	7.5	5.9
Average income (£)........	18	22	27	36	23
Average expenditure (£)....	23	27	29	38	27

* From David Davies, *The Case of Labourers in Husbandry* (Bath, 1795).

as non-quantitative historical data had traditionally been summarized.

Two developments opened the modern era of budgetary

---

[3] I shall not discuss the substantive findings. Comparisons of early and modern budget studies will be made in a forthcoming monograph of the National Bureau of Economic Research.

[4] See the various budget studies reported in the first dozen or so volumes of the *Journal of the Royal Statistical Society*.

studies. The first was the wave of unrest, largely socialistic in aspiration, that swept Europe in the late 1840's and culminated in the Revolutions of 1848. The agitation and violence of the working classes led to an increasing concern for their economic condition and thus to the collection of economic

TABLE 2*

BUDGETS OF ENGLISH WORKING FAMILIES, 1794

INCOME CLASS	No. OF FAMILIES	AVERAGE INCOME (£)	AVERAGE EXPEND-ITURE (£)	PER CENT OF TOTAL EXPENDITURES				
				Rent	Food	Fuel	Clothes	Miscellaneous
			Agricultural Workers					
15–25.........	16	23	30	6.3	69.6	4.9	11.2	8.1
25–30.........	16	28	36	4.4	75.1	4.8	7.1	8.7
30–35.........	15	32	40	3.1	75.3	4.1	9.7	7.8
35–40.........	5	38	42	5.6	76.9	4.8	5.6	7.1
40 and over....	8	45	63	4.3	76.6	3.6	9.5	6.0
All.......	60	......	......	4.6	74.5	4.4	9.0	7.6
			Nonagricultural Workers					
15–25.........	4	22	26	8.8	68.9	7.4	6.0	8.8
25–35.........	6	28	30	5.4	73.3	7.9	4.9	8.5
35–40.........	6	36	37	5.2	78.6	6.5	1.6	8.2
40 and over....	10	51	55	6.0	73.3	3.8	6.2	10.7
All.......	26	......	......	6.0	73.9	5.4	5.0	9.6

* From Sir Frederick Morton Eden, *The State of the Poor* (London, 1797).

data, including budgetary data. Studies of budgets were made in Saxony and Prussia in 1848, and in 1855 a Belgian study, by Édouard Ducpetiaux, was published with full details on almost two hundred budgets.[5]

The second development was the popularization of statis-

---

[5] *Budgets économiques des classes ouvrières en Belgique* (Brussels, 1855).

tical analyses of collections of social data. The contributions to the mathematical theory of probability by Laplace, Cournot, Poisson, Gauss, and others provided an expanding technique of analysis. Adolphe Quételet was the chief exponent of the application of statistical techniques to social data. He was the lucid and energetic (and naïve) expositor of the view that the caprice and irregularity of individual acts and phenomena disappear when aggregates of such data are combined:[6]

> It seems to me that that which relates to the human species, considered en masse, is of the order of physical facts; the greater the number of individuals the more the individual will is effaced and leaves predominating the series of general facts which depend on the general causes, in accordance with which society exists and maintains itself. These are the causes we seek to ascertain, and, when we shall know them, we shall determine effects for society as we determine effects by causes in the physical sciences.[7]

Although Quételet did not concern himself with economic problems, he forcibly illustrated his thesis in many fields. His most famous creation was *l'homme moyen,* of interest chiefly to biometricians and politicians, but he demonstrated many regularities in marriage, suicide, etc. If one could show that crimes against property reach their peak in December, that

---

[6] See especially *Physique sociale* (Paris, 1869) and *Letters on The Theory of Probabilities* (London, 1849). For some important ideological currents of the time see the remarkable articles by F. A. Hayek, "The Counter-revolution of Science," *Economica,* N.S., Vol. VIII (1941).

[7] In *Recherches sur le penchant au crime,* quoted by F. H. Hankins, *Adolphe Quételet as Statistician* (New York: Columbia University, 1908), pp. 87–88.

suicides reach their peak at from six to eight in the morning, and the like, it was natural to seek corresponding regularities in economic behavior. Ernst Engel, who later expressed his admiration for Quételet by calling the equivalent expenditure unit a "quet," now made this application to consumer behavior.

Engel.—The first and most famous of all statistical analyses of budgets was made in 1857.[8] It rested on Ducpetiaux's data for 153 Belgian families, which had been classified into three social-economic groups: (1) families dependent upon public assistance; (2) families just able to live without such assistance; and (3) families in comfortable circumstances. Engel's summary of these data is reproduced in Table 3, and I have added data to indicate the great overlap in the incomes of these classes.

On the basis of this study (and of Le Play's studies of a few families), Engel proposed a law of consumption: "The poorer a family, the greater the proportion of its total expenditure that must be devoted to the provision of food."[9] This was the first empirical generalization from budget data.

This investigation had an astonishing aftermath. On the basis of the Belgian figures, Engel estimated rather roughly the consumption of the corresponding three classes of families in Saxony. In 1875 Carroll Wright, then Commissioner of Labor

---

8 "Die Productions- und Consumtionsverhältnisse des Königreichs Sachsen," reprinted with separate pagination as an appendix to Engel's *Die Lebenskosten belgischer Arbeiter-Familien* (Dresden, 1895). The essay was addressed to the population problem. Engel used the budgetary data to estimate the aggregate consumption of Saxony and compared the composition of this consumption with that of production (estimated from occupational data on the labor force). He argued that the optimum social structure required that the distribution of laborers among industries be proportional to the distribution of consumer expenditures and that, given this condition, the absolute size of the population was unimportant.

9 *Ibid.*, pp. 28–29. Engel also asserted that the wealthier a nation, the smaller the proportion of food to total expenditure.

Statistics in Massachusetts, reproduced this hypothetical table, attributed it to Prussia, and assigned to the three social-economic classes of families, expenditure ranges of $225 or $300, $450 to $600, and $750 to $1,100, respectively.[10] He then gave the following, excessively free translation of Engel's law.

TABLE 3*

PERCENTAGE COMPOSITION OF BELGIAN WORKMEN'S
FAMILY BUDGETS, 1853

CATEGORY OF EXPENDITURE	FAMILY TYPE		
	I (On Relief)	II (Poor but Independent)	III (Comfortable)
Food........................	70.9	67.4	62.4
Clothing (including cleaning)......	11.7	13.2	14.0
Housing......................	8.7	8.3	9.0
Heat and light.................	5.6	5.5	5.4
Tools and work supplies..........	0.6	1.2	2.3
Education, religion, etc..........	0.4	1.1	1.2
Taxes.......................	0.2	0.5	0.9
Health, recreation, insurance, etc...	1.7	2.8	4.3
Personal services...............	0.2	0.2	0.4
Total......................	100.0	100.0	100.0
Average income (francs)..........	565	797	1,198
Average expenditure (francs)......	649	845	1,214
Minimum expenditure (francs).....	370	440	541
Maximum expenditure (francs)....	1,256	1,769	2,823

* "Die Productions- und Consumtionsverhältnisse des Königreichs Sachsen," in Engel, *Die Lebenskosten belgischer Arbeiter-Familien* (Dresden, 1895), p. 27. The table contains some errors; I have added the last four lines of the table.

10 *Sixth Annual Report of the Bureau of Labor Statistics* (Boston, 1875), p. 438. On the basis of one of Engel's hypothetical tables, which gave food expenditures as a percentage of *income* (*op. cit.*, p. 30), the mean income of the first class is $250 and that of the second class a trifle over $600; the table extends no farther. Marshall probably got the class intervals from Wright; he gave them as £45–£60, £90–£120, and £150–£200. The first two classes correspond exactly with $5 = £1. But Marshall did not repeat a numerical mistake Wright made in copying the table (see *Principles of Economics* [8th ed.; London, 1920], p. 115 n.).

The distinct propositions are:

First, That the greater the income, the smaller the relative percentage of outlay for subsistence.

Second, That the percentage of outlay for clothing is approximately the same, whatever the income.

Third, That the percentage of outlay for lodging, or rent, and for fuel and light, is invariably the same, whatever the income.

Fourth, That as the income increases in amount, the percentage of outlay for "sundries" becomes greater.[11]

The comedy was not yet finished. In 1881 Engel gave income limits for the three classes of families in his hypothetical table for Saxony, and apparently took them from Wright![12] In 1895, Engel said of Wright's study that "the confirmation [of Engel's law] was complete."[13] In fact, Wright accepted the first (and only Engel) law and the fourth "law," but said: "As regards fuel, the law is quite generally verified; but its propositions as regards clothing and rents are plainly disproved."[14]

When Engel finally (in 1895) analyzed Ducpetiaux's data by income class rather than by social-economic class, the percentage of income or total expenditures spent on clothing rose and that spent on housing and fuel and light fell, as income or total expenditure rose, and thus there was no conflict with Wright's findings. Wright's "translation," for which I can find

---

11 *Op. cit.* He substantially reproduced this passage in *Eighteenth Annual Report of the Commissioner of Labor* (Washington, 1903), p. 101.

12 The income classes were 300–400 thaler, 600–800 thaler, and 1,000–1,500 thaler; see "Das Rechnungsbuch der Hausfrau," *Zeitschrift des Königlich preussischen statistischen Bureaus,* XXI (1881), 389. It has been suggested that Wright got the income classes by correspondence; if true, then Engel got them by divination.

13 *Die Lebenskosten,* p. 29.

14 *Sixth Annual Report,* p. 441.

no satisfactory explanation, still forms the basis of most present-day statements about "Engel's laws."

Before we leave Engel, mention should be made of two further contributions of great value. In *Der Preis der Arbeit* (Berlin, 1866), he analyzed the cost of raising a boy and training him for his father's occupation and showed that differentials in this cost relative to the father's earnings agreed with differentials in family sizes.[15] Subsequently he returned to a more precise investigation of the cost of raising a child and presented a scale by which families could be reduced to equivalent adults.[16] He proposed to call the unit of comparison the "quet"; a later generation in its wisdom prefers the word "ammain."

Schwabe.—Hermann Schwabe, the director of the Berlin statistical bureau, proposed a second "law" in 1868.[17] He had salary and rent data for 4,281 public employees receiving less than 1,000 thaler a year, and income and rent data for 9,741 families with incomes in excess of 1,000 thaler. For each group he found the percentage of income (or salary) spent on rent declined as income rose, and proposed the law: "The poorer anyone is, the greater the amount relative to his income that he must spend for housing."[18]

The law seemed to contemporaries less obviously true than Engel's, and a considerable literature arose about it. Ernst

---

15 "A hundred manual workers of our first example could on average raise 260 children, a hundred trained workers of our second example could raise only 234 and a hundred of the third example [the professional bureaucracy] only 214" (*Der Preis der Arbeit*, pp. 62–63).

16 *Der Werth des Menschen* (Berlin, 1883). This was called Part I; Part II, on the earnings-value of a man, never appeared.

17 "Das Verhältniss von Miethe und Einkommen in Berlin," in *Berlin und seine Entwickelung für 1868* (Berlin, 1868), pp. 264–67. This was the second annual volume of the statistical yearbook of Berlin.

18 *Ibid.*, p. 266.

Hasse found that it held for Leipzig in 1875,[19] and E. Laspeyres confirmed it for Hamburg.[20] Engel also accepted Schwabe's law.[21]

Wright.—The 1875 study by Carroll Wright, to which we have already referred, was for its time a model of full reporting and careful analysis. It surveyed 397 families of workingmen in Massachusetts. Their average income was $763, of which the husbands, on the average, earned $575 and children

TABLE 4*

PERCENTAGE COMPOSITION OF BUDGETS OF MASSACHUSETTS WORKMEN'S FAMILIES, 1875

CATEGORY OF EXPENDITURE	INCOME OF FAMILY ($)				
	300–450	450–600	600–750	750–1,200	1,200 and Over
Subsistence....	64	63	60	56	51
Clothing........	7	10.5	14	15	19
Rent..........	20	15.5	14	17	15
Fuel..........	6	6	6	6	5
Sundry........	3	5	6	6	10

* Carroll Wright, *Sixth Annual Report of the Bureau of Labor Statistics* (Boston, 1875), p. 441.

almost the entire remainder. Two of Wright's tables are reproduced as Tables 4 and 5.

The now familiar pattern of savings disclosed by Table 5

[19] "Das Verhältniss zwischen Wohnungsmiethe und Einkommen in Leipzig im Sommer 1875," *Zeitschrift des Königlich sächsischen statistischen Bureaus,* XXI (1875), 70–73. He found that about half the families had to be excluded because they sublet rooms.

[20] "Verhältniss der Miethe zum Einkommen in Leipzig, verglichen mit Hamburg und Berlin," *Zeitschrift des Königlich sächsischen statistischen Bureaus,* XXII (1876), 24–29.

[21] "Die Wohnungsnoth," *Zeitschrift des Königlich preussischen statistischen Bureaus,* XII (1872), 382.

led Wright to the generalization: "That the higher the income, generally speaking, the greater the saving, actually and proportionately."[22] He interpreted the negative savings as a proof of poverty, like countless equally mistaken successors, and recommended that a minimum-wage law be instituted. It is illustrative of the caprice of fame—or of the importance of

TABLE 5*

SAVINGS OF MASSACHUSETTS WORKMEN'S
FAMILIES, 1875 (IN DOLLARS)

Income Class	Average Income	Average Surplus
300– 400............	359	− 33
400– 500............	461	− 8
500– 600............	555	− 5
600– 700............	653	+ 10
700– 800............	754	+ 20
800– 900............	850	+ 32
900–1,000............	950	+ 58
1,000–1,100............	1,039	+ 50
1,100–1,200............	1,190	+106
1,200–1,300............	1,243	+129
1,300–1,400............	1,366	+172
1,500–1,600............	1,537	+229
1,800 and over........	1,820	+276

* Wright, *Sixth Annual Report*, p. 380.

calling a generalization a "law"—that this documented generalization on savings elicited almost no attention, while Schwabe's less well-demonstrated generalization on rent took its place among the empirical laws.

And here, at the very threshold of the era of budget studies, we must abandon their history. Their number and scope increased incessantly, and their history even to 1914 would require—and deserve—monographic treatment. The emphasis upon empirical generalizations of Engel's type diminished, and, indeed, the leading figures in this subsequent work were

---

22 *Sixth Annual Report*, p. 385.

usually less interested in the strictly economic than in the social implications of the studies. In order to give a taste of the progressive refinement in both data and techniques of analysis, however, I shall describe the analyses of Del Vecchio and Ogburn.

Del Vecchio and Ogburn.—Gustavo del Vecchio borrowed his techniques from Gini, who had employed them in a demand study we shall notice later. In substance, they consist of (i) the assumption that the relationship between food expenditures and income is, $c = a + b \log_{10} Y$, where c is expenditure on food and Y is income (or total expenditure)—a form suggested by the Weber-Fechner law; (ii) the fitting of this form of curve to various bodies of budgetary data; and (iii) the calculation of an "index of elasticity of consumption," which is 2.3 times the now popular income elasticity.[23]

Del Vecchio applied the technique to some 50 budget studies and found that his index fell between 1 and 2 in almost every case and that 1.55 was a good estimate of its average value. (In terms of income elasticities, the range is from 0.4 to 0.8 with a mean value of about 0.6.) He also deduced that the index increases with income, that it increases with the number of children in the family (not holding family income constant), and that it is larger if alcohol is included in food. A few sample calculations also suggest that the index is larger for housing and clothing than for food. This short summary does less than justice to Del Vecchio's work,[24] but it suggests how far the analysis of budgets had proceeded by 1912.

The application to budget data of correlation and curve-fitting techniques took place almost simultaneously with their

[23] "Relazioni fra entrata e consumo," *Giornale degli economisti,* 3d ser., XLIV (1912), 111–42, 228–54, 389–439. These steps are described in more detail below (p. 220).

[24] His discussion of the choice between income and total expenditure (*ibid.,* pp. 236–37) should at least be mentioned, although here, I think, he reached the right conclusion for the wrong reasons.

application to demand curves (see below). As an early, excellent example of this work we may cite William Ogburn's analysis of two hundred family budgets gathered in the District of Columbia in 1916.[25] Ogburn calculated (from the ungrouped data) the relationship between the proportion of each expenditure category to total expenditure and (1) family income, and (2) family size, which was reduced to a single number by the use of an "equivalent adult" scale. The income

TABLE 6*

INCOME ELASTICITIES FOR DISTRICT
OF COLUMBIA FAMILIES, 1916

Expenditure Category	Elasticity
Food	0.67
Rent	0.93
Fuel and light	0.73
Clothing	1.36
Husband's clothing	1.41
Wife's clothing	1.83
Children's clothing	1.07
Sundries	1.48
Life insurance	0.95
Religion	1.67
Furniture	1.40
Education	1.87
Amusement	1.90
Liquor and tobacco	0.51
Sickness	0.88

* William Ogburn, "Analysis of the Standard of Living in the District of Columbia in 1916," *Publications of the American Statistical Association*, XVI (1918–19), calculated from his Tables VI and VIII.

elasticities (evaluated at the mean income of $1,145) listed in Table 6 can be derived from his regression equations. He compared his results with Wright's version of Engel's laws and found the second and third laws to be disproved.

Conclusion.—We have seen that, by the 1870's, budget

---

25 "Analysis of the Standard of Living in the District of Columbia in 1916," *Publications of the American Statistical Association*, XVI (1918–19), 374–92.

studies began to take on the characteristics of an established area of work, and thereafter they increased enormously in volume and improved substantially in quality. Yet it was not until the 1930's that income came to be analyzed systematically in economic theory. How can we explain this long delay in incorporating income in the formal theory?

The delay was not due to the theorists' ignorance of the empirical work; I believe that almost every prominent economic theorist after 1890 was more or less acquainted with the work on family budgets (and also with the work on national income). Nor do I believe that the theorists had any tendency to regard their theoretical system as "closed" or to believe that the introduction of income called for a radical reconstruction of their entire theoretical system. When income was introduced into consumer theory by Slutsky and Hicks and Allen, their work was wholly in harmony with the line of development the theory of utility had been taking.

A large part of the explanation for the delay seems to lie in the widespread belief that real income does not fluctuate much in the short run. Even so well-informed an economist as Marshall could write:

> Next come the changes in the general prosperity and in the total purchasing power at the disposal of the community at large. The influence of these changes is important, but perhaps less so than is generally supposed. For when the wave of prosperity is descending, prices fall, and this increases the resources of those with fixed incomes at the expense of those whose incomes depend on the profits of business. The downward fluctuation of prosperity is popularly measured almost entirely by the conspicuous losses of this last class; but the statistics of the total consumption of such commodities as tea, sugar, butter, wool, etc. prove that the total pur-

chasing power of the people does not meanwhile fall very fast.[26]

This attitude rested on an unsystematic survey of facts rather than on Say's law; and when the extent of short-run fluctuations in real income was demonstrated—roughly in the 1920's in this country—economists were quick to take account of them.

A second factor is that there exists a very considerable set of problems in which income is not an important variable (even if it is known to fluctuate widely). In the analysis of the allocative effects of monopoly, for example, income is unimportant. Similarly, it is possible to deal informatively with freight-rate structures or tariffs or excises on particular commodities or the detailed policies of labor unions, without paying much attention to income. Economists before the First World War were concerned primarily with this kind of problem.

Neither of these explanations is a justification; but, before one starts to allocate blame among the theoreticians, he should also seek to answer the complementary question: Why did not the empirical workers in the field of budget studies seek to construct a theory that gave better expression to their findings?

One cannot say that the empirical workers had (or now have) an aversion to generalizations: in fact, they frequently make bold, and sometimes reckless, generalizations. But they do not give these generalizations the abstract and systematic formulation that characterizes conventional economic theory. As a result, the generalizations seem closely bound to the specific empirical researches on which they are based, and they lend themselves much less to cumulative refinement and elaboration and to widening areas of application. The empirical generalizations therefore fail to achieve the continuity and the widespread influence of the formal theories. Thus Engel's law

---

26 *Op. cit.*, pp. 109–10.

of food consumption gained neither generality nor content in the half-century after it was announced.

Whether this explanation is true or not, I consider it an unhappy division of labor in which one class of scientists collects materials and another class tries to extract their meaning. And if the explanation is correct, the empirical workers who are pioneering new areas can learn more from theorists than how to rationalize their previous findings—they can learn the manner in which to formulate their generalizations so that they will influence the trend of economic thinking.

II. DEMAND THEORY

The first recognition of an inverse relationship between the price and quantity of a commodity must have occurred thousands of years ago, and—to move somewhat closer to the present—the relationship has been known to every economist in the history of the science. Systematic and cumulative work on demand theory began only in the 1870's, however, when Fleeming Jenkin, Jevons, Walras, Marshall, and others began to develop the demand function or curve as an integral part of the theory of price formation.

Empirical work on demand also goes back a fairly long time, and, like the theoretical work, it was also casual and noncumulative in nature. We shall briefly summarize this early empirical work before turning to the modern work on statistical demand curves.

Early work.—The first "empirical" demand schedule was published in 1699 by Charles Davenant in *An Essay upon the Probable Methods of Making a People Gainers in the Balance of Trade.*[27] It was presented with admirable brevity:

> We take it, that a defect in the harvest may raise
> the price of corn in the following proportions:

---

[27] (London, 1699), p. 83.

	Defect		Above the Common Rate	
	1 Tenth			3 Tenths
	2 Tenths			8 Tenths
	3 Tenths	Raises the price		1.6 Tenths
	4 Tenths			2.8 Tenths
	5 Tenths			4.5 Tenths

A century later these calculations were attributed to Gregory King by Lord Lauderdale,[28] without any known basis;[29] and since then they have usually been known as Gregory King's "law." Innumerable economists have since commented, generally favorably, upon the law.[30]

The first real empirical investigation of demand may have been made in the early nineteenth or even in the eighteenth century. Data on imports and their prices, for example, were already available, and no sophisticated technique is necessary to form at least an estimate of the relationship between quantity and price. The earliest analysis of which I know, however, was made in 1861. Dr. Engel, of budget fame, was its author.[31] He calculated the average harvest of rye in Prussia from 1846–47 to 1860–61, the average price from 1816 to 1860, and measured the percentage deviation of price and harvest in each year from these averages (Table 7). Engel pointed out that fluctuations in harvests lead to more than proportional fluctuations in consumption, if the carry-over does not vary, because a fairly constant amount must be set aside for seed. He sum-

---

28 *An Inquiry into the Nature and Origin of Public Wealth* (Edinburgh, 1804), p. 51 n.

29 See *Two Tracts by Gregory King* (Baltimore: Johns Hopkins Press, 1936), pp. 6–7.

30 Wicksteed first found its exact equation, in 1889: $60p = 1,500 - 374q + 33q^2 - q^3$, if we let a normal harvest (q) be 10 and its price (p) be 1 (see *Commonsense of Political Economy* [London, 1934], II, 737).

31 "Die Getreidepreise, die Ernteerträge und die Getreidehandel in preussischen Staate," *Zeitschrift des Königlich preussischen statistischen Bureaus*, I (1861), 249–89.

marized the data in a peculiar manner, as one can see from the table, and concluded: "If there is any general relationship between yield and price to be derived from these numbers, it is, that a decrease in yield of 1 percent causes a rise in price of 2½ percent, and an increase in yield of 1 percent leads to a fall in price of 2 per cent. . . . King's law has no claim to validity."[32] With this he dropped the investigation, satisfied with the conclusion that there could be no universally valid relationship between price and quantity.

TABLE 7*

HARVESTS AND PRICES OF RYE
PRUSSIA, 1846–61

Crop Year	Percentage Deviation from Average Harvest	Percentage Deviation from Average Price
1846–47....................	− 43	+ 93
1847–48....................	+ 22	0
1848–49....................	+ 4	− 33
1849–50....................	+ 7	− 36
1850–51....................	− 10	− 10
1851–52....................	− 22	+ 26
1852–53....................	− 19	+ 21
1853–54....................	− 16	+ 70
1854–55....................	− 2	+ 61
1855–56....................	− 34	+107
1856–57....................	0	+ 23
1857–58....................	+ 1	+ 2
1858–59....................	− 17	+ 12
1859–60....................	− 23	+ 19
1860–61....................	− 1	+ 20
Sum of minus percentages.....	−187	+454
Sum of positive percentages....	+ 34	− 80
Sum........................	−153	+374

* Ernst Engel, "Die Getreidepreise . . . ," *Zeitschrift des Königlich preussischen statistischen Bureaus,* I (1861), 276.

─────────

[32] *Ibid.*, p. 276. It is not obvious that King's law is disproved; it has an elasticity of demand of $-^3/_7$ at the normal harvest level, which is close to Engel's estimate.

Fourteen years later Étienne Laspeyres carried the discussion a trifle further, in his brilliant plea for a discipline of economic statistics.[33] He took Engel's data for potatoes in Saxony and averaged pairs of the ranked fourteen observations to obtain a demand schedule (Table 8). Laspeyres's chief purpose was to demonstrate that even averages of two observations could yield discernible regularities in economic data.

TABLE 8*

HARVESTS AND PRICES OF
POTATOES, SAXONY, AS
PER CENT OF 14-YEAR
AVERAGE

Harvest	Price
66.	139
83.	113
96.	107
103.	104
110.	90
113.	77
129.	72

* Étienne Laspeyres, *Die Kathedersocialisten und die statistischen Congresse* (Berlin, 1875), p. 39.

Substantial refinements in technique were made by Henry Farquhar, a statistician of the Census Bureau, in his study of the demand for potatoes.[34] He calculated the per capita production of potatoes from 1867 through 1888, and compared the annual changes in production with the annual changes in the per capita value of the crop:

Fourteen times out of twenty, an increased crop
is followed by a diminished total value, and *vice
versa*. The amount of this change of total value is

---

[33] *Die Kathedersocialisten und die statistischen Congresse* (Berlin, 1875), esp. pp. 38–39.

[34] A. B. and H. Farquhar, *Economic and Industrial Delusions* (New York, 1891).

approximately 16 cents per capita for every bushel per capita by which the year's crop is larger or smaller. In another calculation I noted the percentage by which product and value respectively increased or lessened, in proceeding from year to year: and I thus found that for every one per cent. by which the crop varied, the total value varied about three tenths of one per cent. in the opposite direction. The price of a bushel therefore varied 1.3 per cent.[35]

This was apparently the first use of either per capita figures or relative changes (link relatives) in demand studies.

Although I have discovered no other examples of empirical demand functions in the nineteenth century, it is probable that some were made after, and possibly even before, Engel's essay. But their discovery will not invalidate the statement that this was a period of isolated, non-cumulative work. The era of continuous and influential work on demand began only after the turn of the century.

The rise of statistics.—The immediate stimulus to the modern era of demand studies was the birth of modern statistics. In the 1880's and 1890's, Galton, Edgeworth, Pearson, and Yule developed correlation analysis and curve-fitting techniques. It cannot be said that the statistical analysis of demand functions had to await these developments: the method of least squares had been developed long before, and numerous other methods of fitting curves to empirical data were available. Yet the brilliant work of Galton and the prodigious labors of Pearson inevitably called wide attention to the growing stock of available statistical techniques.

Fast on the heels of the theory of correlation came a series of statistical studies on economic subjects, and in the course of

[35] *Ibid.*, pp. 207–8.

these studies the problems posed by economic time series were partially formulated and solved. R. H. Hooker, in a study of the relationship between the marriage rate and exports, employed a nine-year moving average to eliminate periodic fluctuations in the series.[36] A year later J. P. Norton, in his remarkable study of the New York money market, fitted growth curves to his series to eliminate trend, and even calculated a "supply curve" of call loans.[37] Hooker soon dealt with the elimination of longer-term movements in series which had no periodic fluctuations, and he recommended correlation of first differences.[38] He illustrated the technique by correlating United States corn production and the Iowa farm price of corn; the correlation between the series (from 1870 to 1904) was —.28, but the correlation between the first differences was —.84, "indicating that the amount of maize produced in the United States is much the most important factor in the price paid in Iowa."[39] He did not give the regression equation.

To abandon a chronological account for a moment, Warren Persons carried Hooker's technique a trifle further in 1910.[40] Persons correlated first differences in average farm prices and corn production for 1866–1906, obtaining a correlation coefficient of —.833 and the regression equation,

$$p_t - p_{t-1} = -0.0254(q_t - q_{t-1}) + 1.32 \text{ .}^{41}$$

---

[36] "Correlation of the Marriage-Rate with Trade," *Journal of the Royal Statistical Society*, LXIV (1901), 485–92.

[37] *Statistical Studies in the New York Money-Market* (New York, 1902), esp. p. 90.

[38] "On the Correlation of Successive Observations, Illustrated by Corn Price," *Journal of the Royal Statistical Society*, LXVIII (1905), 696–703.

[39] *Ibid.*, p. 703.

[40] "The Correlation of Economic Statistics," *Publications of the American Statistical Association*, XII (1910–11), 287–322.

[41] *Ibid.*, p. 314. If we treat the constant as a trend factor, the demand function would be,

$$p = -0.0254\,q + 1.32t + \text{constant} \text{ .}$$

Persons also correlated relative changes in price and quantity and found a slightly lower correlation coefficient (—.794). He did not explicitly link his work with the economist's demand curve.

Early statistical demand curves.—The first modern statistical demand studies were made by Rodolfo Benini, the Italian statistician, in 1907.[42] In addition to estimating the demand for coffee by crude procedures,[43] he made the first application of multiple correlation to demand. His demand function for coffee in Italy was:

$$q = 476 - 0.4732(p_c - 307) - 4.49(p_s - 112.87),$$

where q is per capita quantity of coffee in grams and p_c and p_s are the prices of coffee and sugar, respectively, in lire. Benini was properly embarrassed by this equation, for it indicated that the price of sugar has more influence on the consumption of coffee than does the price of coffee (the demand elasticity is about —0.3; the cross-elasticity about —1). He invoked, for perhaps the first time in this connection, the now traditional defense that the results were only a first approximation and expressed the hope that the introduction of substitutes like alcohol into the equation would eliminate the paradox.

---

[42] "Sull'uso delle formole empiriche nell'economia applicata," *Giornale degli economisti*, 2d ser., XXXV (1907), 1053–63. Slightly different equations are given in "Una possibile creazione del metodo statistico," *ibid.*, XXXVI (1908), 11–34.

[43] Benini estimated the demand function for coffee in Italy, using data for 1880–81 to 1905–06. He ranked the years by price and then divided the data into a number of classes equal to the number of constants to be estimated and selected constants such that the function passed through the averages for the classes. One demand function was

$$q = 487.52 - 0.51681p - 0.001427p^2,$$

where q is per capita consumption (in grams) and p is (price — 300) in lire. He also estimated a constant elasticity curve,

$$qp^{0.384} = 4,282,$$

a form apparently suggested to him by Pareto's income law.

Corrado Gini, the distinguished statistician, soon followed with an extensive study of empirical demand functions.[44] He had a very general conception of the problem: "The consumption of a commodity depends upon many factors in addition to its price: such as the income of the consumers, their tastes, the organization and skill of the sellers, the prices of substitutes and complements."[45] Unfortunately, he imposed on his studies the assumption that the relationship between quantity and price was semilogarithmic. This was superficially justified by reference to the Weber-Fechner law, with price identified with stimulus, and quantity purchased identified with response or sensation.

Gini proceeded to estimate numerous demand functions, of which that for tea in the United Kingdom may serve as an example. Using a peculiar and inefficient method of curve-fitting,[46] he found this function to be

$$q = 11.5933 - 7.63 \log p ,$$

where q is per capita consumption of tea (in pounds) and p is the price including import duty (in hundredths of the pound sterling). Gini then introduced a coefficient of sensitivity, defined as the regression coefficient (7.63) divided by the mean

---

[44] "Prezzi e consumi," *Giornale degli economisti*, 3d ser., XL (1910), 99–114, 235–49.

[45] *Ibid.*, p. 99. We shall pass over his discussion of the effects of the form of organization of sellers; the example—cartels versus competition—displays some confusion in attributing an effect beyond that operating through price.

[46] The procedure was as follows: (i) group the annual data into three to six classes to eliminate minor fluctuations; (ii) average the logarithms of prices for each class and average the corresponding quantities; (iii) calculate the mean deviations of the quantities and logarithms of prices; and (iv) determine the regression coefficient as

$$\frac{\text{Mean deviation in consumption}}{\text{Mean deviation in logarithms of price}} .$$

consumption (5.18); it was 2.3 times the elasticity of demand.[47] Experiments were made in the elimination of trend and—by methods which were praiseworthy only for their novelty—in the estimation of complementarity.[48]

The comparison of coefficients of sensitivity suggested to Gini that they were smaller, the more urgently necessary the commodity: in Italy, they were .4 for salt, 1.0 for coffee, and 1.5 for petroleum. They may also decline with wealth: the coefficient for coffee was 0.4 in the United Kingdom and 1.0 in Italy. He suggested also that the sensitivity declines when a commodity becomes complementary to other goods. He proposed also other questions for future study: for example, whether sensitivity varies inversely with the proportion of income spent upon the commodity. Gini's work was notable for its breadth of vision.

In the same year, A. C. Pigou proposed his first method of deriving statistical demand curves.[49] Relative price elasticities could be derived from budgetary data, he believed, on the special assumptions that the utility function was additive (i.e., the

---

[47] Let $q = a + b \log_{10} p$. Then,

$$\frac{dq}{dp} = \frac{b \log_{10} e}{p} = 0.4343 \frac{b}{p},$$

and

$$\eta_{qp} = \frac{dq}{dp} \frac{p}{q} = 0.4343 \frac{b}{q} = 0.4343 S,$$

where S is Gini's measure of sensitivity.

[48] He estimated that the sweet-toothed Italians used 2 pounds of sugar with each pound of coffee. But when he fitted a curve to the consumption of coffee, and the composite price (price of coffee + 2 price of sugar), the fit was poor. The fit improved when he reduced the weight of the price of sugar by three-fourths, from which he concluded that one cannot attribute an importance to the price of complements proportional to their cost. This conclusion is impeccable, but the demonstration would have been more persuasive if he had used a more meaningful technique.

[49] "A Method of Determining the Numerical Value of Elasticities of Demand," *Economic Journal*, XX (1910), 636–40.

utility of one commodity is independent of the quantities of others) and the marginal utility of income was constant with respect to small changes in income. But the procedure yielded only relative income elasticities,[50] and, of course, the absolute income elasticities could be calculated directly from budgetary data. Apparently, the method was never employed except in Pigou's own illustrative calculations.

Marcel Lenoir.—The first comprehensive treatment of statistical demand curves was made by Lenoir in his fine doctoral dissertation, *Études sur la formation et le mouvement des prix.*[51] Lenoir was the first economist to give a logical justification for the identification of observed price-quantity data with the points on the economist's demand curve, and his empirical work was unusually imaginative.

Lenoir's work falls into two parts: an exposition of the theory of supply and demand and a set of empirical studies. The theoretical studies are built upon a modern exposition of indifference curves, which we need not consider here. This section culminates in a set of interpretations of observable price movements:

> For certain commodities, the influence of [supply] or [demand] will dominate. For a widely consumed food, produced by cultivation, such as wheat, one may assume that in a given country the demand changes only slowly and remains almost unchanged for periods of several years. But the supply curve varies from one year to the next with the state of the harvests. The point [of intersection of supply and demand curves] then moves along a

---

[50] Milton Friedman, "Professor Pigou's Method for Measuring Elasticities of Demand from Budgetary Data," *Quarterly Journal of Economics,* L (1935–36), 151–63.

[51] Paris, 1913.

given demand curve, and the price varies inversely with the supply . . . —subject, however, to the influences exercised by the state of general economic conditions.

If we consider, on the other hand, a commodity such as coal or castings, produced and largely consumed by industries, the demand is likely to vary more rapidly. Supply changes here only as a result of changes in the means of production, which will be made rather slowly under the pressure of demand, and almost always supply tends to increase. The demand, however, is more capricious, and its influence is predominant in short periods of time. Price and production-consumption then move together. . . .

For short periods . . . we may consider as negligible, at least to a first approximation, all the influences other than the variability of harvests, for agricultural products, and all the influences other than the variations of demand, for the purchases by industries.[52]

In the long run, however, one may no longer treat the supply and demand curves as independent, and it becomes much more difficult to estimate them from observations on prices and quantities. Even here, however, one may make allowances for changes in technology or consumers' tastes or in the value of money. Lenoir concentrates chiefly on the short run.

This argument is illustrated graphically, and we may reproduce one part of it. Let D_1 and S_1 be the initial supply and demand curves, and A the price in the initial period.[53] A sudden increase in demand, such as takes place for an industrial good, will shift the demand curve to D_2 and the price to B. The

[52] *Ibid.*, pp. 57–58, 60.   [53] *Ibid.*, p. 58.

profits of producers rise so that they expand their plants and are joined by new producers; the supply curve shifts to S_2, and the price falls to C. A further increase in demand to D_3 lifts the price to E, but then a crisis in the market may be followed by a collapse of demand to D_4, and to a new price of G. If stocks of the commodity are held, the supply curve may be subject to oscillations; for example, when the demand falls, the price may move along the temporary supply curve S_t. Thus in industrial markets one can, at best, estimate the supply curve S_2 from price-quantity information.

After an informed discussion of statistical methodology,[54] Lenoir analyzed the price histories of four commodities: coal, cotton, wheat, and coffee. The first three commodities were not analyzed from the viewpoint of demand theory (because they were not consumer goods), but his studies reveal much imagination. The coal study is interesting for its recognition of the effects of inventories: a close correlation ($r = -.71$) is found between stocks in a year and price in the succeeding year.[55] The price of wheat is found to be closely correlated with the previous, not the current, harvest before 1860 and more closely with the current harvest thereafter.[56] The influence of general price movements is emphasized for all three commodities. Coal production is shown to be closely correlated with economic cycles and is thereafter used as an index of business conditions: it proves to be fairly closely correlated with the price of each

---

[54] Lenoir wishes to decompose an observation for a given year into a steadily changing component and the short-run oscillations about it. In general, this is done by employing a 9-year moving average, which is held to correspond tolerably well to the average of the cycles in economic life, but sometimes trend lines are employed. I am also passing over his analysis of the quantity of money.

[55] *Op. cit.*, p. 93.

[56] *Ibid.*, pp. 107–11. The change is attributed to improvements in predicting the current harvest.

commodity.[57] For each commodity, several periods are compared, and generally also English and other foreign comparisons are made.

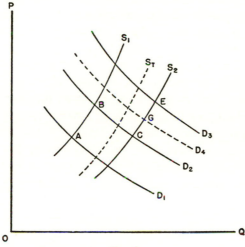

Fig. 1

Coffee was chosen to illustrate the derivation of demand functions. Consumption was expressed in per capita units, and the price was taken inclusive of all taxes. Two equations were calculated, and each was presented in absolute and relative terms:

Period 1847–69:

$$q = 833 + 43.5(t - 1,858) - 1.44(p - 227),$$

$$\frac{q - 833}{833} = 0.052(t - 1,858) - .39\frac{p - 227}{227}.$$

Period 1873–96:

$$q = 1,649 + 32.7(t - 1,884.5) - 2.73(p - 347),$$

$$\frac{q - 1,649}{1,649} = 0.020(t - 1,884.5) - .57\frac{p - 347}{347},$$

57 *Ibid.*, pp. 111, 131, 134.

where q is per capita consumption, p is price, and t is time. In each period the second equation expresses the price and quantity as percentages of the average for the period, so the regression coefficients are the elasticities of demand, i.e., —.39 and —.57.[58] The partial correlation coefficient between p and q (holding t constant) was —.54 in the first period and —.85 in the second period.

Lenoir deserves to be called the founder of the work on statistical demand curves in the modern sense. Although his statistical work was excellent for the time, his basic contribution was a theory of the relationship between the economist's demand curve and the statistical demand curve. Prior to his time, these curves were identified intuitively, but now one could specify a class of demand functions for which the identification was legitimate. It was most unfortunate that this excellent work passed unnoticed, and had to be rediscovered in the 1920's.

Before we turn to the last important figure of the period, Henry Moore, we should notice the well-known study of Robert Lehfeldt.[59] Lehfeldt's chief energies were devoted to the rectification of the data, and his work here was very good, but his final results were marred by a peculiar method of estimating elasticity. Since the elasticity of demand is

$$\eta = \frac{d(\log q)}{d(\log p)},$$

it is equal to the ratio of the first differences of the logarithms of quantity and price. But, since $\Delta \log p$ may be close to zero and lead to erratically large estimates of the elasticity (for example, —9.5 in 1906 in his study), he approximated the

---

58 *Ibid.*, pp. 141–42.

59 "The Elasticity of Demand for Wheat," *Economic Journal,* XXIV (1914), 212–17.

mean elasticity by the ratio of the standard deviations of the first differences of the logarithms. The elasticity was estimated to be —0.6 for 1888–1911. Of course, this last step was a masterpiece of inefficient estimation.[60]

Henry Moore.—Four developments had proceeded far enough by the time he wrote, Moore believed, to pave the way for the construction of a quantitative economic theory. The rigorous and comprehensive formulation of economic theory, especially by Marshall and Pareto; the accumulation of basic economic data, largely in response to growing governmental activity; the improvements in statistical theory; and the invention of mechanical calculators—these were the requisites for a statistical economics. Economists should now "(1) bring to the test of representative facts the hypotheses and theorems of pure economics; and (2) . . . supply data, in the form of general facts and empirical laws, for the elaboration of dynamics economics."[61]

Moore delayed little with the first task, the testing of received hypotheses; instead, he moved to bold theorizing—but, true to his creed, it was bold quantitative theorizing. *Economic Cycles* (1914) contains his first work on demand curves.[62] Although he identified his demand curves with those of the economic theorists, he gave no justification for doing so. He criticized the theorists for assuming other things to remain equal,

---

[60] Henry Schultz analyzed the procedure in the Appendix to *Statistical Laws of Demand and Supply* (Chicago, 1928). The analysis, however, rests upon a confusion: Schultz thought that Lehfeldt calculated the standard deviations of the logarithms of quantities and prices, but Lehfeldt calculated the standard deviations of the first differences of these logarithms.

[61] *The Laws of Wages* (New York: Macmillan Company, 1911), p. 23.

[62] Benini's work was summarized in an earlier article, "The Statistical Complement of Pure Economics," *Quarterly Journal of Economics*, XXIII (1908–9), 1–33.

but then proposed the method of link relatives precisely to eliminate other things that had not remained equal in the data he wished to employ:

> The relative change in the amount of the commodity that is bought may be correlated with the relative change in the corresponding price, and the resulting appropriate regression equation will give the statistical law of demand for the commodity. By taking the relative change in the amount of the commodity that is demanded, instead of the absolute quantities, the effects of increasing population are approximately eliminated; and by taking the relative change in the corresponding prices instead of the corresponding absolute prices, the errors due to a fluctuating general price level are partially removed.[63]

Regressions are so calculated for corn, hay, oats, and potatoes (in each case for the period 1866–1911); for example, the linear and nonlinear equations for corn were

$$p = -0.8896q + 7.79 \, (r = -0.789),$$

$$p = 0.94 - 1.0899q + 0.02391q^2 - 0.999234q^3,$$

where p and q are the percentage changes in price and quantity, respectively.

Moore claimed high accuracy for the predictions from such functions. He submitted them to only one test,[64] and, instead, rested the claim on the fact that the standard errors of estimate

---

63 *Economic Cycles: Their Law and Cause* (New York: Macmillan Company, 1914), p. 69.

64 The valid test was to predict the 1912 price of corn, given its output: the equation predicted 52.7 cents against an actual price of 48.7 cents (*ibid.*, pp. 77–78).

were small, i.e., upon the fact that the regression curves fit the data well. Nor did he apply any internal tests, such as examining the effects of changing the period of time covered. The identification of production with consumption, the neglect of the effects of exports, and similar shortcomings also marred the work.

Under the legitimate title, "A New Type of Demand Curve," Moore derived his famous positively sloping demand curve for pig iron, "our representative producer's good."[65] For the period 1870–1911, he found its equation to be

$$p = 0.5211q - 4.58 \, (\, r = 0.537 \,),$$

where p and q have the previous meaning. "The dogma of the uniformity of the law of demand is an idol of the static state."[66] Moore embraced this finding so eagerly, one feels, because it fit into his theory of cycles: lower yields (which are almost as highly correlated as lower quantities with price increases) reduce the volume of trade; this leads to lower prices of producers' goods; and then crop prices fall.[67]

In his review, Lehfeldt had no kind words for *Economic Cycles*. The demand equations, while correct, were not those of economic theory, because "they do not eliminate the variation of 'other things,' viz., of population and the general price level."[68] This criticism was unfair, for the device of link relatives was employed precisely for this purpose. Lehfeldt's criticism of the demand curve for pig iron, however, contains a clear and probably independent statement of the logical basis for deriving demand curves:

---

[65] *Ibid.*, p. 113.   [66] *Ibid.*

[67] This last link between the price of producers' goods (which was identified with the price level, or at least the strategic part of the price level) and the level of demand for crops was made, not through income explicitly, but through a comparison of demand curves in periods of secularly rising and falling wholesale prices (*ibid.*, pp. 100–102).

[68] Review of *Economic Cycles*, in *Economic Journal*, XXV (1915), 411.

The author thinks he has discovered a new type of demand curve, sloping the opposite way to the usual kind! But the curve (for pig-iron) on p. 115 is not a demand curve at all, but much more nearly a supply curve. It is arrived at by the intersection of irregularly fluctuating demands on supply conditions, that, on the whole, may be regarded as steady except for a secular growth, whereas the whole line of argument with regard to crops is based on considering the intersection of irregular supply (due to fluctuations of weather) with a steady demand.[69]

In another review, Marco Fanno characterized the positively sloping demand curve as "un errore grossolano," for the same reason.[70] Moore made no answer, but this type of demand curve did not reappear in his subsequent work.

In *Forecasting the Yield and the Price of Cotton* (1917), Moore challenged more broadly the theoretical formulation of the demand relationship. He listed five factors which Marshall held constant, to obtain his "one universal rule to which the demand curve conforms," and proceeded to investigate one factor, the general price level, by multiple-correlation analysis. He found the demand function for cotton to be

$$p = -0.97q + 1.60Q + 7.11 ,$$

where p, q, and Q are the percentage changes in the price of cotton, the quantity of cotton, and the wholesale price index, respectively. In this case the total and partial correlations between price and quantity were almost identical (-0.819 and -0.808, respectively), and, in general, "many of the hypothetical relationships have no significance which needs to be regarded in a practical situation."[71] But even if the relationships

---

[69] *Ibid.*

[70] Review in *Giornale degli economisti*, 3d ser., LII (1916), 151–54.

[71] *Forecasting*, p. 161.

are numerous and important, "when the method of multiple correlation is thus applied to economic data it invests the findings of deductive economics with 'the reality and life of fact'; it is the Statistical Complement of Deductive Economics."[72]

Moore's later work contained only minor developments in the technique of deriving demand curves. He proposed the concept of flexibility of demand (price), defined as the reciprocal of the ordinary demand elasticity,[73] and also generalized the elasticity notion by replacing the derivative by the partial derivative in the case of functions of several variables.[74] The supply curve of cotton was calculated by correlating the link relatives of acreage with the link relative of price for the preceding year.[75] In his later work Moore fitted trends to the data and expressed prices and quantities as trend relatives, rather than using link relatives.[76]

Moore was the single most influential economist in the popularization of statistical demand analysis. I have made clear that this influence was not attributable to priority or to excellence, for in both respects Moore must bow to Lenoir. Moore's influence was favored by extraneous circumstances: European scholars were diverted by the First World War from such exploratory work. Yet it would be unjust to deny Moore several important claims. Few economists have ever been so

---

[72] *Ibid.*, p. 173.

[73] "Empirical Laws of Demand and Supply and the Flexibility of Prices," *Political Science Quarterly*, XXIV (1919), 553–54, 556; "Elasticity of Demand and Flexibility of Prices," *Journal of the American Statistical Association*, XVIII (1922), 8 ff.

[74] "Partial Elasticity of Demand," *Quarterly Journal of Economics*, XL (1925–26), 396–97.

[75] "Empirical Laws . . . ," p. 560. This function was then converted into an ordinary supply curve by the use of sample data on the effect of yields on costs of production.

[76] The data for potatoes, 1881–1913, are so analyzed in "Elasticity of Demand . . . ," pp. 13 ff.

neat, so explicit, and so purposeful in their writing: the reader knows what Moore is about and how he thinks, even when he is following a blind path. His bold assumption that relatively simple techniques would reveal important and reliable empirical relationships that might be fitted into a great analytical system was imaginative, and we should not let the subsequent flowering of this attitude obscure the fact that in Moore's time it was also courageous. A more profound theorist and statistician like Edgeworth shrank from the complexity of empirical demand curves, and a vast literature bears testimony to how intensively one can discuss concrete prices and quantities without reaching demand functions. Against this setting, Moore's work takes on stature.

Conclusion.—We have seen that serious work on the estimation of empirical demand curves began just before the First World War. Yet, putting aside Cournot's work as uninfluential, demand curves became common in economic literature after 1870. Fleeming Jenkin made good use of them to display Thornton's bizarre criticisms of the "law of supply and demand"; and Jevons, Walras, Marshall, and others multiplied their use.

The delay of a generation in empirical work on demand curves was due to the general failure to recognize that economic *functions,* as well as quantities, could be determined empirically. John Neville Keynes's treatise on methodology may be taken as an authoritative statement of economists' views in the 1890's:

> The functions of statistics in economic theory are, first, to suggest empirical laws, which may or may not be capable of subsequent deductive explanation; and, secondly, to supplement deductive reasoning by checking its results, and submitting them to the test of experience. Statistics play a still more important part in the applications of econom-

ic science to the elucidation and interpretation of particular concrete phenomena.[77]

Here there was no realization of the possibility of empirically deriving economic functions; in fact, the reader was warned not to confuse the two types.[78]

We owe to the development of statistical theory the realization of a possible quantification of economic functions. Some of the early workers on demand curves were statisticians—Benini, Gini, and Persons—and Moore studied at Pearson's laboratory. On the whole, one must say that economists were quick to perceive the relevance of statistical developments and to enlarge their area of work, so eager, in fact, that until recently it was easy to outrage a statistician by defining his science as a branch of economics.[79]

Perhaps no other science receives as much criticism from both its own members and outsiders as does economics, and one of the ever fashionable criticisms is that economists are slow to take account of highly relevant work in other disciplines. Modern statistics had such a development, and, judged by its fruitfulness, it was of undeniable importance in economic study. The speed and generality with which the new techniques were adopted by economists left no occasion for complaint.

Studies in the history of economics usually culminate in apology or criticism. I seize this opportunity to end one such study on a note of pride.

---

[77] *The Scope and Method of Political Economy* (4th ed.; London: Macmillan Company, 1930), pp. 343–44.

[78] *Ibid.*, p. 340 n.: "The use of diagrams for statistical purposes should be clearly distinguished from their employment in economic theory as discussed in a previous chapter."

[79] I myself think it odd of the statistician to react so violently to excessive praise.

8

Perfect Competition,
Historically Contemplated

No concept in economics—or elsewhere—is ever defined fully, in the sense that its meaning under every conceivable circumstance is clear. Even a word with a wholly arbitrary meaning in economics, like "elasticity," raises questions which the person who defined it (in this case, Marshall) never faced: for example, how does the concept apply to finite changes or to discontinuous or stochastic or multiple-valued functions? And of course a word like "competition," which is shared with the whole population, is even less likely to be loaded with restrictions or elaborations to forestall unfelt ambiguities.

Still, it is a remarkable fact that the concept of competition did not begin to receive explicit and systematic attention in the main stream of economics until 1871. This concept—as pervasive and fundamental as any in the whole structure of classical and neoclassical economic theory—was long treated with the kindly casualness with which one treats of the intuitively obvious. Only slowly did the elaborate and complex concept of

Reprinted from *The Journal of Political Economy,* Vol. LXV (February, 1957).

perfect competition evolve, and it was not until after the First World War that it was finally received into general theoretical literature. The evolution of the concept and the steps by which it became confused with a perfect market, uniqueness of equilibrium, and stationary conditions are the subject of this essay.

I. THE CLASSICAL ECONOMISTS

"Competition" entered economics from common discourse, and for long it connoted only the independent rivalry of two or more persons. When Adam Smith wished to explain why a reduced supply led to a higher price, he referred to the "competition [which] will immediately begin" among buyers; when the supply is excessive, the price will sink more, the greater "the competition of the sellers, or according as it happens to be more or less important to them to get immediately rid of the commodity."[1] It will be noticed that "competition" is here (and usually) used in the sense of rivalry in a race—a race to get limited supplies or a race to be rid of excess supplies. Competition is a process of responding to a new force and a method of reaching a new equilibrium.

Smith observed that economic rivals were more likely to strive for gain by under- or overbidding one another, the more numerous they were:

> The trades which employ but a small number of hands, run most easily into such combinations.
>
> If this capital [sufficient to trade in a town] is divided between two different grocers, their competition will tend to make both of them sell cheaper, than if it were in the hands of one only; and if it were divided among twenty, their competition would be just so much the greater, and the chance

[1] *The Wealth of Nations* (New York: Modern Library ed.), pp. 56–57.

of their combining together, in order to raise the price, just so much the less.[2]

This is all that Smith has to say of the number of rivals.

Of course something more is implicit, and partially explicit, in Smith's treatment of competition, but this "something more" is not easy to state precisely, for it was not precise in Smith's mind. But the concept of competition seemed to embrace also several other elements:

1. The economic units must possess tolerable knowledge of the conditions of employment of their resources in various industries. "This equality [of remuneration] can take place only in those employments which are well known, and have been long established in the neighbourhood."[3] But the necessary information was usually available: "Secrets . . . , it must be acknowledged, can seldom be long kept; and the extraordinary profit can last very little longer than they are kept."[4]

2. Competition achieved its results only in the long run: "This equality in the whole of the advantages and disadvantages of the different employments of labour and stock, can take place only in the ordinary, or what may be called the natural state of those employments."[5]

3. There must be freedom of trade; the economic unit must be free to enter or leave any trade. The exclusive privileges or corporations which exclude men from trades, and the restrictions imposed on mobility by the settlement provisions

---

2 *Ibid.*, pp. 126 and 342.   4 *Ibid.*, p. 60.

3 *Ibid.*, p. 114.   5 *Ibid.*, p. 115.

of the poor law, are examples of such interferences with "free competition."

In sum, then, Smith had five conditions of competition:

1. The rivals must act independently, not collusively.
2. The number of rivals, potential as well as present, must be sufficient to eliminate extraordinary gains.
3. The economic units must possess tolerable knowledge of the market opportunities.
4. There must be freedom (from social restraints) to act on this knowledge.
5. Sufficient time must elapse for resources to flow in the directions and quantities desired by their owners.

The modern economist has a strong tendency to read more into such statements than they meant to Smith and his contemporaries. The fact that he (and many successors) was willing to call the ownership of land a monopoly—although the market in agricultural land met all these conditions—simply because the total supply of land was believed to be fixed is sufficient testimony to the fact that he was not punctilious in his language.[6]

Smith did not state how he was led to these elements of a concept of competition. We may reasonably infer that the conditions of numerous rivals and of independence of action of

---

[6] *Ibid.*, p. 145. Perhaps this is not the ideal illustration of the laxness of the period in the use of the competitive concept, for several readers of this paper have sympathized with this usage. But, to repeat, competition is consistent with a zero elasticity of supply: the fact of windfall gains from unexpected increases in demand is characteristic of all commodities with less than infinitely elastic supplies.

these rivals were matters of direct observation. Every informed person knew, at least in a general way, what competition was, and the essence of this knowledge was the striving of rivals to gain advantages relative to one another.

The other elements of competition, on the contrary, appear to be the necessary conditions for the validity of a proposition which was to be associated with competition: the equalization of returns in various directions open to an entrepreneur or investor or laborer. If one postulates equality of returns as the equilibrium state under competition, then adequacy of numbers and independence of rivals are not enough for equilibrium. The entrepreneur (or other agents) must know what returns are obtainable in various fields, he must be allowed to enter the fields promising high rates of return, and he must be given time to make his presence felt in these fields. These conditions were thus prerequisites of an analytical theorem, although their reasonableness was no doubt enhanced by the fact that they corresponded more or less closely to observable conditions.

This sketch of a concept of competition was not amplified or challenged in any significant respect for the next three-quarters of a century by any important member of the English school. A close study of the literature, such as I have not made, would no doubt reveal many isolated passages on the formal properties or realism of the concept, especially when the theory was applied to concrete problems. For example, Senior was more interested in methodology than most of his contemporaries, and he commented:

> But though, under free competition, cost of production is the regulator of price, its influence is subject to much occasional interruption. Its operation can be supposed to be perfect only if we suppose that there are no disturbing causes, that capital and labour can be at once transferred, and without loss,

from one employment to another, and that every
producer has full information of the profit to be
derived from every mode of production. But it is
obvious that these suppositions have no resemblance to the truth. A large portion of the capital
essential to production consists of buildings, machinery, and other implements, the results of much
time and labour, and of little service for any except
their existing purposes. . . . Few capitalists can estimate, except upon an average of some years, the
amounts of their own profits, and still fewer can
estimate those of their neighbours.[7]

Senior made no use of the concept of perfect competition
hinted at in this passage, and he was wholly promiscuous in his
use of the concept of monopoly.

Cairnes, the last important English economist to write in the
classical tradition, did break away from the Smithian concept
of competition. He defined a state of free competition as one
in which commodities exchanged in proportion to the sacrifices (of labor and capital) in their production.[8] This condition
was amply fulfilled, he believed, so far as capital was concerned, for there was a large stock of disposable capital which
quickly flowed into unusually remunerative fields.[9] The condition was only partly fulfilled in the case of labor, however,
for there existed a hierarchy of occupational classes ("non-
competing industrial groups") which the laborer found it most
difficult to ascend.[10] Even the extra rewards of skill beyond
those which paid for the sacrifices in obtaining training were

---

[7] N. W. Senior, *Political Economy* (New York, 1939), p. 102.

[8] *Some Leading Principles of Political Economy Newly Expounded* (London: Harper and Brothers, 1874), p. 79.

[9] *Ibid.*, p. 68.

[10] *Ibid.*, p. 72.

a monopoly return.[11] This approach was not analytically rigorous—Cairnes did not tell how to equate the sacrifices of capitalists and laborers—nor was it empirically fruitful.

Cairnes labeled as "industrial competition" the force which effects the proportioning of prices to psychological costs which takes place to the extent that the products are made in one non-competing group, and he called on the reciprocal demand theory of international trade to explain exchanges of products between non-competing groups. Hence we might call industrial competition the competition within non-competing groups, and commercial competition that between non-competing groups. But Sidgwick and Edgeworth attribute the opposite concepts to Cairnes: commercial competition is competition within an industry, and industrial competition requires the ability of resources to flow between industries.[12] Their nomenclature seems more appropriate; I have not been able to find Cairnes's discussion of commercial competition and doubt that it exists.[13]

II. THE CRITICS OF PRIVATE ENTERPRISE

The main claims for a private-enterprise system rest upon the workings of competition, and it would not have been unnatural for critics of this system to focus much attention on the competitive concept. They might have argued that Smith's assumptions were not strong enough to insure optimum results or that, even if perfect competition were formulated as the

---

[11] *Ibid.*, p. 85. Thus Cairnes tacitly labeled all differences in native ability as "monopolistic."

[12] Henry Sidgwick, *Principles of Political Economy* (London: Macmillan and Company, 1883), p. 182; F. Y. Edgeworth, *Papers Relating to Political Economy* (London, 1925), II, 280, 311.

[13] Karl Marx once distinguished interindustry from intraindustry competition in *Theorien über den Mehrwert* (Stuttgart: J. H. W. Dietz, 1905), II, Part 2, 14 n.

basis of the theory, certain deviations from optimum results (such as those associated with external economies) could occur. The critics did not make this type of criticism, however, possibly simply because they were not first-class analysts; and for this type of development we must return to the main line of theorists, consisting mostly of politically conservative economists.

Or, at another pole, the critics might simply have denied that competition was the basic form of market organization. In the nineteenth century, however, this was only a minor and sporadic charge.[14] The Marxists did not press this point: both the labor theory of value and the doctrine of equalization of profit rates require competition.[15] The early Fabian essayists were also prepared to make their charges rest upon the deficiencies in the workings of competition rather than its absence.[16] The charge that competition was non-existent or vanishing did not become commonplace until the end of the nineteenth century.

---

[14] For example, Leslie repeatedly denied that resource owners possessed sufficient knowledge to effect an equalization of the rates of return (see T. E. Cliffe Leslie, *Essays in Political and Moral Philosophy* [London, 1888], pp. 47, 48, 81, 158–59, 184–85).

[15] See especially Volume III of *Das Kapital* and also F. Engels, *The Condition of the Working-Classes in England,* reprinted in Karl Marx and Friedrich Engels, *On Britain* (London, 1954), pp. 109 ff. The Marxian theory of the increasing concentration of capital was a minor and inconsistent dissent from the main position (see *Capital* [Modern Library ed.], pp. 684 ff.).

[16] See *Fabian Essays* (Jubilee ed.; London, 1948), especially those by Shaw and Webb. But the attention devoted to monopoly was increasing, and the essay by Clarke argued that "combination is absorbing commerce" (*ibid.,* p. 84). A few years later the Webbs used a competitive model in their celebrated discussion of "higgling in the market" and then went on to describe the formation of monopolistic structures as defences erected against the competitive pressures the Webbs did not quite understand (see *Industrial Democracy* [London: G. Allen & Unwin, 1920], Part III, chap. ii).

The critics, to the extent that they took account of competition at all, emphasized the evil tendencies which they believed flowed from its workings. It would be interesting to examine their criticisms systematically with a view to their treatment of competition; it is my impression that their most common, and most influential, charge was that competition led to a highly objectionable, and perhaps continuously deteriorating, distribution of income by size.[17] In their explanations of the workings of a competitive economy the most striking deficiency of the classical economists was their failure to work out the theory of the effects of competition on the distribution of income.

III. THE MATHEMATICAL SCHOOL

The first steps in the analytical refinement of the concept of competition were made by the mathematical economists. This stage in the history of the concept is of special interest because it reveals both the types of advances that were achieved by this approach and the manner in which alien elements were introduced into the concept.

When an algebraically inclined economist seeks to maximize the profits of a producer, he is led to write the equation

$$\text{Profits} = \text{Revenue} - \text{Cost}$$

and then to maximize this expression; that is, to set the derivative of profits with respect to output equal to zero. He then faces the question: How does revenue (say, pq) vary with output (q)? The natural answer is to *define* competition as that situation in which p does not vary with q—in which the demand curve facing the firm is horizontal. This is precisely what Cournot did:

---

[17] A second main criticism became increasingly more prominent in the second half of the nineteenth century: that a private-enterprise system allowed or compelled large fluctuations in employment. For some critics (e.g., Engels), competition was an important cause of these fluctuations.

> The effects of competition have reached their
> limit, when each of the partial productions D_k [the
> output of producer k] is *inappreciable,* not only
> with reference to the total production $D = F(p)$,
> but also with reference to the derivative $F'(p)$, so
> that the partial production D_k could be subtracted
> from D without any appreciable variation resulting
> in the price of the commodity.[18]

This definition of competition was especially appropriate in
Cournot's system because, according to his theory of oligopoly,
the excess of price over marginal cost approaches zero as the
number of like producers became large.[19] Cournot believed
that this condition of competition was fulfilled "for a multitude of products, and, among them, for the most important
products."[20]

Cournot's definition was enormously more precise and ele-

---

[18] *Mathematical Principles of the Theory of Wealth* (New York, 1929), p.
90. It is sufficient to assume that D_k is small relative to D if one assumes
that the demand function is continuous, for then "the variations of the demand will be so sensibly proportional to the variations in price so long as
these last are small fractions of the original price" (*ibid.,* p. 50).

[19] Let the revenue of the firm be $q_i p$, and let all firms have the same
marginal costs, MC. Then the equation for maximum profits for one firm
would be

$$p + q_i \frac{dp}{dq} = MC \, .$$

The sum of n such equations would be

$$np + q \frac{dp}{dq} = nMC \, ,$$

for $nq_i = q$. This least equation may be written,

$$p = MC - \frac{p}{nE} \, ,$$

where E is the elasticity of market demand (*ibid.,* p. 84).

[20] *Ibid.,* p. 90.

gant than Smith's so far as the treatment of numbers was concerned. A market departed from unlimited competition to the extent that price exceeded the marginal cost of the firm, and the difference approached zero as the number of rivals approached infinity. But the refinement was one-sided: Cournot paid no attention to conditions of entry and so his definition of competition held also for industries with numerous firms even though no more firms could enter.

The role of knowledge was made somewhat more prominent in Jevons' exposition. His concept of competition was a part of his concept of a market, and a perfect market was characterized by two conditions:

> [1.] A market, then, is theoretically perfect only when all traders have perfect knowledge of the conditions of supply and demand, and the consequent ratio of exchange; . . .
>
> [2.] . . . there must be perfectly free competition, so that anyone will exchange with any one else upon the slightest advantage appearing. There must be no conspiracies for absorbing and holding supplies to produce unnatural ratios of exchange.[21]

One might interpret this ambiguous second condition in several ways, for the pursuit of advantages is not inconsistent with conspiracies. At a minimum, Jevons assumes complete independence of action by every trader for a corollary of the perfect market is that "in the same market, at any moment, there cannot be two prices for the same kind of article."[22] This rule

---

21 *Theory of Political Economy* (1st ed.; London, 1871), pp. 86 and 87.

22 *Ibid.,* p. 92. This is restated as the proposition that the last increments of an act of exchange (i.e., the last exchange in a competitive market) must be proportional to the total quantities exchanged, or that dy exchanges for

of a single price (it is called the "law of indifference" in the second edition) excludes price discrimination and probably requires that the market have numerous buyers and sellers, but the condition is not made explicit. The presence of large numbers is clearly implied, however, when we are told that "a single trader . . . must buy and sell at the current prices, which he cannot in an appreciable degree affect."[23]

The merging of the concepts of competition and the market was unfortunate, for each deserved a full and separate treatment. A market is an institution for the consummation of transactions. It performs this function efficiently when every buyer who will pay more than the minimum realized price for any class of commodities succeeds in buying the commodity, and every seller who will sell for less than the maximum realized price succeeds in selling the commodity. A market performs these tasks more efficiently if the commodities are well specified and if buyers and sellers are fully informed of their properties and prices. Possibly also a perfect market allows buyers and sellers to act on differing expectations of future prices. A market may be perfect and monopolistic or imperfect and competitive. Jevons' mixture of the two has been widely imitated by successors, of course, so that even today a market is commonly treated as a concept subsidiary to competition.

---

dx in the same proportion that y exchanges for x, or

$$\frac{dy}{dx} = \frac{y}{x}.$$

It would have been better for Jevons simply to assert that, if x_i exchanges for y_i, then for all i

$$\frac{x_i}{y_i} = \frac{p_y}{p_x}.$$

23 *Ibid.*, p. 111. In the Preface to the second edition, where on most subjects Jevons was farseeing, the conceptual treatment of competition deteriorated: "Property is only another name for monopoly. . . . Thus monopoly is limited by competition . . ." (*Theory* [4th ed.], pp. xlvi–xlvii).

Edgeworth was the first to attempt a systematic and rigorous definition of perfect competition. His exposition deserves the closest scrutiny in spite of the fact that few economists of his time or ours have attempted to disentangle and uncover the theorems and conjectures of the *Mathematical Psychics,* probably the most elusively written book of importance in the history of economics. For his allegations and demonstrations seem to be the parents of widespread beliefs on the nature of perfect competition.

The conditions of perfect competition are stated as follows:

> The *field of competition* with reference to a contract, or contracts, under consideration consists of all individuals who are willing and able to recontract about the articles under consideration. . . .
>
> There is free communication throughout a *normal* competitive field. You might suppose the constituent individuals collected at a point, or connected by telephones—an ideal supposition [1881], but sufficiently approximate to existence or tendency for the purposes of abstract science.
>
> A *perfect* field of competition professes in addition certain properties peculiarly favourable to mathematical calculation; . . . The conditions of a *perfect* field are four; the first pair referrible to the heading *multiplicity* or continuity, the second *dividedness* or fluidity.
>
> I. An individual is free to *recontract* with any out of an indefinite number, . . .
>
> II. Any individual is free to *contract* (at the same time) with an indefinite number; . . . This condition combined with the first appears to involve the indefinite divisibility of each *article* of contract (if any X deal with an indefinite number of Ys he must give each an indefinitely small portion of x); which might be erected into a separate condition.

III. Any individual is free to *recontract* with another independently of, *without the consent* being required of, any third party, . . .

IV. Any individual is free to *contract* with another independently of a third party; . . .

The failure of the first [condition] involves the failure of the second, but not *vice versa;* and the third and fourth are similarly related.[24]

The natural question to put to such a list of conditions of competition is: Are the conditions necessary and sufficient to achieve what intuitively or pragmatically seems to be a useful concept of competition? Edgeworth replies, in effect, that the conditions are both necessary and sufficient. More specifically, competition requires (1) indefinitely large numbers of participants on both sides of the market; (2) complete absence of limitations upon individual self-seeking behavior; and (3) complete divisibility of the commodities traded.[25]

The rationale of the requirement of indefinite numbers is as follows. With bilateral monopoly, the transaction will be indeterminate—equilibrium can be anywhere on the contract curve.[26] If we add a second buyer and seller, it is shown that the range of permissible equilibriums (the length of the tenable contract curve) will shrink.[27] By intuitive induction, with infinitely many traders it will shrink to a single point; a single price must rule in the market.[28]

---

[24] *Mathematical Psychics* (London: C. Kegan Paul & Company, 1881), pp. 17–19.

[25] Edgeworth's emphasis upon recontract, the institution which allows tentative contracts to be broken without penalty, is motivated by a desire to assure that equilibrium will be achieved and will not be affected by the route by which it is achieved. It will not be examined here.

[26] *Ibid.,* pp. 20 ff.

[27] *Ibid.,* pp. 35 ff.   [28] *Ibid.,* pp. 37–39.

Before we discuss this argument, we may take account also of the condition that individual traders are free to act independently. Edgeworth shows that combinations reduce the effective number of traders and that "combiners *stand to gain*."[29] In effect, then, he must assume that the individual trader not only is free to act independently but will in fact do so.

The proof of the need for indefinite numbers has serious weaknesses. The range of indeterminacy shrinks only because one seller or buyer tries to cut out the other by offering better terms.[30] Edgeworth fails to show that such price competition (which is palpably self-defeating) will occur or that, if it does occur, why the process should stop before the parties reach a unique (competitive) equilibrium. Like all his descendants, he treated the small-numbers case unsatisfactorily.

It is intuitively plausible that with infinite numbers all monopoly power (and indeterminacy) will vanish, and Edgeworth essentially postulates rather than prove this. But a simple demonstration, in case of sellers of equal size, would amount only to showing that

$$\text{Marginal revenue} = \text{Price} + \frac{\text{Price}}{\text{Number of sellers} \times \text{Market elasticity}}$$

and that this last term goes to zero as the number of sellers increases indefinitely.[31] This was implicitly Cournot's argument.

But why do we require divisibility of the traded commodity?

---

29 *Ibid.*, p. 43.

30 ". . . It will in general be possible for *one* of the Ys (without the consent of the other) to *recontract* with the two Xs, so that for all those three parties the recontract is more advantageous than the previously existing contract" (*ibid.*, p. 35).

31 Let one seller dispose of q_i, the other sellers each disposing of q. Then the seller's marginal revenue is

$$\frac{d(p q_i)}{d q_i} = p + q_i \frac{dp}{dQ} \frac{dQ}{d q_i},$$

> Suppose a market, consisting of an equal number
> of masters and servants, offering respectively wages
> and service; subject to the condition that no man
> can serve two masters, no master employ more than
> one man; or suppose equilibrium already estab-
> lished between such parties to be disturbed by any
> sudden influx of wealth into the hands of the mas-
> ters. Then there is no *determinate,* and very gen-
> erally *unique,* arrangement towards which the sys-
> tem tends under the operation of, may we say, a law
> of Nature, and which would be predictable if we
> knew beforehand the real requirements of each, or
> of the average, dealer; . . .[32]

Consider the simple example: a thousand masters will each
employ a man at any wage below 100; a thousand laborers will
each work for any wage above 50. There will be a single wage
rate: knowledge and numbers are sufficient to lead a worker to
seek a master paying more than the going rate or a master to
seek out a worker receiving less than the market rate. But any
rate between 50 and 100 is a possible equilibrium.[33]

It is not the lack of uniqueness that is troublesome, however, for a market can be perfectly competitive even though
there be a dozen possible stable equilibrium positions.[34]

---

where Q is total sales, and $dQ/dq_i = 1$. Letting $Q = nq_i = nq$, and writing
E for

$$\frac{dQ}{dp}\frac{p}{Q},$$

we obtain the expression in the text.

[32] *Mathematical Psychics,* p. 46.

[33] Of course, let there be one extra worker, and the wage will be 50; one
extra master, and it will be 100.

[34] Since chance should operate in the choice of the equilibrium actually
attained, it is not proper to say, as Edgeworth does (in a wider context),
that the dice will be "loaded with villainy" (*ibid.,* p. 50).

Rather, the difficulty arises because the demand (or supply) functions do not possess continuous derivatives: the withdrawal of even one unit will lead to a large change in price, so that the individual trader—even though he has numerous independent rivals—can exert a perceptible influence upon price.

The element of market control arising out of the non-continuity is easily eliminated, of course. If the article which is traded is divisible, then equalities replace inequalities in the conditions of equilibrium: the individual trader can no longer influence the market price. A master may employ a variable amount of labor, and he will therefore bid for additional units so long as the wage rate is below his marginal demand price. A worker may have several employers, and he will therefore supply additional labor so long as any employer will pay more than his marginal supply price. "If the labour of the assistants can be sold by the hour, or other sort of differential dose, the phenomenon of determinate equilibrium will reappear."[35] Divisibility was introduced to achieve determinateness, which it fails to do, but it is required to eliminate monopoly power.

Divisibility had a possible second role in the assumptions, which, however, was never made explicit. If there are infinitely many possessors of a commodity, presumably each must have only an infinitesimal quantity of it if the existing total stock is to be finite. But no economist placed emphasis upon the strict mathematical implications of concepts like infinity, and this word was used to convey only the notion of an indefinitely large number of traders.

The remainder of the mathematical economists of the period

---

[35] *Collected Papers Relating to Political Economy* (London, 1925), I, 36. One might also seek to eliminate the indeterminateness by appeal to the varying demand-and-supply prices of individual traders; this is the path chosen by Hicks in "Edgeworth, Marshall, and the Indeterminateness of Wages," *Economic Journal*, XL (1930), 45–51. This, however, is a complicated solution; one must make special hypotheses about the distribution of these demand-and-supply prices.

did not extend, or for that matter even reach, the level of precision of Edgeworth. Walras gave no adequate definition of competition.[36] Pareto noticed the possible effects of social controls over purchases and sales.[37] Henry Moore, in what may have been the first article on the formal definition of competition,[38] listed five "implicit hypotheses" of competition:

I. Each economic factor seeks a maximum net income.

II. There is but one price for commodities of the same quality in the same market.

III. The influence of the product of any one producer upon the price per unit of the total product is negligible.

IV. The output of any one producer is negligible as compared with the total output.

V. Each producer orders the amount of his product without regard to the effect of his act upon the conduct of his competitors.[39]

This list of conditions is noteworthy chiefly because it marked an unsuccessful attempt to revert to the narrower competitive concept of Jevons.

IV. MARSHALL

Marshall as usual refused to float on the tide of theory, and his treatment of competition was much closer to Adam Smith's

---

36 *Elements of Pure Economics*, trans. Jaffé (Homewood, Ill.: R. D. Irwin, 1954), pp. 83 and 185. It is indicative that the word "competition" is not indexed.

37 *Cours d'économie politique* (Lausanne, 1896, 1897), §§ 46, 87, 705, 814; cf. also *Manuel d'économie politique* (2d ed.; Paris, 1927), pp. 163, 210, 230.

38 "Paradoxes of Competition," *Quarterly Journal of Economics*, XX (1905–6), 209–30. Most of the article is concerned with duopoly.

39 *Ibid.*, pp. 213–14. The fifth statement is held to be a corollary of III and IV; but see p. 260 below.

than to that of his contemporaries. Indeed, Marshall's exposition was almost as informal and unsystematic as Smith's in this area. His main statement was:

> We are investigating the equilibrium of normal demand and normal supply in their most general form: we are neglecting those features which are special to particular parts of economic science, and are confining our attention to those broad relations which are common to nearly the whole of it. Thus we assume that the forces of demand and supply have free play in a perfect market; there is no combination among dealers on either side, but each acts for himself: and there is *free competition;* that is, buyers compete freely with buyers, and sellers compete freely with sellers. But though everyone acts for himself, his knowledge of what others are doing is supposed to be sufficient to prevent him from taking a lower price or paying a higher price than others are doing; . . .[40]

If this quotation suggests that Marshall was invoking a strict concept of competition, we must remember that he discussed the "fear of spoiling the market" and the firms with negatively sloping demand curves in the main chapters on competition[41] and that the only time perfect competition was mentioned was when it was expressly spurned.[42]

Soon he yielded a bit to the trend toward refinement of the concept. Beginning with the third (1895) edition, he explicitly

---

[40] *Principles of Economics* (1st ed.; London, 1890), p. 402. A comparison with the corresponding passage in the eighth edition (*op. cit.,* p. 341) will reveal the curious changes which were later made in the description of competition.

[41] *Principles* (8th ed.; London, 1929), pp. 374 and 458.

[42] *Ibid.,* p. 540.

introduced the horizontal demand curve for the individual firm as the normal case and gave it the same mathematical formulation as did Cournot.[43] But these were patchwork revisions, and they were not carried over into the many passages where looser concepts of competition had been employed.

Marshall's most significant contribution was indirect: he gave the most powerful analysis up to his time of the relationship of competition to optimum economic organization (Book V, chap. xiii, on the doctrine of maximum satisfaction). There he found the competitive results to have not only the well-known qualification that the distribution of resources must be taken as a datum, and the precious exception that only one of several multiple stable equilibriums could be the maximum,[44] but also a new and possibly extremely important exception, arising out of external economies and diseconomies. The doctrine of external economies in effect asserts that in important areas the choices of an individual are governed by only part of the consequences, and inevitably the doctrine opens up a wide range of competitive equilibriums which depart from conventional criteria of optimum arrangement. It was left for Pigou to elaborate, and exaggerate, the importance of this source of disharmonies in *Wealth and Welfare*.

V. THE COMPLETE FORMULATION
CLARK AND KNIGHT

Only two new elements needed to be added to the Edgeworth conditions for competition in order to reach the modern concept of perfect competition. They pertained to the mobility of resources and the model of the stationary economy, and both were presented, not first,[45] but most influentially, by John Bates Clark.

---

43 *Ibid.*, pp. 517 and 849–50.

44 Both of these qualifications were of course recognized by predecessors such as Walras and Edgeworth.

45 In the mathematical exposition of theory it was natural to postulate stable supply and demand functions, and therefore stable technologies and

Clark, in his well-known development of the concept of a static economy, ascribed all dynamic disturbances to five forces:

1. Population is increasing.
2. Capital is increasing.
3. Methods of production are improving.
4. The forms of industrial establishments are changing: . . .
5. The wants of consumers are multiplying.[46]

The main purpose of his treatise was to analyze the stationary economy in which these forces were suppressed, and for this analysis the assumption of competition was basic:

> There is an ideal arrangement of the elements of society, to which the force of competition, acting on individual men, would make the society conform. The producing mechanism actually shapes itself about this model, and at no time does it vary greatly from it.
>
> We must use assumptions boldly and advisedly, making labor and capital absolutely mobile, and letting competition work in ideal perfection.[47]

Although the concepts of a stationary economy and of competition are completely independent of each other, Clark somehow believed that competition was an element of static analysis:

> The statement made in the foregoing chapter that a static state excludes true entrepreneurs' profits

---

tastes, so one could trace a gradually expanding concept of the stationary economy in Walras, Auspitz and Lieben, and Irving Fisher.

[46] *The Distribution of Wealth* (New York: Macmillan Company, 1899), p. 56.

[47] *Ibid.*, pp. 68 and 71.

does not deny that a legal monopoly might secure
to an entrepreneur a profit that would be permanent as the law that should create it—and that, too,
in a social condition which, at first glance, might
appear to be static. The agents, labor and capital,
would be prevented from moving into the favored
industry, though economic forces, if they had been
left unhindered, would have caused them to move
to it. This condition, however, is not a true static
state, as it has been defined. . . . Industrial groups
are in a truly static state when the industrial agents,
labor and capital, show a *perfect mobility, but no
motion.* A legal monopoly destroys at a certain
point this mobility. . . .[48]

I shall return to this identification of competition with stationary equilibrium at a later point.

The introduction of perfect mobility of resources as an
assumption of competition was new, and Clark offers no real
explanation for the assumption. One could simply eliminate
his five dynamic influences, and then equilibrium would be
reached after a time even with "friction" (or less than instantaneous mobility). Clark was aware of this possible approach but
merely said that "it is best to assume" that there is no friction.[49]
The only gain in his subsequent work, of course, is the avoidance of an occasional "in the long run."

Mobility of resources had always been an implicit assumption of competition, and in fact the conditions of adequate
knowledge of earning opportunities and absence of contrived
barriers to movement were believed to be adequate to insure
mobility. But there exist also technological limitations to the
rate at which resources can move from one place for industry
to another, and these limitations were in fact the basis of

---

[48] *Ibid.,* p. 76; cf. also p. 78.   [49] *Ibid.,* p. 81.

Marshall's concept of the short-run normal period. Once this fact was generally recognized, it became inevitable that mobility of resources be given an explicit time dimension, although of course it was highly accidental that instantaneous mobility was postulated.

The concept of perfect competition received its complete formulation in Frank Knight's *Risk, Uncertainty and Profit* (1921). It was the meticulous discussion in this work that did most to drive home to economists generally the austere nature of the rigorously defined concept[50] and so prepared the way for the widespread reaction against it in the 1930's.

Knight sought to establish the precise nature of an economy with complete knowledge as a preliminary step in the analysis of the impact of uncertainty. Clark's procedure of eliminating historical changes was shown to be neither necessary nor sufficient: a stationary economy was not necessary to achieve complete competitive equilibrium if men had complete foresight; and it was not sufficient to achieve this equilibrium, because there might still be non-historical fluctuations, owing, for example, to drought or flood, which were imperfectly anticipated.[51] Complete, errorless adjustments required full knowledge of all relevant circumstances, which realistically can be possessed only when these circumstances do not change; that is, when the economy is stationary.

The assumptions necessary to competition are presented as part of a list that describes the pure enterprise economy, and I quote those that are especially germane to competition:

---

50 Although Pigou was not concerned with the formal definition of competition, he must also be accounted an influential figure in the popularization of the concept of perfect competition. In his *Wealth and Welfare* (1912), he devoted individual chapters to the effects of immobility (with incorrect knowledge as one component) and indivisibility upon the ability of a resource to receive an equal rate of return in all uses (*ibid.*, Part II, chaps. iv and v).

51 *Risk, Uncertainty and Profit* (New York: Houghton Mifflin, 1921), pp. 35–38.

2. We assume that the members of the society act with complete "rationality." By this we do not mean that they are to be "as angels, knowing good from evil"; we assume ordinary human motives . . . ; but they are supposed to "know what they want" and to seek it "intelligently." . . . They are supposed to know absolutely the consequence of their acts when they are performed, and to perform them in the light of the consequences. . . .

4. We must also assume complete absence of physical obstacles to the making, execution, and changing of plans at will; that is, there must be "perfect mobility" in all economic adjustments, no cost involved in movements or changes. To realize this ideal all the elements entering into economic calculations—effort, commodities, etc.—must be continuously variable, divisible without limit. . . . The exchange of commodities must be virtually instantaneous and costless.

5. It follows as a corollary from number 4 that there is perfect competition. There must be perfect, continuous, costless intercommunication between all individual members of the society. Every potential buyer of a good constantly knows and chooses among the offers of all potential sellers, and conversely. Every commodity, it will be recalled, is divisible into an indefinite number of units which must be separately owned and compete effectually with each other.

6. Every member of the society is to act as an individual only, in entire independence of all other persons. . . . And in exchanges between individuals, no interests of persons not parties to the exchange are to be concerned, either for good or for ill. Individual independence in action excludes all forms of

collusion, all degrees of monopoly or tendency to monopoly. . . .

9. All given factors and conditions are for the purposes of this and the following chapter and until notice to the contrary is expressly given, to remain absolutely unchanged. They must be free from periodic or progressive modification as well as irregular fluctuation. The connection between this specification and number 2 (perfect knowledge) is clear. Under static conditions every person would soon find out, if he did not already know, everything in his situation and surroundings which affected his conduct. . . .

The above assumptions, especially the first eight, are idealizations or purifications of tendencies which hold good more or less in reality. They are the conditions necessary to perfect competition. The ninth, as we shall see, is on a somewhat different footing. Only its corollary of perfect knowledge (specification number 2) which may be present even when change takes place is necessary for perfect competition.[52]

This list of requirements of perfect competition is by no means a statement of the *minimum* requirements, and in fact no one is able to state the minimum requirements.

Consider first complete knowledge. If each seller in a market knows any *n* buyers, and each seller knows a different (but overlapping) set of buyers, then there will be perfect competition if the set of *n* buyers is large enough to exclude joint action. Or let there be indefinitely many brokers in any market, and let each broker know many buyers and sellers, and also let each buyer or seller know many brokers—again we have

---

[52] *Ibid.*, pp. 76–79; cf. also p. 148.

perfect competition. Since entrepreneurs in a stationary economy are essentially brokers between resource owners and consumers, it is sufficient for competition if they meet this condition. That is, resource owners and consumers could dwell in
complete ignorance of all save the bids of many entrepreneurs.
Hence knowledge possessed by any one trader need not be
complete; it is sufficient if the knowledge possessed by the
ensemble of individuals in the market is in a sense comprehensive.

And now, mobility. Rigid immobility of every trader is compatible with perfect competition if we wish to have this concept denote only equilibrium which is not affected by the
actions of individual traders: large numbers (in any market)
and comprehensive knowledge are sufficient to eliminate monopoly power. If we wish perfect competition to denote also
that a resource will obtain equal returns in all possible uses,
mobility becomes essential, but not for all resources. If one
resource were immobile and all others mobile, clearly the
returns of all resources in all uses could be equalized. Even if
all resources were immobile, under certain conditions free
transport of consumers' goods would lead to equalization of
returns.[53] Even in the general case in which mobility of resources is required, not all the units of a resource need be
mobile. If some units of each resource are mobile, the economic system will display complete mobility for all displace-
ments up to a limit that depends upon the proportion of mobile units and the nature of the displacement.

The condition that there be no costs of movement of resources is not necessary in order to reach maximum output for
an economy; under competition only those movements of resources will take place for which the additional return equals

---

53 See P. A. Samuelson, "International Factor-Price Equalization Once
Again," *Economic Journal*, LIX (1949), 181–97; and S. F. James and I. F.
Pierce, "The Factor Price Equalization Myth," *Review of Economic Studies*,
XIX (1951–52), 111–22.

or exceeds the cost of movement. But costless movement is necessary if equality is to obtain in the return to a resource in all uses: if the movement between *A* and *B* costs $1.00 (per unit of time), the return to a resource at *A* can vary within $1.00 of either direction of its return at *B*. Equilibrium could be reached anywhere within these limits (but would be uniquely determined), and this equilibrium would depend upon the historical distribution of resources and consumers.

Next, divisibility. It is not enough to have a large number of informed traders in a market: price must change continuously with quantity if an individual trader is to have only an imperceptible influence upon the market rate, and this will generally require divisibility of the commodity traded. Infinite divisibility, however, is not necessary to eliminate significant control over price by the individual trader, and divisibility of time in the use of a resource is a substitute for divisibility in its quantity. Divisibility, however, is not sufficient to insure uniqueness of equilibriums; even in the simpler problems one must also require that the relevant economic functions display strict monotonicity, but this has nothing to do with competition.

And homogeneity. The formal condition that there be many producers of *a* commodity assumes homogeneity of this commodity (Knight's assumption 5). Certain forms of heterogeneity are of course unimportant because they are superficial: potatoes need not be of the same size if they are sold by the pound; laborers do not have to be equally efficient if the differences in their productivity are measurable. As these examples may suggest, heterogeneity can be a substitute for divisibility.

The final assumption, concerning collusion, is especially troublesome. If one merely postulates the absence of collusion, then why not postulate also that even two rivals can behave in such a way as to reach competitive equilibrium? Instead, one usually requires that the number of traders be large enough so that collusion will not appear. To determine this number, one must have a theory of the conditions under which collusion occurs. Economists have generally emphasized two barriers to collusion. The first is imperfect knowledge, especially of the consequences of rivalry and of the policy which would maximize profits for the group, and of course neither of these difficulties would arise in the stationary economy with perfect knowledge. The second barrier is the difficulty of determining the division of profits among colluders, and we simply do not know whether this difficulty would increase with the number of traders under the conditions we are examining. Hence it seems essential to assume the absence of collusion as a supplement to the presence of large numbers: one of the assumptions of perfect competition is the existence of a Sherman Act.

It is therefore no occasion for complaint that Knight did not state the minimum requirements for perfect competition; this statement was impossible in 1921, and it is impossible today. The minimum assumptions for a theoretical model can be stated with precision only when the complete theory of that model is known. The complete theory of competition cannot be known because it is an open-ended theory; it is always possible that a new range of problems will be posed in this framework, and then, no matter how well developed the theory was with respect to the earlier range of problems, it may require extensive elaboration in respects which previously it glossed over or ignored.

The analytical appeal of a definition of competition does not depend upon its economy of assumptions, although gratuitously wide assumptions are objectionable.[54] We wish the definition to specify with tolerable clarity—with such clarity as

---

[54] They are objectionable chiefly because they mislead some user or abusers of the concept as to its domain of applicability. That dreadful list of assumptions of perfect competition which textbooks in labor economics so often employ to dismiss the marginal productivity theory is a case in point.

the state of the science affords—a model which can be used by practitioners in a great variety of theoretical researches, so that the foundations of the science need not be debated in every extension or application of theory. We wish the definition to capture the essential general content of important markets, so the predictions drawn from the theory will have wide empirical reliability. And we wish a concept with normative properties that will allow us to judge the efficiency of policies. That the concept of perfect competition has served these varied needs as well as it has is providential.

VI. CONCLUDING REFLECTIONS

If we were free to redefine competition at this late date, a persuasive case could be made that it should be restricted to meaning the absence of monopoly power in a market. This is an important concept that deserves a name, and "competition" would be the appropriate name. But it would be idle to propose such a restricted signification for a word which has so long been used in a wide sense, and at best we may hope to denote the narrower concept by a suggestive phrase. I propose that we call this narrower concept *market competition.*

Perfect market competition will prevail when there are indefinitely many traders (no one of which controls an appreciable share of demand or supply) acting independently in a perfect market. A perfect market is one in which the traders have full knowledge of all offer and bid prices. I have already remarked that it was unfortunate that a perfect market was made a subsidiary characteristic of competition, for a perfect market may also exist under monopoly. Indeed, in realistic cases a perfect market may be more likely to exist under monopoly, since complete knowledge is easier to achieve under monopoly.

Market competition can exist even though resources or traders cannot enter or leave the market in question. Hence market competition can rule in an industry which is not in long run competitive equilibrium and is compatible with the existence of large profits or losses.

It is interesting to note that Chamberlin's definition of "pure" competition is identical with my definition of market competition: "competition unalloyed with monopoly elements."[55] But Chamberlin implied that pure competition could rule in an imperfect market; the only conditions he postulated were large numbers of traders and a standardized commodity. The conditions are incomplete: if one million buyers dealt with one million sellers of a homogeneous product, each pair dealing in ignorance of all others, we should simply have one million instances of bilateral monopoly. Hence pure competition cannot be contrasted with perfect competition, for the former also requires "perfect" knowledge (subject to qualifications I have previously discussed), and for this reason I prefer the term "market competition."

The broad concept of perfect competition is defined by the condition that the rate of return (value of the marginal product) of each resource be equal in all uses. If we wish to distinguish this concept from market competition, we may call it (after the terminology attributed to Cairnes) *industrial competition*. Industrial competition requires (1) that there be market competition within each industry; (2) that owners of resources be informed of the returns obtainable in each industry; and (3) that they be free to enter or leave any industry. In addition, the resources must be infinitely divisible if there is to be strict equality in the rate of return on a resource in all uses.

An industrial competitive equilibrium will obtain continuously if resources are instantaneously mobile or in the long run if they move at a finite time rate. Since the concept of long-run competitive equilibrium is deeply imbedded in modern economic theory, it seems most desirable that we interpret indus-

---

55 *The Theory of Monopolistic Competition* (1st ed.; Cambridge, Mass.: Harvard University Press, 1933), p. 6.

trial competition as a long-run concept. It may be noticed that a time period did not have to figure explicitly in the pre-Marshallian theory because that theory did not separate and devote special attention to a short-run normal period in which only a portion of the resources were mobile: the basic classical theory was a long-run theory.

The concept of industrial competition has a natural affinity to the static economy even though our definition does not pay any explicit attention to this problem. Rates of return on resources will be equalized only if their owners have complete knowledge of future returns (in the case of durable resources), and it seems improper to assume complete knowledge of the future in a changing economy. Not only is it misleading to endow the population with this gift of prophecy but also it would often be inconsistent to have people foresee a future event and still have that event remain in the future.

One method by which we might seek to adapt the definition to a historically evolving economy is to replace the equalization of rates of return by *expected* rates of return. But it is not an irresistibly attractive method. There are troublesome questions of what entrepreneurs seek to maximize under these conditions and of whether risk or uncertainty premiums also enter into their calculations. A more important difficulty is that this formulation implies that the historically evolving industry is in equilibrium in long-run normal periods, and there is no strong reason to believe that such long-run normal periods can be defined for the historically evolving industry. If all economic progress took the form of a secularly smooth development, we could continue to use the Marshallian long-run normal period, and indeed much progress does take this form. But often, and sooner or later always, the historical changes come in vast surges, followed by quiescent periods or worse, and it is harder to assume that the fits and starts can be foreseen with tolerable confidence or that they will come frequently enough to average out within economically relevant time periods.

It seems preferable, therefore, to adapt the concept of competition to changing conditions by another method: to insist only upon the absence of barriers to entry and exit from an industry in the long-run normal period; that is, in the period long enough to allow substantial changes in the quantities of even the most durable and specialized resources. Then we may still expect that some sort of expected return will tend to be equalized under conditions of reasonably steady change, although much work remains to be done before we can specify exactly what this return will be.[56]

The way in which the competitive concept loses precision when historically changing conditions are taken into account is apparent. It is also easily explained: the competitive concept can be no better than the economic theory with which it is used, and until we have a much better theory of economic development we shall not have a much better theory of competition under conditions of non-repetitive change.

The normative role of the competitive concept arises from the fact that the equality of rate of return on each resource in all uses which defines competition is also the condition for maximum output from given resources. The outputs are measured in market prices, and the maximum is relative to the distribution of ownership of resources. This well-known restriction of the competitive optimum to production, it may be remarked, should be qualified by the fact that the effects of competition on distribution have not been studied. A competitive system affects the distribution of the ownership of resources, and—given a stable distribution of human abilities— a competitive system would probably lead eventually to a stable income distribution whose characteristics are unknown.

---

[56] It is worth noticing that even under static conditions the definition of the return is modified to suit the facts and that mobility of resources is the basic competitive requirement. Thus we say that laborers move so that the net advantages, not the current money return, of various occupations are equalized. The suggestion in the text is essentially that we find the appropriate definition of net advantages for the historically evolving economy.

The theory of this distribution might have substantial normative value.

The vitality of the competitive concept in its normative role has been remarkable. One might have expected that, as economic analysis became more precise and as the range of problems to which it was applied widened, a growing list of disparities between the competitive allocation of resources and the maximum-output allocation would develop. Yet to date there have been only two major criticisms of the norm.[57] The first is that the competitive individual ignores external economies and diseconomies, which—rightly or wrongly—most economists are still content to treat as an exception to be dealt with in individual cases. The second, and more recent, criticism is that the competitive system will not provide the right amount (and possibly not the right types) of economic progress, and this is still an undocumented charge. The time may well come when the competitive concept suitable to positive analysis is not suitable to normative analysis, but it is still in the future.

Finally, we should notice the most common and the most important criticism of the concept of perfect competition—that it is unrealistic. This criticism has been widespread since the concept was completely formulated and underlies the warm reception which the profession gave to the doctrines of imperfect and monopolistic competition in the 1930's. One could reply to this criticism that all concepts sufficiently general and sufficiently precise to be useful in scientific analysis must be abstract: that, if a science is to deal with a large class of phenomena, clearly it cannot work with concepts that are faithfully descriptive of even one phenomenon, for then they will be grotesquely undescriptive of others. This conventional line

---

[57] In a wider framework there have of course been criticisms of the competitive norm with respect to (i) the ability of individuals to judge their own interests and (ii) the ability of a competitive system to achieve a continuously high level of employment of resources.

of defense for all abstract concepts is completely valid, but there is another defense, or rather another form of this defense, that may be more persuasive.

This second defense is that the concept of perfect competition has defeated its newer rivals in the decisive area: the day-to-day work of the economic theorist. Since the 1930's, when the rival doctrines of imperfect and monopolistic competition were in their heyday, economists have increasingly reverted to the use of the concept of perfect competition as their standard model for analysis. Today the concept of perfect competition is being used more widely by the profession in its theoretical work than at any time in the past. The vitality of the concept is strongly spoken for by this triumph.

Of course, this is not counsel of complacency. I have cited areas in which much work must be done before important aspects of the definition of competition can be clarified. My fundamental thesis, in fact, is that hardly any important improvement in general economic theory can fail to affect the concept of competition. But it has proved to be a tough and resilient concept, and it will stay with us in recognizable form for a long time to come.

9

Bernard Shaw,
Sidney Webb,
and the Theory
of Fabian Socialism

The transition of public policy in England from one of relatively pure *laissez faire* to one of collectivism began in the first half of the nineteenth century, and presumably has not yet reached its end. The shift in public opinion and in effective electoral power which lies behind the shift of policy, therefore, cannot have been initiated by the Fabian socialists, who began their labors in 1884. Yet they are commonly credited with a leading role in persuading the intellectual classes of England of the undesirability of organizing economic life on the basis of private enterprise.

The two leading theoreticians of Fabian socialism were Shaw and Webb—indeed one is inclined to say that they were the only theoreticians in the first decades of the Society. Webb's

Reprinted from the *Proceedings of the American Philosophical Society,* Vol. CIII (June, 1959).

labors in both economic scholarship and politics are well known; at least in this country, there is some tendency to underestimate Shaw's part, simply because his other activities eventually overshadowed as well as displaced his Fabian period. Shaw felt differently:

> Now gentlemen, I am really a political economist. I have studied the thing. I understand Ricardo's law of rent; and Jevons' law of value. I can tell you what in its essence sound economy means for any nation.[1]

The propriety of this claim is better judged at a later point.

I propose to discuss only two aspects of the Fabian movement. The first aspect is the early work in economic theory by Shaw which commands our interest because of its importance as well as its authorship. The second aspect is the precise nature of the theoretical critique of capitalism to which Shaw and Webb devoted their immense talents and energies in the first two decades of the Fabian Society.

I. THE EARLY SHAW

Bernard Shaw was first persuaded of the need for radical economic reform, he tells us, when—in 1882—he accidentally drifted into a London hall and heard one of Henry George's influential lectures for a tax on the rent of land.[2] The study of *Progress and Poverty* soon led Shaw toward socialism. Shaw's incomplete novel, *An Unsocial Socialist,* revealed that within a year after hearing George the conversion to socialism was

---

[1] Shaw, G. B., "The Case for Equality," p. 11, an address delivered on the first of May, 1913 (1st ed; London, 1913), National Liberal Club Political and Economic Circle, *Transactions,* pt. 85; reprinted in *The Socialism of Shaw,* ed. with introduction by J. Fuchs (New York: Vanguard, 1926), p. 58.

[2] Archibald Henderson, *George Bernard Shaw: Man of the Century* (New York: Appleton-Century-Crofts, 1956), p. 215.

complete. Shaw's hero, a Sydney Trefusis, abandoned his wife and his inheritance—both of admirable dimensions—to devote his days to long speeches on the iniquities of capitalism and to inciting the rural proletariat to trespass. That this prince of prigs did not choke off socialism in England is itself one indication that the novel was not widely read.

The criticisms of Henry George by English Marxists drove Shaw to the French edition of Volume I of *Das Kapital*. He was captivated without being persuaded of the validity of all its economic theory. These doubts spilled into print in a letter to a weekly, *Justice,* entitled "Who Is the Thief?"[3] It is a tribute to Shaw's penetration that he had found for himself a crucial flaw in Marx's labor theory of value.

Marx's central argument was that the capitalists, by their control over capital equipment and the means of subsistence, forced a worker who added ten shillings of value to ten shillings of material, to work for only three shillings (his assumed subsistence requirement), yielding up seven shillings of surplus value.

> But mark what must ensue. Some rival capitalist, trading in tables on the same principle, will content himself with six shillings profit for the sake of attracting custom. He will sell the table for nineteen shillings; that is, he will allow the purchaser one shilling out of his profit as a bribe to secure his custom. The first capitalist will thus be compelled to lower his price to nineteen shillings also, and presently the competition of brisk young traders, believing in small profits and quick returns, will bring the price of tables down to thirteen shillings and sixpence.[4]

---

[3] Signed G. B. S. Larking. Reprinted by R. W. Ellis in *Bernard Shaw and Karl Marx: A Symposium, 1884–1889* (New York: Random House, for R. W. Ellis: Georgian Press, 1930).

[4] *Ibid.,* pp. 5–6.

But if the worker is being robbed of 7 shillings, then the purchaser is committing thirteen-fourteenths of the theft—every English consumer is the thief. The criticism received no reply.

The assumptions of competition and of surplus value are indeed incompatible, and even today I would like to amend Shaw's argument in only two respects. The competition of capitalists would also take place in the labor market, and force wages up. And, secondly, the customer-thieves are, of course, chiefly the workmen and their families.

The distrust of Marx's value theory was strengthened by an attack made by Philip H. Wicksteed.[5] Using the recently developed marginal utility theory, Wicksteed showed that Marx's theory was illogical. It was illogical because Marx insisted that only socially necessary labor governs values, which introduced surreptitiously the very quality of utility which he had denied as a universal attribute of commodities. The theory was incomplete because it could not cope with the value of commodities which were not freely reproducible (such as old masters) or were monopolized. Wicksteed's own radical leanings (which diminished subsequently) were perhaps revealed by the fact that he did not comment upon the crucial flaw in Marx's theory—the denial of productivity to resources other than labor.

Shaw took upon himself the writing of a good-natured rejoinder to Wicksteed.[6] Ignoring Marx, he rashly attacked the marginal utility theory, a task for which he was unprepared. The attack centered upon the fact that the amount of utility obtained from an increment of a commodity fluctuates widely over time for one man, and varies widely among men, without any corresponding variation in the value of the commodity. The criticism failed to distinguish positions of equilibrum

---

5 Wicksteed was adding to his careers in the Unitarian ministry and literature—he was the translator of Dante—that of economist.

6 G. B. Shaw, *The Jevonian Criticism of Marx* (1885), reprinted in Ellis, *op. cit.*

from those of disequilibrium, and Wicksteed had no trouble in disposing of it.[7]

The debate now shifted to a small discussion group, the Hampstead Historic Club, where Shaw and Webb, as well as other critics of capitalism, were joined by two economists, Wicksteed and Edgeworth. For two years Shaw was subjected to training in economic theory by two of the world's leading theoreticians—although one may conjecture that with students such as he the professors learned a fair amount about debating. He emerged a complete convert to Jevons and Ricardo—an odd set of intellectual parents considering Jevons' vast dislike for Ricardo's theory.

The conversion was announced by three notices on *Das Kapital* in *The National Reformer* (1887).[8] They express a deep appreciation of the powerful influence of Marx's denunciation of the injustice of capitalism and of his presentation of a law of historical evolution which gives little more time to capitalistic society. The crucial weakness of the Marxian theory of value proves to be the same point that Wicksteed made, that only relative utilities can account for the observed phenomena of value, and this is tacitly recognized when Marx refers to socially necessary labor.[9]

It will suffice merely to mention Shaw's remaining work, because we shall consider its theoretical content below. The essays on the economic theory of and the transition to socialism in *Fabian Essays* (1889) were his. Thereafter, his economic

---

[7] Wicksteed, "A Rejoinder," reprinted in Ellis, *op. cit.* Shaw subsequently wrote that his reply proved nothing but his incompetence (Ellis, *op. cit.*, p. 138 n.)

[8] Shaw, reprinted in Ellis, *op. cit.* The essays contain a remarkable vilification of H. M. Hyndman, the Colonel Blimp of English Marxism.

[9] Apropos of the "transformation" problem of which there was promised a solution in the third volume of *Das Kapital,* Shaw observes that "scientific socialism" means cashing a promissory note of Mr. Engels, dated "London, an Marx' Geburtstag, 5 mai, 1885" (Ellis, *op. cit.*, p. 108).

writings took the form chiefly of Fabian pamphlets,[10] although he also wrote a book on municipal trading.[11] The much later *Intelligent Woman's Guide to Socialism* contains nothing new on our main subject.

Sydney Webb's prodigious literary output seldom lacked relevance to economic theory, but only a few early items are germane to our inquiry.[12] They will be considered in the Fabian critique of the basic logic of a capitalistic (private enterprise) system, to which we now turn.

II. THE ECONOMIC THEORY OF FABIANISM

The main Fabian indictment of private enterprise rested squarely upon the classical theory of the rent of land.

> On Socialism the analysis of the economic action of Individualism bears as a discovery, in the private appropriation of land, of the source of those unjust privileges against which Socialism is aimed. It is practically a demonstration that public property in land is the basic economic condition of Socialism.[13]

---

10 They are identified in E. R. Pease, *History of the Fabian Society,* Appendix IV (new and revised edition; New York: International Publishers, 1926); some are reprinted in *The Socialism of Shaw.*

11 *The Commonsense of Municipal Trading,* Fabian Socialist Series No. 5 (London: A. C. Fifield, 1908). Although the volume is of more interest to political scientists than to economists, it has some remarkably bold analyses resting on the differences between social and private costs. Shaw places extraordinary weight upon the ability of cities to borrow at low interest rates.

12 There seems to be no doubt that Beatrice did not contribute to the work on economic theory. Perhaps one reason was her haste: "I went straight to the club and read right through Marshall's six hundred pages— got up, staggering under it. It is a great book, nothing new—showing the way, not following it." (Diary, July 27, 1890, quoted in Margaret Cole, *Beatrice Webb* [New York: Harcourt, Brace, 1946].)

13 Shaw, in *Fabian Essays,* p. 24 (Jubilee edition; London: George Allen & Unwin, 1950), p. 24.

The crux of this theory is the assumption that, in a settled country, the effective supply of land is fixed. No degree of expansion of the demand for the products of land would call forth an additional acre of land—putting aside normally trifling amounts due to drainage, irrigation, and the like. The aggregate income of the landowners will therefore wax with the growth of population and wealth.

This doctrine had provided the main theoretical support for free trade in grain—the repeal of the Corn Laws in effect greatly increased the supply of land available to meet the demands of British consumers.[14] This was the main goal of policy of the Ricardian school, and one might have expected that once the goal was achieved, the landowner and the rent theory would have receded from the stage of public controversy.

For a time after the repeal of the Corn Laws the criticisms of the private ownership of land abated, but they revived in the latter decades of the century. John Stuart Mill threw his immense prestige behind the Land Tenure Reform Association,[15] and he was succeeded by A. R. Wallace, the co-discoverer of the Darwinian theory. The importance of the absentee rents in the Irish agitation contributed to this revival. The interest in land taxation or nationalization became almost universal after Henry George's triumphal lecture tours beginning in 1882.[16]

---

14 Of course economists defended free trade in grain also—as perhaps one should say, directly—on the principle of comparative cost, but this more general theory had no special relevance to the politically strategic commodity, food, nor did it necessarily have a prospering beneficiary, that is, a villain.

15 John Stuart Mill, *Dissertations and Discussions* (Papers on Land Tenure [London: L. J. Parker & Son, 1859]), p. 5. Mill recognized the validity of the landowners' claim to compensation for any differential taxation, and proposed that only future increments of land values be taken by the state.

16 E. P. Lawrence, *Henry George in the British Isles* (East Lansing: Michigan State Univ. Press, 1957).

Shaw restated the Ricardian rent theory without appreciable modification so far as land is concerned, embellishing it only with his handsome prose. Shaw's piece on the economics of socialism in the Fabian essays was a straightforward repro-duction, on a non-rigorous level, and his tract on *The Impos-sibility of Anarchism,* where anarchism virtually means com-petitive private enterprise, turns on the fact that it is intrinsic to economic life that some land is more valuable than others.[17] Webb's acceptance was as complete.[18]

How could one seriously make a heavy indictment of private property in land when free trade had made wheat—and land—cheap? Late Victorian England was an odd place to offer heavy criticism of feudalism. The answer is a complex one. In the first place, the facts were largely ignored and, when recognized, misinterpreted. The famous Fabian Tract, *Facts for Socialists,* estimates rents to be £200,000,000 or one-sixth of the nation's income in the mid-eighties. Aside from a myriad of minor errors, which the incredibly complex English income tax law invited,[19] the Fabians blithely included the value of all build-ings in that of land. The true rent of land (urban as well as rural) surely did not exceed £60 million, or a mere 5 per cent of income. Moreover, agricultural rents had been declining in absolute amount since the 1870's, and as a share of national income they had probably been declining since 1810. One careful student set the pure agricultural land rents at £6 mil-lion at the end of the century.[20]

---

17 Fabian Tract No. 45 (4th edition, 1893). Also *Fabian Essays,* pp. 165, 167.

18 The rate of interest and the laws of distribution, *Quarterly Journal of Economics,* II (1887–88), 188–209; also, "The Rate of Interest," *ibid.,* pp. 469–72.

19 J. C. Stamp, *British Incomes and Property* (London: P. S. King & Son, 1916).

20 J. R. Thompson, "An Inquiry into the Rent of Agricultural Land," *Journal of the Royal Statistical Society,* LXX (1907), 587 ff.

One could divert attention to urban rents, and the Duke of Bedford made a regular appearance in Fabian publications. Shaw asserted that "town rents have risen oppressively,"[21] and Webb was no doubt the author of *The Unearned Increment*, which dilated upon the unearned increment in London, which even his one-sided manipulations raised only to £6 million per year in the twenty-five years up to 1895.[22]

But no amount of literary skill or empirical absent-mindedness can make a Duke of Bedford the arch-villain of capitalism. It was necessary to generalize the indictment, and the attempt was made by both men. They sought to include interest on capital with rent on land, and they denounced the unequal distribution of income. Both criticisms, however, had to be based upon the theory of rent, or a second, independent theoretical basis had to be found for explaining the workings of a capitalistic system. The second alternative was not chosen: it is not only intellectually inelegant, but psychologically ineffective, to use several unrelated theoretical principles to launch a program of reform.

Shaw's endeavors to extend the theory of rent to interest, that is, to identify the returns to capital and labor—were relatively crude. The basic method was that of assertion:

> Colloquially, one property with a farm on it is said to be land yielding rent; whilst another, with a railway on it, is called capital yielding interest. But economically there is no distinction between them when they once become sources of revenue . . . shareholder and landlord live alike on the produce extracted from their property by the labor of the proletariat.[23]

---

21 G. B. Shaw, "The Impossibility of Anarchism," p. 9 n.

22 Tract No. 30, 1895.

23 *Fabian essays*, p. 19. He subsequently refers to "a form of rent called interest, obtained by special adaptations of land to production by the application of capital . . ." (*ibid.*, p. 25).

This argument is, in effect, that all capital instruments incorporate land in some degree—the unique location and resources of a railroad or a water company are similar to those of agricultural or urban land. Of course this is true, and "land" is in fact only an abbreviation, in the classical economics, for non-producible, non-human resources. But this element of land hardly dominates the vast mass of capital of an economy, which is both fluid in form and augmentable in quantity, and therefore not obedient to such classical theorems as that the rent of a piece of land increases with economic progress. Shaw's dogmatic assertion that capital produces nothing, and interest is a mere exaction, is simple Marxism, wholly inconsistent with the marginal utility theory of value he professed.

Webb's attempt to identify rent and interest took a more sophisticated form. He generalized the rent theory to cover other distributive shares. If rent is the surplus of the yield of resources on good land over the yield on poor land, can one not also say that interest is the surplus of return of resources (including land) on good capital over the yield on decrepit and obsolete capital?

> "Economic interest" is the amount of produce over and above "economic wages" which is obtained through the use of capital, upon land at the margin of cultivation by the skill of the worst worker employed in the industrial community, or upon the better land with greater skill, after deduction of the economic rent of the land and ability.
>
> Economic interest, as here defined, is expressed by a law similar to the Ricardian law of rent.[24]

Webb argues that most interest is the product of "opportunity and chance." The basic theorem that the rates of interest on

---

[24] "The National Dividend and Its Distribution," in S. and B. Webb, *Problems of Modern Industry* (London, New York, and Bombay: Longmans, Green, 1898), pp. 218, 219.

various investments tend to equality, is conceded only for "the last increment of capital employed in each case."[25]

It is true that in one sense the rent theory can be generalized to embrace every form of return—Wicksteed demonstrated in 1894 that the rent theory in this sense is analytically equivalent to the marginal productivity theory.[26] But the rent theory, in this sense, is only a device for isolating the contribution of one productive factor to a product, and has no relevance to the crucial assumption of fixity of supplies which gave the Ricardian rent theory its empirical content.

Without this assumption of fixity of supply, there is little substantive similarity between capital and land. Under competition all forms of investment which yield higher than average rates of return will attract additional investment until the rate of return is equalized on all, not merely on marginal, increments of investment.

One could seek escape from this conclusion by denying the existence of competition—by arguing that monopolies of various sorts had become so ubiquitous and powerful that most interest was a monopoly return.[27] But Webb placed no emphasis upon such a development. On the contrary, he asserts, that "every development toward a freer Individualism must, indeed, inevitably emphasize the power of the owner of the superior instruments of wealth-production to obtain for himself all the advantages of their superiority."

> But the monopoly of which the democracy is here
> impatient is not that of any single individual, but
> that of the class itself. What the workers are ob-

---

25 *Ibid.*, p. 220.

26 Philip Henry Wicksteed, *Coordination of the Laws of Distribution* (London: Macmillan, 1894).

27 It would still not be a rent, in the sense that a reduction in this monopoly return brought about by price fixing or taxation would usually lead to a reduction in the monopolist's output.

jecting to is . . . the creation of a new feudal class
of industry, . . . who compete, it is true, among
themselves, but who are nevertheless able, as a class,
to preserve a very real control over the lives of
those who depend upon their own daily labor.[28]

In Webb's scheme, indeed monopoly was not even an evil.
In *Industrial Democracy* he presents the famous picture of
"higgling in the market."[29] The search of consumers for bar-
gains forces down retailers' prices, retailers in turn are compelled to drive down wholesalers' prices, and so on until the
competitive pressure "finally crushes the isolated workman at
the bottom of the pyramid."[30] Monopolies are devices to obtain some relief from this unrelenting pressure, and, if they
succeed in diminishing competition, they treat their workers
a *little* better. Here monopoly is a modestly benevolent phenomenon.

In this later volume, Webb alleges a further resemblance
between land and capital, but it appears to be *ad hoc:* the
supply of savings is held to be virtually independent of the
rate of interest.[31] But even if this were wholly true, it would
not yield the Ricardian conclusion that the capitalist necessarily benefits from every advance of society—what happened
would depend upon the supply of capital over time.[32]

---

28 *Problems of Modern Industry*, p. 237. Also *Fabian Essays*, p. 55.

29 *Ibid.*, Part III, Ch. II.

30 *Op. cit.*, p. 671.

31 *Ibid.*, pp. 622 ff.

32 In *Capital and Land* (Fabian Tract No. 7 [7th ed., 1908]) a wholly different criticism of private receipt of interest is advanced by Sidney Oliver.
It is to the effect that savings are invested to form concrete capital goods,
and when these goods wear out, the goods which replace them are in some
mysterious sense not due to the original savings. Shaw uses this argument
also in *The Intelligent Woman's Guide to Socialism and Capitalism* (Garden
City, N.Y.: Garden City Publ. Co., *ca*. 1928; London: Constable, 1928).

Both Webb and Shaw seek to extend the rent theory even farther, to include the "rent of ability" of superior workers.[33] It is a most unusual feature of Fabian socialism that it attacked large labor incomes as well as property incomes. Much of the superior earnings of professional men and artists was attributed to the unequal distribution of income, which allowed a few men to prosper by catering to the whims of the rich. Even more was attributed to the "monopoly" of education by the children of property-owning families. The chief remedy proposed was widespread education (which was already developing rapidly), supplemented if necessary by a progressive income tax.

In one respect the analogy between labor and land was closer than that between capital and land: there are natural differences in quality of both men and acres, unlikely to be eliminated under any social system. But the fixity of supply of land finds no parallel in population, and both classical economists and almost all socialists concurred in the absence of any secular increase in wage rates as a society progressed economically. The Fabian doctrine of rents of ability tended both to blur the ethical differences they alleged between wages and other incomes, and to alienate the professional classes from their doctrines, and perhaps these are the reasons this aspect of their theory received little elaboration or emphasis. Still, the socialization of the labor force was latent in this doctrine, and the various hints of compulsion which were dropped[34] are in keeping with the anti-democratic tendencies both Shaw and Webb made explicit in later years.

The final indictment of capitalism, that it generated a cruel

---

[33] Thus Webb says the Ricardian theory must be extended "to all the instruments of production, as well as to the varying efficiencies of every kind of human labour" ("The Rate of Interest," *loc. cit.*, p. 472; for Shaw's statement, see *Fabian Essays*, pp. 183 ff.).

[34] For example, *Fabian Essays*, pp. 55–57. See also E. Halévy, *L'ère des tyrannies* (3rd ed., Paris: Gallimard, *ca.* 1938), pp. 217–18.

and inhuman distribution of income, was no doubt the most influential. The street corner orator was especially clear in Shaw when he reached this theme:

> A New York lady, for instance, having a nature of exquisite sensibility, orders an elegant rosewood and silver coffin, upholstered in pink satin, for her dead dog. It is made: and meanwhile a live child is prowling barefooted and hunger-stunted in the frozen gutter outside.[35]

This sort of diatribe—adorned by frequent references to such strange capitalistic institutions as compulsory prostitution —must have been especially effective at the lips of one of the most formidable debaters of his time.

The denunciation of inequality may be viewed as an ethical judgment, to be accepted or rejected according to one's taste. This is not a very useful view, however, for equality is not a basic ethical value in any important western philosophy.[36] One surely wishes to distinguish nominal from real inequality: the difference between the average earnings of a twenty-five-year-old lawyer and one twice his age is devoid of ethical significance. If policies are to have purpose and effectiveness, one must isolate the sources of inequality, be they education, natural inheritance, luck, thrift, property inheritance, or a par-

---

[35] *Fabian Essays*, p. 21.

[36] For every Shavian parable on the inequities of inequality, one could contrive a counter-parable on the inequities of equality; e.g., "Dr. John Upright, the young physician, devoted every energy of his being to the curing of the illnesses of his patients. No hours were too long, no demand on his skill or sympathies too great, if a man or child could be helped. He received £2,000 net each year, until he died at the age of 41 from overwork. Dr. Henry Leisure, on the contrary, insisted that even patients with broken legs be brought to his office only on Tuesdays, Thursdays, and Fridays, between 12:30 and 3:30 P.M. He preferred to take three patients simultaneously, so he could advise while playing bridge, at which he cheated. He received £2,000 net each year, until he retired at the age of 84."

ticular government policy. One should seek to quantify the subtle and ambiguous concept of inequality, discover whether it is increasing or decreasing, and invent and analyze alternative methods of dealing with objectionable inequality.

Shaw and Webb discharged a portion, but only a very small portion, of the duties of a responsible proponent of an egalitarian program. Shaw advanced, in fact, three basic arguments for equality of income. The first was simply that there is no other objective basis for distribution:

> Now . . . suppose you think there should be some other standard applied to men, I ask you not to waste time arguing about it in the abstract, but bring it down to a concrete case at once. Let me take a very obvious case. I am an exceedingly clever man. There can be absolutely no question at all in my case that in some ways I am above the average of mankind in talent. You laugh; but I presume you are not laughing at the fact, but only because I do not bore you with the usual modest cough. . . . Now pick out somebody not quite so clever. How much am I to have and how much is he to have? I notice a blank expression on your countenances. You are utterly unable to answer the question. . . .
>
> It is now plain that if you are going to have any inequalities of income, they must be arbitrary inequalities.[37]

This argument cannot be taken as seriously as it was given. Equality is an unambiguous rule of distribution only when it is applied as unmeaning arithmetic, giving equal sums of income to the day-old baby, the adult worker, and the jailed felon. Conversely, a competitive market does determine, not how much more clever Shaw was than contemporary drama-

---

[37] "The Case for Equality," in *The Socialism of Shaw*, pp. 53–54.

tists, but how much more he produced of what people desired.

Shaw's second argument for equality was professedly "economic":

> . . . if you allow the purchasing power of one class
> to fall below the level of the vital necessities of sub-
> sistence, and at the same time allow the purchas-
> ing power of another class to rise considerably
> above it into the region of luxuries, then you find
> inevitably that those people with that superfluity
> determine production to the output of luxuries,
> while at the same time the necessities that are
> wanted at the other end cannot be sold, and are
> therefore not produced. I have put it as shortly as
> possible; but that is the economic argument in
> favor of equality of income.[38]

That an unequal distribution of income will lead to an unequal distribution of consumption, however, is not an argument for equality. If one believes, as almost everyone always
has, that no living person should be denied subsistence (and
perhaps much more), then he should favor raising consumption of some people, but the belief does not lead to egalitarianism.

Shaw's final argument for egalitarianism was eugenic; economic barriers prevented marriage from taking place when-
ever biological urges dictated:

> Just consider what occurs at the present time. I
> walk down Oxford Street, let me say, as a young
> man. I see a woman who takes my fancy. I fall in
> love with her. It would seem very sensible, in an
> intelligent community, that I should take off my
> hat and say to this lady: "Will you excuse me; but

---

[38] *Ibid.,* p. 60.

you attract me very strongly, and if you are not already engaged, would you mind taking my name and address and considering whether you would care to marry me?" Now I have no such chance at present. Probably when I meet that woman, she is either a charwoman and I cannot marry her, or else she is a duchess and she will not marry me.[39]

Of this argument I will say only that Shaw was utterly sincere, and that it did not become a Fabian article of faith.

Webb based his analysis of inequality much more directly upon the rent theory.

Nor is there any doubt or dispute as to the causes of this inequality. The supersession of the Small by the Great Industry has given the main fruits of invention and the new power over Nature to a comparatively small proprietary class, upon whom the mass of the people are dependent for leave to earn their living. When it suits any person having the use of land and capital to employ the worker, this is done only on the condition that two important deductions, rent and interest, can be made from his product, for the benefit of two, in this capacity, absolutely unproductive classes—those exercising the bare ownership of land and capital.[40]

That "the most virtuous artisan cannot dodge the law of rent"[41] is the anchor of this indictment of inequality.

The net effect of rent upon the distribution of income among families in late Victorian England is not known. If it

---

[39] *Ibid.,* pp. 63–64.

[40] "The Difficulties of Individualism," in *Problems of Modern Industry,* pp. 235–36.

[41] *Ibid.,* p. 260.

parallels modern American experience—and there should be at least a family resemblance—the wealthiest classes received a much more than proportionate share of rents, and so, too, did the lowest income classes, and the intermediate classes received a less than proportionate share.[42] Elimination of rents, therefore, would reduce income inequality at the top of the income distribution and increase it at the lower end. But no matter what one did with rents, the distribution of income would change little.

Only if one includes interest on capital are the possibilities of redistribution large, and here the rent theory was of no avail: one must contrive an entirely new reason for rejecting private property in capital. Of course such reasons can be contrived, but the Fabians did not meet this demand.

III. CONCLUSION

Reformers seldom proportion criticism carefully to evil, but the Fabians must be among the most extreme in their concentration upon a minor and uncharacteristic aspect of capitalism as its major flaw. There is a non-functional income to productive resources in fixed supply, and it is roughly—but only very roughly—approximated by rent of land, but it was already trifling in their time and it was on balance (including urban rents) declining relative to national income.

One expects blind slogans and high emotions to carry a mass movement, but the particular clientele of the Fabians was the educated class of Great Britain. That they were as successful as they are reputed to be[43] is suggestive of a proposition for

---

[42] See D. Gale Johnson, "Rent Control and the Distribution of Income," *Proceedings of the American Economic Association*, May, 1951, pp. 568–82.

[43] Their influence is a difficult question, to which no established answer has yet been given. They are credited with much long-run influence, but little immediate impact, by H. Pelling, *The Origins of the Labour Party, 1880–1900* (London: Macmillan, 1954; New York: St Martin's Press, 1954).

which I believe there is much support: that social problems are the creation of the "intellectual." The intrinsic importance of a complaint against a social system, as judged by later opinion, has little to do with its effectiveness in shifting opinion. If enough able and determined men—and the number in the Fabian group was almost unbelievably small—denounce and denounce again a deficiency, that deficiency becomes grave.[44]

It is less unusual of the Fabian theoreticians that they were not good economists—popular reformers have seldom been. In economics Shaw was merely a clever dilettante. No short sentence could do justice to Webb's large talents, but they did not include a strong command of economic theory. Their limitations prevented them from constructing a coherent program of economic reform, but it apparently did not decrease the effectiveness of their criticisms of the existing order. Had the leading economists of the period subjected this literature to critical review—instead they simply ignored it—I doubt whether the control over land use would have been an element of modern English socialism.

---

[44] Of course, to the possibly decisive extent that the distribution of income, rent, theory aside, was the successful element of their indictment, they were only one of many streams of nineteenth-century criticism, and their influence must be assessed correspondingly lower.

10

Stuart Wood and the Marginal Productivity Theory

Stuart Wood has two claims to economic fame: he appears to have been the first person to receive a Ph.D. in economics in America and he was one of the independent discoverers of the marginal productivity theory. The latter claim, at least, is substantial: he shares this discovery with economists of the stature of Marshall, Wicksell, Barone, and J. B. Clark. I shall first present a few biographical details and then summarize Wood's economic writings.

I. BIOGRAPHICAL DETAILS

Stuart Wood was born in Philadelphia on May 30, 1853, and died there on March 2, 1914.[1] His father, Richard Davis Wood,

---

Reprinted from *The Quarterly Journal of Economics,* August, 1947.

[1] The sources of information are various: obituaries; university records; correspondence with associates; etc. I am particularly indebted to Mr. C. B. Suttle of Philadelphia, who was Wood's secretary during the latter years of his life.

was a prominent banker, manufacturer, and railroad builder, and he eventually followed into the former two industries.

Wood was apparently privately tutored before entering Haverford College in 1866 at the age of thirteen,[2] where he had been preceded by his five older brothers. His academic record was very good: his annual average grades were 98.0, 98.3, 98.9, and 99.6—although one should add that grades over 100 were not unknown. The following three years were spent chiefly in travel, including a year of study of philosophy at an unknown German university.

In 1873 Wood entered the Graduate School of Harvard University. He was in residence for two years, and wrote (in longhand) a 133-page thesis entitled "A Review of the 'Principles of Social Science' by Henry C. Carey." In 1875, a month after becoming twenty-two, he received a Ph.D., the first in economics at Harvard. His work in economics, under Professor Dunbar, had included readings of Blanqui's *History of Political Economy*, Smith's *Wealth of Nations*, and Carey's *Social Science*. It was eight years later before a second Ph.D. in economics was conferred by Harvard—on F. W. Taussig.

Even before completing his academic work, Wood had entered his father's manufacturing business. In 1874 he formed a partnership with four of his brothers, to continue as iron founders and machinists (with mills at Florence and Millville, N.J.) and as commission merchants and dealers and finishers in cotton and other goods. He specialized in the financial end of the business. He also became privately interested in several public utilities (Millville Gas and Water Co., Tampa Water Works Co., Macon Gas and Water Co., etc.), banks (Vineland National Bank, N.J., and the Market Street National Bank, of Philadelphia) and acquired large acreages of undeveloped coal

---

2 His record at Haverford College gives only the Westtown Friends School (at Westtown, Pa.) as earlier training; the records of this latter school indicate that he attended only for five months in 1863.

and timber lands in West Virginia and property suburban to Philadelphia.

He must have had more than average energy, for in addition to these numerous business activities, he dabbled in politics,[3] was manager of the Pennsylvania Institute for Deaf and Blind, treasurer of several learned societies, and active in the American Economic Association. He joined this association in 1886 shortly after it was founded and was a member until his death. He was long a member of the Council, a body much like, and in the course of time not much smaller than, the Legion of Honor.[4] He attended numerous meetings of the Association (at one of which he played host to the entire group), helped finance early journalistic ventures of the Association, and was a vice-president in 1901.

His active writing in economics fell in a short span of time (1888 to 1891). It is reported that only early and extensive business entanglements prevented him from entering academic life, for which, as we shall see, he had talents not common in faculties of economics at that time.

II. ECONOMIC WRITINGS

Stuart Wood's doctoral dissertation, it must be reported, was an undistinguished performance. It was a selective summary and a non-selective criticism of Henry C. Carey's *Principles of Social Science*. Bits of the analysis were fresh, but on the whole Wood was content to repeat J. S. Mill and his predecessors. The style was flowery, the tone superior,[5] and the standard of

---

[3] In 1884 he organized the Independent Republican movement in Pennsylvania to support Cleveland.

[4] When he was first appointed in 1886, the Council had forty members; by 1903 this number had grown to 166.

[5] The following passage is an exaggerated example:

"Before examining Mr. Carey's own theory, I now turn to what he says about Mr. Malthus. He attempts in an early chapter to refute him offhand in a very few words,—words which demonstrate either Mr. Carey's own complete and stupid misapprehension of Mr. Malthus' meaning, or else his

craftsmanship low.[6] Yet few who, after a decent interval, have reread their own theses will fail to have some sympathy for these shortcomings. And for Wood there was the extenuation of youth—the thesis was written when he was twenty-one.

Our real interest, however, is in his later essays. They fall into the two fields of the marginal productivity theory and the history of doctrine.

The Marginal Productivity Theory. The marginal productivity theory was presented in two essays which appeared in 1888 and 1889.[7] It is assumed in these essays that the supply of labor is fixed, and the investigation then turns on the manner in which the price of labor acts on the quantity of labor demanded so as to lead to an equilibrium with full employment.[8] The fundamental determinant of the demand for labor is immediately stated to be the substitution relationship between capital and labor. Wood is concerned chiefly with two problems: (1) the manner in which one productive factor is substituted for the other; and (2) the determination of the rates of wages and interest.

Substitution of one factor for the other takes place in two

---

wilful misinterpretation of it,—which refutes nothing but that silly claim for fairness which Mr. Carey has the impudence to put forward in his preface" (pp. 66–67).

6 Compare the light-hearted accusation of plagiarism:
"Many of Mr. Carey's views, in fact, are closely related to those of List, and although I have not been at the pains to examine with accuracy the question of priority, all the circumstances seem to point very strongly to liberal plagiarism on the part of the former" (pp. 51–52).

7 "A New View of the Theory of Wages," *Quarterly Journal of Economics*, III (1888–89), 60–86, 462–80; and "The Theory of Wages," Publications of the American Economic Association, IV (1889), 5–35. The latter paper was presented at the same meeting at which J. B. Clark first presented his version of the theory, in "Possibility of a Scientific Law of Wages," *ibid.*, pp. 39–69.

8 "New View," pp. 61–63; "Theory of Wages," pp. 6–9.

general ways. The first method of substitution is inter-industrial:

> All articles are produced by the coöperation of labor and of capital, but it may be that no two articles are produced by exactly the same proportions of them. As consumption happens to be of those articles into whose production labor enters more largely, or of those other articles into whose production the use of capital enters more largely, just in such proportion does it occasion a large or a small demand for labor.[9]

The technical relationships between capital and labor and the conditions of demand together determine the equilibrium position:

> If the price of labor be excessively high, the price of those commodities into which labor most largely enters will also be high, and the demand for them will slacken. Employers will withdraw capital from their production in order to embark it in industries using a greater proportion of auxiliary capital. The demand for labor and its price will fall, and the use of auxiliary capital will grow at its expense until equilibrium is restored.[10]

This method of inter-industrial substitution had already been formulated with greater precision by Walras and Wieser, and later Cassel made it the fundamental part of his theory of production.

The new and important element in Wood's theory, however, is his second method of substitution. It may be termed intra-firm:

---

[9] "Theory of Wages," p. 11.   [10] "New View," p. 84.

Of the vast number of processes which are carried on by machinery, the greater number perhaps could be executed as well by hand labor. Machinery is preferred simply because the cost of production is lessened by its use. Also, in many processes now executed by hand, machinery would be equally efficient; but it is not used, because it would involve a greater cost of production. In these cases, opportunities for labor or for auxiliary capital to supplant the one the other only occur when either the price of labor or the cost of using machinery changes. In some cases, a great change only will afford such opportunities: in other cases, a small change will suffice. But there are other cases in which the cost is equal, or very nearly equal, whether labor is employed or auxiliary capital. In such cases, the slightest change in the price of labor immediately affects the demand for it.[11]

Wood comes close to the modern concept of a marginal rate of substitution; he speaks, in fact, of the "rate of interchange" between factors.[12] There is a strong temptation to attribute clairvoyance to him when he states that "Labor and capital are interchangeable and are used indifferently where . . . each may be said to be at its final relative utility,"[13] for the marginal rate of substitution of capital for labor (in the Hicks-Allen terminology) is the ratio of the marginal productivity of labor to that of capital. Again, diminishing returns (to capital and labor) are stated primarily in terms of a scale of the quantities of capital necessary to supplant one laborer in various occupa-

---

11 *Ibid.*, pp. 67–68.

12 *Ibid.*, pp. 73, 463, 476; "Theory of Wages," pp. 19, 30, 34.

13 "Theory of Wages," p. 29 (italicized by Wood).

tions.[14] With such an approach, it is not surprising to find also an excellent statement of what is commonly called Marshall's "law of substitution":

> In productive industry, every form of investment is open to the employer. . . . In all cases, he is governed by one and the same motive—namely, the desire for gain; and, according to his expectations as to the comparative profit to be reaped, he turns capital into one field or into another. He does not buy labor until he has compared the profit to be got by so doing with that obtainable by a different outlay. . . . If labor commands a high price, he economizes in its use and employs more auxiliary capital.[15]

Let us turn now to Wood's second problem, the determination of the rates of interest and wages. Given the supplies of the productive factors, the tastes of consumers, and the state of technology—the list is his—the wage rate and the interest rate are determined by three conditions: (1) full employment of capital and labor;[16] (2) equalization of marginal utilities of various commodities per dollar's worth of expenditure;[17] and

---

14 "New View," pp. 68, 464; "Theory of Wages," especially the graph on page 31 and the accompanying discussion.

15 "New View," pp. 63–64.

16 *Ibid.*, pp. 63, 480; "Theory of Wages," pp. 13–14.

17 "New View," p. 84: "Equilibrium can only exist in the price of labor and in the price of using capital when it is impossible to augment the sum of gratifications by supplanting industries employing a large proportion of one by industries employing a large proportion of the other. Among the industries between which desire is evenly balanced, there are some in which labor predominates, and some in which capital predominates. The price of labor which will produce any gratification in the former industries equals the cost of using capital to produce in the latter other gratifications equally esteemed by human desire." See also "Theory of Wages," p. 9.

(3) the marginal productivity theorem: "the relative final utilities [marginal productivities] of labor and of capital fix their relative prices, and the wages of labor and the interest on capital are the same in all their employments as they are here."[18] All of the essentials of the theory of general equilibrium are present in this analysis.

An interesting application of the theory is made to international trade.[19] Wood is one of the few nineteenth century economists (Sismondi and Longfield must also be named) to explain the existence and nature of international (and interregional) trade directly by differences between countries in the relative supplies and prices of capital and labor:

> Each country will devote itself to the growth of that crop for which it is best suited, and will supply its wants of other things by exchange. If the people of the country which grows oranges [which require much capital] wish for flax [which requires much labor], they will obtain it by giving oranges in exchange to the people of the flax-growing country. . . . Thus the needs of each country will be supplied in the cheapest manner. The demand for labor, however, will be far greater in the flax-growing country relatively to the demand for capital, and should the supplies of labor and of capital be the same in both countries, wages will be higher where flax is grown and interest where oranges are grown.[20] If in any two countries the relative prices paid for labor and for the use of capital differ, then

---

18 "Theory of Wages," p. 14; also "New View," pp. 63, 66.

19 Considerable attention is also paid to the absolute and relative shares of capital and labor, but the discussion does not get beyond a listing of determinants—a position at which it still tends to come rest. See "New View," pp. 72–73, 463–78; "Theory of Wages," pp. 17–29.

20 "Theory of Wages," p. 21.

such industries as require most labor tend towards
the country where labor is relatively cheapest, while
such as require most auxiliary capital gravitate to
the country where labor is relatively dearest and
where interest is lowest.[21]

We need not subject Wood's theory to a detailed criticism.
There are obvious defects in his exposition: for example, the
implicit assumption that there are two homogeneous factors of
production, labor and capital, and consequently such entities
as "the" wage rate and "the" interest rate. The only point that
seems worth elaborating here, however, is his peculiar concept
of the nature of substitution. The essence of this concept is
that production consists of integral processes which must be
carried on exclusively by one of the two factors.[22] This is an
unduly narrow view: Wood considers only what might be
called the extensive margin of substitution between capital
and labor, and overlooks the equally important possibilities of
substitution within any process. But even a partial generalization of the substitution relationships among productive factors
marked a major advance over the classical theory. And up to
that time probably no other non-mathematical economist had
shown equal insight into the interplay between production
functions, demand conditions, and the supplies of productive
factors.

The History of Doctrine. Stuart Wood's first—and only vol-

---

21 "New View," p. 468.

22 "Theory of Wages," p. 14: "The relative advantages of labor and of
capital vary so greatly in their different uses, that whatever may be their
hire at any time, it will in most of their employments be impossible to substitute one for the other, unless a vast change should occur in the relative
price of using them." "New View," p. 69: ". . . at whatever point this equality of costs exists, labor and auxiliary capital will be employed indifferently; while one one side of it labor alone will be used and on the other side
capital exclusively, . . ."

untary—contribution to the history of ideas was a critical history of the wages-fund doctrine.[23] This historical survey was the most complete to appear down to that time, and it remains today an unusually illuminating and convincing appraisal.

The views of James Mill, McCulloch, Senior, and J. S. Mill are summarized and criticized because of their failure to face the problem of what determines the wages-fund. Torrens, and more particularly Cairnes, went farther: They assumed that the quantity of fixed capital and of materials (circulating capital not spent on labor) was determined by the size of the laboring population (since the proportion between capital and labor was fixed in each industry), and therefore the wages-fund is a residual.[24] Wood's criticism of this theory deserves full quotation:

> But, unfortunately, Cairnes, in his turn, fails to inquire into the causes of the existing industries and methods.
>
> One set of these causes is to be found in the character of the natural resources of any country, another in the state of the arts, and a third in the nature of human desires. If all of these things were invariable, or if, at least, none of them varied under the influence of price, then Cairnes's explanation would exhaust the causes which go to make up the rate of wages; . . . For then the national industries and their prevailing methods of production would be really fixed independently of the rate of wages, and would decide what stock of implements and materials must be assigned to each laborer. . . .

---

23 "A Critique of Wages Theories," Annals of the American Academy of Political and Social Science. I (1890), 426–61.

24 *Ibid.*, pp. 446, 453. Wood forgets the indeterminate deduction from total capital for the capitalists' consumption.

> But the price of labor does affect the choice of the
> industries and methods which prevail. It influences
> desire, because it affects the relative price of the ob-
> jects of desire, in so far as labor enters into their
> production in different proportions. It therefore
> affects the choice between the industries which pro-
> duce different kinds of goods, by reason of its influ-
> ence on the desire for these goods. It also affects the
> choice between different methods of producing the
> same goods, by enhancing or cheapening the cost of
> those methods into which labor more largely enters,
> as compared with those into which the use of fixed
> capital enters more largely. In these ways the price
> of labor does potently affect the demand for labor,
> and no explanation of the phenomena of wages will
> hold good which ignores this fact.[25]

Thornton's refutation of the wages-fund theory by the argument that the demand curve for labor has zero elasticity is
properly rejected on essentially the same ground of substitution between factors.[26]

Only two points in Wood's appraisal of the wages-fund doctrine are seriously objectionable. The first is a positive error:
he suggested that the classical economists believed that the size
of the wages-fund was independent of labor's productivity,[27]
when of course it was generally recognized that increases in

---

25 *Ibid.*, pp. 452–53.

26 Wood points out the terminological confusion whereby the classical
economists and Thornton secured contradictory conclusions from the same
premise, that the demand for labor was fixed (independent of its price). By
demand for labor, the classical economists meant the quantity of commodities offered in exchange for labor, Thornton meant the quantity of labor
demanded (*ibid.*, p. 460).

27 "No assiduity on the part of the laborers, no improvement in production, could raise wages, and just as surely, no degree of neglect or indolence
could lower them" (*ibid.*, p. 450).

productivity would lead to a larger future wages-fund. The second point is an oversight, in this as in his previous essays: Wood never questioned the realism or usefulness of the concept of an "average wage rate." But it cannot be disputed that he seized upon the greatest single defect in the classical theory of production and distribution, the failure to discover the relationship of substitution among productive factors.

Wood's final publication in economics was a review of Augusto Graziani's "Studii sulla Teorica Economica delle Macchine."[28] Graziani had criticized von Thünen's marginal productivity theory and extended the criticism to Wood's version, which had been presented "without too much novelty of reasoning."[29] Wood vehemently denied the accusation of plagiarism which he read into this passage, but the text supports Graziani's rejoinder that no insinuation of plagiarism was intended. Graziani's criticisms of the marginal productivity theory were wrong; the episode acquires some significance only because of a sequel.

In the September, 1894, issue of the *Journal of Political Economy* there appeared the anonymous note which is reproduced on page 299.[30] The note is too brief to permit of an unambiguous interpretation, but its wording and format are calculated to suggest plagiarism to most readers. Wood never replied to the note.

We may reject the implication. Casual analogies are not a sufficient basis for so grave a charge. Brief study would reveal

---

28 Turin: Fratelli Bocca, 1891. The review was "Note on Professor Graziani's Economic Theory of Machinery," Annals of the American Academy of Political and Social Science, II (1891), 522–30; to which a reply was made by Graziani, "The Economic Theory of Machines," *ibid.*, pp. 838–41.

29 The disputed passage is on pp. 57–58 of Graziani's book, translated (with minor inaccuracies) in Wood's review, p. 526.

30 II (1894), 574. The present quotation follows the published note, which contains twenty-six minor errors. It has been impossible to determine the authorship of the note.

that Wood's theory differs in important respects from that of the eccentric Lord Lauderdale. The latter, it is true, emphasized the substitution of capital for labor. But he argued that only a monopolist can secure for his capital goods a price equal to the wages of the displaced labor;[31] under competition the return on machinery is set by "the proportion betwixt the quantity of machines that can be easily procured, and the demand for them."[32] Nor does Lauderdale see the possibility of substituting labor for capital. As the third set of parallel quotations in the note indicates, Lauderdale usually wrote as if the quantity of capital was governed by the state of the arts;[33] Wood placed this ultimate technological limitation on the use of capital in the background and focussed attention on the prices of the factors. But even if the theories of Wood and Lauderdale were similar in details, Wood's high character and his total lack of professional incentives would make plagiarism unthinkable.

NOTES

An interesting coincidence between Lauderdale's *Public Wealth,* published early in the century, and a recent study on wages, appears below, in parallel columns:

| S. Wood, "New View of the Theory of Wages," *Quarterly Journal of Economics,* October, 1888, and July, 1889. | Lauderdale, *Public Wealth* [Edinburgh, 1804]. |

---

[31] *An Enquiry into the Nature and Origin of Public Wealth* (Edinburgh, 1804), pp. 168–69, 179.

[32] *Ibid.,* p. 167; also p. 179.

[33] *Ibid.,* pp. 214–15, 219–21, 228; on p. 252, however, he inconsistently says that increases of capital may force capitalists to supplant labor "at a cheaper rate."

The price of a given amount of labor is equal to the price which is paid for the use of such amount of auxiliary capital as can replace it in those operations where the two things can be indifferently employed with equal pecuniary advantage (October, 1888, p. 68).

We have seen that capital and labor compete with each other for employment, being able often to supplant each other (p. 85).

If a man can be hired for one hundred and ten dollars to do a certain piece of work, and if, when interest is at six per cent, a machine can be hired for one hundred and twenty dollars that will do the same work, then so long as the rate of interest remains at six per cent labor will be employed, but if interest falls to five per cent then the machine will be employed (p. 64).

The absolute limit to the increase of capital would be attained when its amount should be at the maximum

That the profit of stock employed in machinery is paid out of a fund that would otherwise be destined to pay the wages of the labor it supplants is evident (p. 167). . . . He [the owner of machinery] has only to charge a little less than the wages of the labor which the machine supplants.

Supposing one man with a loom should be capable of making three pair of stockings a day, and that it should require six knitters to perform the same work with equal elegance in the same time, it is obvious that the proprietor of the loom might demand . . . the wages of five knitters, . . . but if a stocking loom was only capable of making one pair of stockings in three days . . . it would be thrown aside as useless (p. 165–66).

There must at all times be a point determined by the existing state of knowledge and the art of supplanting which can usefully be employed in connection with the existing supply of labor, in the existing state of nature and art (July, 1889, p. 478).

labor . . . beyond which capital cannot profitably be increased, . . . because . . . when it exceeds that point . . . its value must of consequence diminish in such a manner as effectually to check its augmentation (p. 228).

11

Sraffa's Ricardo[1]

Ricardo was a fortunate man. He lived in a period
—then drawing to a close—when an untutored genius could still
remake economic science. He lived in a nation where two great
problems, inflation and free trade, gave direction and significance to economics. And now, 130 years after his death, he is as
fortunate as ever: he has been befriended by Sraffa—who has
been befriended by Dobb.

Keynes told us, in 1933, that Sraffa, "from whom nothing is
hid," would give us the full works of Ricardo within the year.[2]
The truth of the first part of the statement had as its cost the
falsification of the second, and it has been a splendid bargain.
For Sraffa's *Ricardo* is a work of rare scholarship. The meticulous care, the constant good sense, and the erudition make this
a permanent model for such work; and the host of new mate-

Reprinted from *The American Economic Review*, Vol. XLIII (September, 1953).

[1] Reflections on *The Works and Correspondence of David Ricardo*,
edited by Piero Sraffa with the collaboration of M. H. Dobb, in nine volumes (Cambridge, Eng. and New York: Cambridge University Press, 1952).
References to volume and page will be by roman and arabic numbers, respectively.

[2] *Essays in Biography* (London: Macmillan and Company, 1933), p. 138.

rials seem to suggest that Providence meets half-way the de-
serving scholar. The Royal Economic Society, his patron, displays its justifiable pride in the outcome of this venture by the
excellence of the presentation of the work.

I shall not attempt any general estimate of Ricardo's work.
It does not seem called for: these nine volumes often amplify
and sometimes modify our understanding of his doctrines, but
they do not change it in essentials. This is desirable as well as
inevitable: it would be high tragedy if Ricardo had been forced
to wait more than a century before revealing, his ideas. Moreover, there is little point in the conventional "estimates" of
past economists. One can indeed debate the desirability of the
influence Ricardo exerted on economics, but his vast influence
is undeniable and the debate serves no clear purpose beyond
exciting his heirs and intellectual assignees. I doubt whether
dead professors should be graded—but for those who must have
grades, I think Ricardo's policy recommendations were pro-
foundly good but his theory was not of the highest quality.[3]

Be that as it may, I shall restrict my comments to three subjects: the quality of the edition; Mill's influence on Ricardo;
and Ricardo and Malthus on Say's Law.

I. THE QUALITY OF THE EDITION

Sraffa's edition seems to breathe precision, so it was only
with difficulty that I brought myself to test a small portion of
it. The test consisted of a comparison of roughly one-tenth of
the paragraphs of his text of the *Principles* with the first ed-
tion.[4] The impression of precision is well-founded; I found

---

[3] And T. W. Hutchison flunks him; "Some Questions about Ricardo,"
Economica, XIX (1952), 415–32.

[4] Sraffa will be pleased to learn that his conjecture as to how two Chapter
VIII's appeared in the first edition is verified (I, xxviii). The copy in the
Columbia library has an uncorrected page 220, which continues with the
opening passages of the second Chapter VIII; the corrected pages 219–22
were bound in the index.

only one large error.[5] Any economist who does not appreciate how extraordinary such accuracy is, should spend an hour or two checking published quotations.

Aside from the introduction to Volume I, Sraffa's editorial prefaces and notes serve an informative, rather than an interpretive, function. This severe self-abnegation was wise: the facts are relatively timeless but even the best analysis of a predecessor will change with the interests and knowledge of the science. The editorial notes are superb. They seem unbelievably omniscient; they are never obtrusive or pedantical; and they maintain unfailing neutrality. Their presence not only clarifies much of Ricardo's work but also provides a vast fund of information on the economics of the period.

Others may be as uncomfortable as I at undiluted praise, and perhaps one should criticize Sraffa for the insertion of an erroneous "not" (VIII, 359) or argue the irrelevance of the splendid tale of Mr. —— (III, 427 ff.) in order to emphasize more subtly the superlative quality of the scholarship. But usual rules must bow to unusual events: here is a task that need not be performed again.

II. MILL AND RICARDO

Ricardo's correspondence opens in 1810, a year after he made the public plunge into economics, and closes with the sad letters of his friends describing his death in 1823. In the former year he was 38, Malthus was 44, Say was 43, James Mill was 37, McCulloch was 31, and John Mill, still busy with Greek, was 4.

In the few letters between Say and Ricardo, the Frenchman seems soft and muddled in comparison with the tough-minded Ricardo. Say's approach was fundamentally much more modern than that of his English contemporaries, but he lacked the intellectual power to develop it satisfactorily. The corre-

---

[5] Sraffa fails to report, I, 149, line 24, that "they" was "we" in the first edition.

spondence makes McCulloch out a less servile and uncritical
disciple than legend would have him; for example, he sturdily
opposed, although not on the best grounds, Ricardo's mistaken
theory of the effects of machinery (fixed capital) on wages
(VIII, 381 ff.). The many letters to Trower, an intelligent stock-
broker friend of Ricardo's, provide exercise in exposition to
Ricardo and relaxation to the reader. Trower was an amiable
man, and one imagines with compassion his reception when he
unsuccessfully tried to tell a rural audience, at a time when the
price of corn was catastrophically low, that its troubles were
augmented by decreases in agricultural taxes (IX, 165 n.).

The major interest of the correspondence lies in the letters
of Mill and Malthus, most of which have not previously been
published. The Mill letters illuminate his role in directing
Ricardo's career—they are unimportant on matters of economics since Mill was inactive in economics during most of the
period. The Malthus letters present the debate over a large
number of scientific differences that separated the two leading
English economists of the period. We begin with Mill.

Mill had come to London in 1802 to make his way as a
writer—a move that surely improved the Scotch Presbytery as
well as the literary journals of London.

> The extent of his acquired knowledge and original
> thinking, when he left Scotland at the age of twen-
> ty-nine, will be judged by what he was able to do in
> the next few years. He kept back from the aspiring
> Scotchman's venture upon London, until he had at-
> tained an unusual maturity of intellectual power;
> while possessed of good ballast in the moral part.
> Moreover, we are to conceive of him as a youth of
> great bodily charms. One of my lady informants
> spoke of him with a quite rapturous admiration of
> his beauty. His figure and proportions were fine;
> the short breeches of the time showed a leg of per-

fect form. His features beamed with expression. Nothing was wanting that could prepossess people's favourable regards.[6]

Already in 1804 he wrote a first, very poor pamphlet on foreign trade,[7] and in 1808 a second, very able pamphlet, *Commerce Defended,* so he was already an economist of sorts when his acquaintance with Ricardo began.

Ricardo had a great respect for Mill, and so should we. Mill had an integrity, a strength of purpose, and a public spiritedness that ordinary men can only admire. He married in 1805, apparently not very wisely, and the twenty greatest years of his professional life were devoted to earning a livelihood as a journalist and editor. He lived partly on the bounty of Bentham, a crotchety landlord. Yet over these years he found the time and energy to educate his oldest son in a manner unparalleled in written history, and to write his famous *History of British India.*

Mill was a man of considerable logical power, wanting only that mysterious gift of insight to achieve greatness. His will could shatter Sheffield steel, and his opinions were no softer; here is an example:

> We are as little able to humble Bonaparte, as Bonaparte is to humble us. There is hardly any human event that is less within the reach of chance than the humiliation of Bonaparte by the prolongation of our hostilities. This is a truth in which all men appear at last to be agreed; it is so evident that it seems to defy objection.[8]

---

6 A. Bain, *James Mill* (London, 1882), p. 35.

7 *An Essay on the Impolicy of a Bounty on the Exportation of Grain.*

8 *Commerce Defended* (London, 1808), p. 128.

The portrait of the cold machine of a man drawn in his son's
Autobiography is no doubt a fair-minded picture, but reflects
also the serious human shortcomings of the artist. The letters
show a little more of the human being, although the gal-
lantries to Ricardo's womenfolk are most ponderous. In plain
fact, I disagree with Bain: something was lacking in Mill to
prepossess our favorable regards. But let us get on to Ricardo.

In the late summer of 1815, Mill began to press for a treatise.
Ricardo was settled on his estate, Gatcomb Park, and now
"sufficiently rich to satisfy all my desires, and the reasonable
desires of all those about me" (VI, 262), when Mill's campaign
began.

> When I am satisfied, however, that you can not only
> acquire that reputation [for talents, and profound
> knowledge of an important subject], but that you
> can very greatly improve a science on which the
> progress of human happiness to a singular degree
> depends; in fact that you can improve so important
> a science far more than any other man who is devot-
> ing his attention to it, or likely to do so, for Lord
> knows how many years—my friendship for you, for
> mankind, and for science, all prompt me to give
> you no rest, till you are plunged over head and ears
> in political economy.
>
> I have other projects upon you, however, besides.
> You now can have no excuse for not going into par-
> liament. . . . (VI, 252.)

Within a week Ricardo agreed to make the attempt:

> Whether it be art in you, knowing how effectual
> the desire of distinction is in calling forth exertion
> and talent, to persuade me that I have certain capa-
> bilities, in order by the reward which you display in

such glowing colours, and to which I am feelingly
alive, to stimulate me to exertion and put my
power to the test,—or whether you are really satisfied that I have those capabilities I am not quite
sure,—but of this I am certain that if the latter is
your opinion you are completely deceived. . . . The
experiment shall however be tried,—I will devote as
much time as I can to think and write on my favor-
ite subject. . . . (VI, 262–63.)

The letters now unfold the picture of a strict but kindly
master dealing with a brilliant but unconfident and procrasti-
nating pupil. There are detailed instructions on the high art
of composition (VI, 329, 339), and even on the way to organize
one's time (VI, 340). Ricardo periodically despairs, as in a letter to Trower: "Thus you see that I have no other encourage-
ment to pursue the study of Political Economy than the
pleasure which the study itself affords me, for never shall I be
so fortunate however correct my opinions may become as to
produce a work which shall procure me fame and distinction"
(VI, 315; also VII, 54, 89). But the taskmaster just as often
revives confidence: "For as you are already the best *thinker* on
political economy, I am resolved you shall also be the best
writer" (VI, 340).

By the fall of 1816 Mill is receiving portions of the manuscript, and his reaction could not fail to encourage any author:

My opinion may be given in very few words; for I
think you have made out all your points. There is
not a single proposition the proof of which I think
is not irresistible. . . .

You have, therefore, made great progress toward
the production of a most admirable book. The style
also, is really excellent. . . . And easy then for you
to put the last hand to a work which will gain you
immortal honour (VII, 98–99).

Ricardo expresses his indebtedness in generous terms:

> How very encouraging your letter is! . . . If I am
> successful in my undertaking it will be to you main-
> ly that my success will be owing, for without your
> encouragement I do not think that I should have
> proceeded, and it is to you that I look for assistance
> of the utmost importance to me—the arranging the
> different parts, and curtailing what may be super-
> fluous (VII, 100–101).

In the spring of 1817 the *Principles* appeared, but Ricardo
was given no rest. He must have shivered at Mill's wish to have
a cottage within a couple of miles of Gatcomb Park: "how I
would keep you to it!" (VII, 184.) Ricardo again hesitates at
Mill's bold plans:

> In the first place I am not very persevering, unless
> the object for which I work is steadily before my
> eyes.—I have all the disadvantages too of a neglected
> education, which it is now in vain to seek to repair.
> It would be wise in me to stop where I am and not
> like a desperate gamester venture my gains to the
> fearful odds to which they are exposed. My mind
> often misgives me about the Parliamentary scheme,
> and I think if you knew me as well as I know myself
> you would advise me against it (VII, 190).

Such excuses were to Mill mere literary lace:

> Which of our *educated* sparks has written such a
> book as yours? (VII, 196.)

> You are now, beyond all dispute at the head of
> Political Economy. Does not that gratify your am-
> bition? And who prophesied all this? Tell me that!

And scolded you on, coward that you are? Tell me
that! (VII, 10.)

And so, in the fall of 1818 the seat in Parliament is arranged,
and Ricardo is instructed to write political discourses as practice for his role of legislator.

Should we take these letters at face value and credit Mill
with the existence of Ricardo's treatise? I do not know. We
must recall that Ricardo wrote the two pamphlets on the bullion controversy and the *Essay* (1815) without apparent intervention by Mill, and the *Proposal* (1816) is due chiefly to Pas-
coe Grenfell's solicitation. Interest, leisure, and ambition supported the writing of the *Principles*. Nor is there any evidence
that intellectual humility was an obstacle to publication for
Ricardo. He never deferred to the authority of Malthus, Say,
or even Smith; it is always his literary accomplishments, and
never his beliefs, for which he apologizes (e.g., VII, 140). The
apologies were justified, and a comparison of the early pamphlets with the *Principles* reveals precious little progress in
this respect for which Mill might claim credit. Perhaps Ricardo
had a phobia on literary composition that it took a Mill to
overcome, but perhaps also Mill, with all his fussing and prod-
ding, merely hastened the work.

I shall not follow any farther the schemes of the Scottish im-
presario, but before we leave him, let us hear Ricardo's response to still another plan:

> This scheme would not contribute to my happiness.
> You are mistaken in supposing that because I con-
> sider life on the whole as not a very desirable thing
> to retain after 60, that therefore I am discontented
> with my situation, or have not objects of immediate
> interest to employ me. The contrary is the case—I
> am very comfortable, and am never in want of ob-
> jects of interest and amusement. I am led to set a

light value on life when I consider the many accidents and privations to which we are liable. . . . No
one bears these serious deprivations with a better
temper than myself, yet I cannot help anticipating
from certain notices which I sometimes think I
have, that many more await me. I have not I assure
you seriously quarreled with life,—I am on very
good terms with it, and mean while I have it to
make the best of it, but my observation on the loss
of esteem and interest which old people generally
sustain from their young relatives . . . convinces me
that general happiness would be best promoted if
death visited us on average at an earlier period
than he now does (VIII, 253).

Ricardo got both wishes: he did not become a director of the
East India Company; and within three years he was dead.

III. RICARDO AND MALTHUS: SAY'S LAW

Malthus was already the celebrated author of the *Essay on
Population* and the only professor of political economy in England when his friendship with Ricardo began. They must have
been uncommonly fond of each other to persist in an intimacy
despite great scientific and intellectual differences and despite
their rivalry for the dominance of English economics.

Malthus had one wondrous gift, the intuition to bring to an
explicit level deep problems of economic life. His claims are
vast: he was an independent discoverer of the "principle" of
population; of the theory of rent; and of the fact of a relationship between saving and the level of economic activity. And he
had one great weakness—he could not reason well. He could
not construct a theory that was consistent with either itself or
the facts of the world.

The correspondence should perhaps give us occasion for de-
spair. The leaders of the science, honorable men seeking

earnestly for truth, could hardly ever resolve a difference after the most protracted exchanges, and the pages on pages of dreary repetition of arguments tells us again how odd an instrument the human mind is. It would be admirable training, and in more than economics, for our graduate students to write analyses of one of these disputes.

We could follow their early exchanges over the theory of profits or their final dispute over the measure of value, but most readers will probably prefer a discussion of the controversy over what is called Say's Law. This choice is commended by its impartiality; for neither man held an enviable position.

J. B. Say first presented his law of *débouchés*, without fanfare or details, in 1803. Each individual specializes in production, and the surplus of his product over his needs is exchanged for the surplus products of others.

> This shows, I believe that it is not so much the abundance of money, but rather the abundance of other commodities in general, that facilitates sales.
>
> . . .
>
> In this double exchange, money fills only a transitory function. . . . As a result, when a nation has too much of one kind of product, the way to dispose of it is to produce another kind.[9] [My translation.]

Without elaboration or application this theory could mean little or much; a theory draws much of its content from its enemies.

Mill presented a similar theory in *Commerce Defended;* it is uncertain whether he was an independent discoverer.[10] One

---

[9] *Traité d'Économie Politique* (1st ed. Paris, 1803), I, 153, 154; see also II, 361–63.

[10] He made no claims of originality and he was already acquainted with Say's book (see *Commerce Defended* [London, 1808], p. 76 n.), but also he did not attribute the doctrine to Say.

may say that if Say invented the weapon, Mill was the first to slay a duck. The duck was William Spence, a physiocrat, who argued, *inter alia,* that the expenditure of landlords on luxuries was essential to maintain the markets for agricultural produce (and inferentially, all markets). Mill refuted this argument by showing that savings which were invested would continue to provide a demand for the services of the "sterile" groups.[11]

Mill went on to dispute a notion of the *Economistes* that "there is only . . . a market for a given quantity of commodities, and if you increase the supply beyond that quantity you will be unable to dispose of the surplus."[12] Mill was led to state the law of markets:

> But if a nation's power of purchasing is exactly measured by its annual produce, as it undoubtedly is; the more you increase the annual produce, the more by that very act you extend the national market, the power of purchasing and the actual purchases of the nation. Whatever be the additional quantity of goods therefore which is at any time created in any country, an additional power of purchasing, exactly equivalent, is at the same instant created; so that a nation can never be naturally overstocked either with capital or with commodities; . . .[13]

Mill's statement was different from Say's in one respect: he explicitly introduced the condition that the composition of output be adapted to the tastes of consumers and investors.[14]

11 *Ibid.,* pp. 68 ff. Mill argued parenthetically that the savings would be spent more rapidly than the portion of income reserved for consumption; *ibid.,* pp. 76–77.

12 *Ibid.,* p. 80. 13 *Ibid.,* p. 81.

14 "All that here can ever be requisite is that the goods should be adapted to one another; that is to say, that every man who has goods to dispose of

Ricardo became acquainted with Mill through this pamphlet,[15] and he embraced Mill's version without reservation. In fact Ricardo went considerably beyond the law in his denial that the quantity of money could have any influence on real output. He was called upon in late 1810 to referee for possible publication a manuscript of Bentham's. Bentham made much of the point that if an increase in the stock of money were given to the productive classes (entrepreneurs), they would bid up prices (thus imposing forced savings on fixed income groups) but the amount of investment would be increased. Ricardo commented:

> That money is the causes [*sic*] of riches has been supported throughout the work and has in my view entirely spoiled it (III, 318).

> An augmentation of money in all cases operates to the disadvantage of some and the advantage of others,—it will neither accelerate nor retard the growth of real riches (III, 325).

Ricardo's objections were fundamentally empirical: the lag of wages behind prices would be of only "momentary duration" (III, 319); and it was "mere speculation" whether entrepreneurs would save more of a given real income than the fixed income recipients (III, 333; also VI, 15–16). His empirical judgments, however, were excessively dogmatic, and he treated his conclusion as if it were as certain as an analytical theorem. His objections considerably delayed the publication of Bentham's essay.[16]

---

should always find all those different sorts of goods with which he wishes to supply himself in return." *Ibid.*, pp. 82–83, also p. 85.

15 J. S. Mill, *Principles of Political Economy* (Ashley ed. London: Longmans, Green and Company, 1929), p. 563.

16 It is now to appear in Volume III of Stark's edition of *Bentham's Economic Writings*.

Within a few months Ricardo made this position public, in the *High Price of Bullion* (III, 120–23), and at the same time disputed the possibility of a general glut. Malthus, in reviewing various pamphlets (including both of Ricardo's) on the bullion controversy, dissented from Ricardo's argument that premiums on foreign currencies are due only to overissue of currency. If there is a crop failure, the exchange might move adversely to a country when it imported corn because "the prices of commodities are liable to general depressions from a glut in the market."[17] Ricardo restated Mill's law, with characteristic vigor:

> No mistake can be greater than to suppose *that a nation can ever be without wants for commodities of some sort.* It may possess too much of one or more commodities for which it may not find a market at home . . . but no country ever possessed a general glut of all commodities. It is evidently impossible. If a country possesses every thing necessary for the maintenance and comfort of man, and these articles be divided in the proportions in which they are usually consumed, they are sure, however abundant, to find a market to take them off (III, 108).

Malthus soon sought out Ricardo, and henceforth the controversy continued in their correspondence.

During 1814 and 1815, when Malthus and Ricardo were publishing highly incompatible pamphlets on the corn laws, the former expressed more openly his scepticism of Mill's law.

> In short I by no means think that the power to purchase necessarily involves a proportionate will to

---

17 "Publications on the Depreciation of Paper Currency," *Edinbugh Review,* XXXIV (February, 1811), 345.

purchase; and I cannot agree with Mr. Mill in an ingenious position which he lays down in his answer to Mr. Spence, that in reference to a nation, supply can never exceed demand. A nation must certainly have the power of purchasing all that it produces, but I can easily conceive it not to have the will. . . . It is not merely the proportion of commodities to each other but their proportion to the wants and tastes of mankind that determines prices (VI, 132).

Ricardo would not admit the possibility of a lack of desire:

I go much further than you in ascribing effects to the wants and tastes of mankind,—I believe them to be unlimited. Give men but the means of purchasing and their wants are insatiable. Mr. Mill's theory is built on this assumption. It does not attempt to say what the proportions will be to one another, of the commodities which will be produced in consequence of the accumulation of capital, but presumes that those commodities only will be produced which will be suited to the wants and tastes of mankind, because none other will be demanded (VI, 148).

Malthus did not deny categorically the insatiability of human wants, nor has any married economist since his time, but he repeatedly argued that a taste for luxuries developed only slowly (VI, 155). It is difficult to see why a lack of wants would lead to a glut of markets, however, since men so constituted would simply not produce in excess of their desires and any surplus of productive capacity would be devoted to indolence—the classical economists' word for leisure.[18]

J. B. Say dealt more elaborately, but not much more precise-

---

[18] We find Malthus seriously confused on the nature of income. He insisted that the "true question" was whether prices would fall if output in-

ly, with the law of markets in the second edition of the *Traité* (1814).[19] His formulation was essentially a truism: Assume that money receipts are always promptly spent; then an offer of one commodity is always an implicit demand for another.[20] This truism has properly been labeled Say's Identity. Say goes *beyond* this truism, or contradicts it, when he asserts that some commodities lack a market because insufficient amounts of other commodities are being produced,[21] but he does not introduce any conditions (such as rigid prices) which would bring such a disequilibrium about.

When Ricardo came to write the *Principles,* he developed the law of markets along Mill's line (I, 289 ff.). He too had each recipient of money spend it promptly; "he would not lock it up in a chest" (I, 291). But he asserted that no matter how large the accumulation of capital, all commodities could be sold for prices equal to their costs of production provided the commodities suited consumers' tastes:

> There cannot, then, be accumulated in a country
> any amount of capital which cannot be employed
> productively, until wages rise so high in conse-

---

creased greatly, income remaining constant, and would not accept Ricardo's argument that income inevitably rose under this assumption (VI, 142, 148, 155–56).

19 *Traité d'Économie Politique* (2d ed. Paris, 1814), Vol. I, Ch. 15.

20 "Il est bon de remarquer qu'un produit créé offre, *dès cet instant,* un débouché à d'autres produits pour tout le montant de sa valeur; car tout produit n'est créé que pour être consommé, soit reproductivement, soit improductivement, et même pour être consommé le plutôt possible, puisque toute valeur qui attend, fait perdre à celui qui en est actuellement le possesseur, l'intérêt de cette attente; le marchand a soin de ne pas avoir des marchandises qui doivent rester en magasin, et le consommateur a soin de ne pas en acheter très-long-temps avant le moment d'en faire usage. Un produit est donc toujours, autant que chacun peut, destiné à la plus prompte consommation, Du moment qu'il existe, il cherche donc un autre produit avec lequel il puisse s'échanger" (*ibid.,* pp. 147–48).

21 *Ibid.,* pp. 148–50.

quence of the rise of necessaries, and so little consequently remains for the profits of stock, that the motive for accumulation ceases (I, 290).

Too much of a particular commodity may be produced, of which there may be such a glut in the market, as not to repay the capital expended on it; but this cannot be the case with respect to all commodities; . . . (I, 292).

It follows then from these admissions that there is no limit to demand—no limit to the employment of capital while it yields any profit, . . . (I, 296).

In this form the law of markets is no longer a truism, it is the proposition that general equilibrium of the economy, with prices equal to costs (including "profits"), is compatible with any level of real income. It would be more appropriate to call this the Mill-Ricardo Law than Say's Law.

Ricardo marred this theory by making a concession to Malthus:

There is only one case, and that will be temporary, in which the accumulation of capital with a low price of food may be attended with a fall of profits; and that is, when the funds for the maintenance of labour increase much more rapidly than population;—wages will then be high, and profits low (I, 292–93).

This is consistent with his theory, but he continues:

If every man were to forego the use of luxuries, and be intent only on accumulation, a quantity of necessaries might be produced, for which there could not be any immediate consumption. Of commodities so limited in number, there might un-

doubtedly be a universal glut, and consequently
there might neither be demand for an additional
quantity of such commodities, nor profits on the
employment of more capital. If men ceased to consume, they would cease to produce (I, 293).

The concession is mistaken: if all luxuries were abandoned for
savings, there would be no piling up of necessaries, and for
that matter their quantity might not increase at all. The output of fixed capital would rise as that of luxuries fell.

We should note that Ricardo did not interpret his law of
markets as excluding the possibility of general commercial distress. On the contrary, he devoted a chapter (19) to Sudden
Changes in the Channels of Trade, which he believed could
for a time occasion widespread distress. Beginning in 1815,
however, he made a series of predictions that prosperity would
soon come to England (e.g., VI, 232, 345; VII, 49, 170–71; etc.).
The prediction was continuously wrong, and it was no compliment to his intelligence that after 1820 he blamed the distress on the abundance of harvests.

The controversy reached a climax with the publication of
Malthus' *Principles* (1820). Malthus' theory has been praised
lavishly in recent times, but it does not contain any germs of
a theory of underemployment equilibrium. We may state with
confidence that it does not turn on hoarding: "No political
economist of the present day can by saving mean mere hoarding; . . ."[22] In fact his theory is entirely non-monetary in nature,
and the prominence given to a footnote on the importance of
money is hard to explain and impossible to justify.[23]

---

22 *Principles of Political Economy* (London, 1820), p. 32.

23 The footnote, which has no relevance to the text, is:
Theoretical writers in Political Economy, from the fear of appearing to
attach too much importance to money, have perhaps been too apt to throw
it out of their consideration in their reasonings. It is an abstract truth that
we want commodities, not money. But, in reality, no commodity for which

The fundamental argument is expressed as follows:

> It is undoubtedly possible by parsimony to devote
> at once a much larger share than usual of the pro-
> duce of any country to the maintenance of produc-
> tive labour; and it is quite true that the labourers
> so employed are consumers as well as unproductive
> labourers; and as far as the labourers are con-
> cerned, there would be no diminution of consump-
> tion or demand. But it has already been shewn that
> the consumption and demand occasioned by the
> persons employed in productive labour can never
> alone furnish a motive to accumulation and em-
> ployment of capital; and with regard to the capital-
> ists themselves, together with the landlords and
> other rich persons, they have, by the supposition,
> agreed to be parsimonious, and by depriving them-
> selves of their usual conveniences and luxuries to
> save from their revenue and add to their capital.
> Under these circumstances, I would ask, how is it
> possible to suppose that the increased quantity of
> commodities, obtained by the increased number of
> productive labourers, should find purchasers, with-
> out such a fall of price as would probably sink their
> value below the costs of production, or, at least,
> very greatly diminish both the power and the will
> to save.[24]

---

it is possible to sell our goods at once, can be an adequate substitute for a
circulating medium, and enable us in the same manner to provide for children, to purchase an estate, or to command labour and provisions a year
or two hence. A circulating medium is absolutely necessary to any considerable saving; and even the manufacturer would get on but slowly, if
he were obliged to accumulate in kind all the wages of his workmen . . .
(*ibid.*, pp. 361–62 n.).

[24] *Ibid.*, pp. 352–53 (also II, 301–3).

This theory is wrong. An amount of savings is matched by an amount of capital goods, and the act of saving need exert no downward pressure on the prices of consumption goods. Malthus' error arises from his assumption that capital formation takes the form only of accumulating the necessaries of labor, *i.e.*, all capital is circulating capital.

Ricardo wrote a critique of the *Principles* at McCulloch's request, and a fair share of it is devoted to the theory of gluts. Ricardo accepts Malthus' theory, with one important correction. If saving leads to a large accumulation of necessaries (Ricardo also improperly identifies capital with circulating capital), which is not accompanied by a corresponding increase of population, wages will rise; Malthus on the contrary argues that wages will fall.[25]

> But if a great quantity of commodities will command little labour, every labourer will have the power to consumer a great quantity of commodities. The will to consume exists wherever the power to consume is. Mr. Malthus proves that this power is not annihilated but is transferred to the labourer. We agree with him and say wherever the power and will to consume exists there will necessarily be demand (II, 311).

Malthus fends this attack by introducing rigidity of wages: "We know from repeated experience that the money price of labour never falls till many workmen have been for some time out of work" (IX, 20). Ricardo finds this argument without merit: "I know no such thing, and if wages were previously high, I can see no reason whatever why they should not fall before many labourers are thrown out of work" (IX, 25). Malthus did not pursue this argument.

It is a question of words whether rapid capital accumulation,

---

[25] *Ibid.*, p. 362 (also II, 316–17).

leading to high wages and low profits, should be said to create a glut; certainly all markets still may be in competitive equilibrium, and no commodity need sell for less than cost. Whatever its name, Ricardo admits that this situation may lead to a cessation of capital accumulation, until the increase of population lowers wages and restores profits.

> Mr. Malthus asks "how is it possible to suppose that the increased quantity of commodities, obtained by the increased number of productive labourers should find purchasers, without such a fall of price as would probably sink their value below the cost of production, or, at least, very greatly diminish both the power and the will to save?["] To which I answer that the power and the will to save will be very greatly diminished, for that must depend upon the share of the produce allotted to the farmer or manufacturer. But with respect to the other question where would the commodities find purchasers? If they were suited to the wants of those who would have the power to purchase them, they could not fail to find purchasers, and that without any fall of price (II, 303–4).

> What I wish to impress on the readers mind is that it is at all times the bad adaptation of commodities produced to the wants of mankind which is the specific evil, and not the abundance of commodities (II, 306).

This concession pertains only to rapid *changes* in the amount of savings, and is independent of the level of savings.

Say made a more prolix refutation in his *Letters to Malthus*.[26] Say's letters have considerable merit, and in particular

---

26 *Lettres à M. Malthus* (Paris, 1820). There is a grotesque "translation"; *Letters to Malthus*, reprinted (London: G. Harding, 1936).

they contain a remarkable sketch of the circular flow in an enterprise economy. But they emphasize Say's lack of precision, and at one point he makes a fatal admission:

> Mr. Ricardo claims that, in spite of taxes and other fetters, the extent of industry is always as great as that of the capital employed, and that all savings are always employed because the capitalists do not wish to lose the interest. On the contrary, there are considerable savings that are not invested when it is difficult to find a use for them, or which, once invested, are dissipated in a mistaken undertaking.[27] [My translation.]

Malthus claimed that this concession was "all that I contend for" (VIII, 260), which is not true because Malthus did not make hoarding the basis of his argument. But he was right in saying that Say did not understand his peculiar position: "This important distinction however Say does not make for me, but runs off into an 'Eh! Monsieur!'" (VIII, 261). Ricardo also felt that the *Lettres* "are not very well done" (VIII, 276).

Ricardo once more came against a critic of the Mill-Ricardo theory when he wrote a commentary (IV, 325–56) on William Blake's *Observations on the Effects Produced by the Expenditure of Government* (London, 1823), to which Blake wrote a rejoinder. Blake attributed the postwar distress to "the transition from an immense, unremitting, protracted, effectual demand, for almost every article of consumption, to a comparative cessation of that demand."[28]

> I believe there are at all times some portions of capital devoted to undertakings that yield very slow returns and slender profits, and some portions lying wholly dormant in the form of goods, for which

---

27 *Lettres,* p. 101 n.   28 *Observations,* p. 88.

there is not sufficient demand. I believe, too, that
when capital accumulates rapidly from savings, it is
not always practicable to find new modes of employing it. Now, if these dormant portions and
savings could be transferred into the hands of government in exchange for its annuities, they would
become sources of new demand, without encroach-
ing upon the existing capital.[29]

Blake's discussion contained ample confusion and lacunae, but
Ricardo's rejoinder was not impressive: his mind was closed
on the subject, and he insisted on postulating full employment
in dealing with a theory of unemployment (IV, 356).

We have touched on only a small part of the contemporary
literature bearing on market gluts, but a review of Ricardo's
works is not an appropriate occasion for a full survey. Even
this strand of the literature, however, is enough to tell us that
the analysis rose above the level of bare truisms and blind disregard of commercial fluctuations. The triumph of Ricardo
over Malthus cannot be regretted by the modern economist:
it is more important that good logic win over bad than that
good insight win over poor.

IV. CONCLUSION

One leaves Ricardo with some envy. In his time economics
was at least as pleasant a subject as it is today. The basic
truths of the science seemed almost within grasp: only a few
concepts like the measure of value had still to be tidied up,
or so it seemed. The frustratingly complex economy which
generations of research have uncovered was still hidden in the
future. The truths of economics then led directly to good social policy, which only an unrepresentative, soon to be re-
formed, Parliament sometimes prevented from being translated

---

29 *Ibid.*, pp. 54–55 (and IV, 340).

into immediate action. The possibility that good economics will not inevitably carry the day in a democracy, of which we are acutely aware, also dwelled in the unpredicted future. A diligent economist, to mention a smaller but not negligible attraction, could read all the worthwhile economics appearing and still have time to do work of his own. Indeed, if he were merely to reside in London, "the place in which we meet a succession of clever men . . . and in which we gain instruction by the active opposition which all our speculations whether right or wrong encounter" (IX, 312), he could exchange opinions with a majority of the world's good economists. But we must be content with our compensations, which include things as precious as greater knowledge and greater humility.

We are still to receive from Sraffa a biography of Ricardo. We shall wait for it with the patience which he munificently rewards.

12

Ricardo and the 93 Per Cent Labor Theory of Value

> Mr. Malthus shows that in fact the exchangeable
> value of commodities is not *exactly* proportioned to
> the labour which has been employed on them,
> which I not only admit now, but have never denied.
>
> RICARDO, *Works*, II, 66

Did Ricardo have a labor theory of value—did he
believe that the relative values of commodities are governed
exclusively by the relative quantities of labor necessary to produce them?

A considerable number of historians of economics have given
a flat affirmative answer to this question—a surprisingly large
number considering the fact that there is not the slightest basis
for such an answer.[1] In the course of their expositions one en-

---

Reprinted from *The American Economic Review*, Vol. XLVIII (June,
1958).

[1] Some examples are E. Whitaker, *A History of Economic Ideas* (New
York, 1940), pp. 422–25; P. C. Newman, *The Development of Economic
Thought* (New York: Prentice-Hall, 1952), p. 85; Emile James, *Histoire*

counters quite remarkable statements such as that Ricardo assumed that labor and capital were in a fixed proportion in all industries,[2] or that "Ricardo . . . constantly takes no notice of capital."[3] Presumably these writers did not have access to Ricardo's *Principles*.

More careful historians of doctrine have recognized the several and important departures from a pure labor theory that Ricardo emphatically made. There is, in fact, an almost continuous spectrum of interpretations. At one uninteresting extreme some writers argue that Ricardo simply forgot or did not understand the import of the qualifications he made. A very important group has advanced the view that Ricardo *wished* to hold a labor theory of value—Cannan heads his treatment: "Ricardo's Attempt to Revive the Pure Labour Theory."[4] They hold that under adverse criticism and honest self-examination, Ricardo was gradually forced to introduce in successive editions of the *Principles* a series of qualifications of increasing importance, so that in the end it really was not a labor theory.[5] But Ricardo was not willing to abandon the

---

sommaire de la pensée économique (Paris: Editions Mouth-restien, 1955), pp. 88–89; and C. Gide and C. Rist, *A History of Economic Doctrines* (2nd ed., New York, n.d.), p. 164.

[2] G. Myrdal, *The Political Element in the Development of Economic Theory* (Cambridge, England: Cambridge University Press, 1954), p. 62; similarly W. Stark, *The History of Economics* (New York: Oxford University Press, 1944), p. 36.

[3] J. K. Ingram, *A History of Political Economy* (New York, 1897), p. 125.

[4] *A Review of Economic Theory* (London: Macmillan Company, 1929), p. 172.

[5] This "evolution" in Ricardo's thought was apparently invented by Hollander, "The Development of Ricardo's Theory of Value," *Quarterly Journal of Economics*, XVIII, 1903–4, 455–91. Sraffa has recently shown that it rests upon a misconception; *Works and Correspondence of David Ricardo*, ed. Piero Sraffa (Cambridge, England: Cambridge University Press, 1951), I, xxxvii ff. (Subsequent references to the latter will be given simply by volume and page numbers.)

theory completely: "his heart clung to the pure labour theory,"[6] or he made a "brave show" of "identifying, as far as
might be, value and the amount of labour necessary for production."[7]

In the most sophisticated versions of this view, the formal
exposition of Ricardo's theory is, as I believe, correct and
complete in substance, but there persists a strong implication
that Ricardo attributes more than quantitative importance to
labor in determining values.[8] Thus, after carefully stating
Ricardo's "modifications" of a labor theory, St. Clair says that
Ricardo "sweeps them all into the waste-paper basket"; for "he
never got rid entirely of the idea with which he started, namely, that labour is the only price exacted by Nature for her
gifts."[9]

The only economists to argue at some length that Ricardo
had a cost-of-production theory of value, so far as I know, have
been Marshall, Diehl, and Viner—but who could wish for more
comforting allies?[10]

---

[6] Cannan, *op. cit.*, p. 177.

[7] Alexander Gray, *The Development of Economic Doctrine* (New York:
Longmans, Green and Company, 1931), p. 177.

[8] In addition to O. St. Clair, one may cite A. C. Whitaker, *History and
Criticism of the Labor Theory of Value* (New York: Columbia University
Press, 1904), Ch. 5, pp. 130–31, J. Schumpeter, *History of Economic Analysis*
(New York: Oxford University Press, 1954), pp. 590–95, and H. Biau-
jeaud, *Essai sur la théorie Ricardienne de la valeur* (Paris, 1934).

[9] *A Key to Ricardo* (New York: Macmillan Co., 1957), pp. 40, 348.

[10] Marshall's discussion is in the *Principles of Economics* (8th ed., 1920),
Appendix I. It elicited from the leading historian of the English classical
economics the remark that "Marshall endeavours to show, in defiance of
all evidence, that Ricardo never desired to put forward the pure labour
theory of value" (Cannan, *op. cit.*, p. 177 n.). Viner criticized Cannan's position in his distinguished review of Cannan's book, *Economica*, X (1930),
78–80. Karl Diehl's extensive, but only moderately detailed, account is in
Sozialwissenschaftliche Erläuterungen zu David Ricardo's Grundgesetzen
(Leipzig, 1905), Pt. I, pp. 1–50.
At least two other historians of doctrine asserted what I take to be the

The widespread misinterpretation of a leading doctrine of an economist of the first rank is not only a product of later viewpoints and knowledge, for it occurred already in Ricardo's lifetime. The present essay seeks to set forth precisely what Ricardo's theory of value was, and to examine the interpretation placed upon it by his leading contemporaries.

I. RICARDO'S THEORY OF VALUE

Ricardo's formulation of his theory of value was much influenced by his desire to correct what he believed to be the major errors of Adam Smith's theory. For Smith the long-run value of a commodity equaled its cost of production: the "natural" price of a commodity was the sum of the necessary payments for labor, capital, and land. A rise in the price of one of these factors, and in particular a rise in wages, would lead to a rise in the prices of the commodities in which the factor entered.[11] If the changes in values were to be more than nominal price-level changes,[12] however, this was clearly a superficial analysis: why should the relative values of commodities be affected in any systematic way by the absolute level of input prices? The organization, although not the content, of Ri-

---

correct view but did not argue it: J. M. Ferguson, *Landmarks of Economic Thought* (2nd ed., New York: Longmans, Green and Company, 1950), p. 106; and W. A. Scott, *The Development of Economics* (New York, 1933), pp. 108–13.

[11] *Wealth of Nations* (New York: Modern Library ed.) Bk. I, ch. 7. Ricardo quoted as a striking example of this argument the passage: "By regulating the money price of all the other parts of the rude produce of land, [the price of corn] regulates that of the materials of almost all manufactures. By regulating the money price of labour, it regulates that of manufacturing art and industry. And by regulating both, it regulates that of the complete manufacture. The money price of labour, and of every thing that is the produce either of land or labour, must necessarily either rise or fall in proportion to the money price of corn" (*ibid.*, p. 477).

[12] And Ricardo was not inclined to make this exception since he had a commodity theory of money.

cardo's chapter on value can be interpreted as one which presses the criticism of Smith's theory to the utmost limits.

The analysis is limited to useful goods, produced in free competition, and the element of rent is temporarily put aside (and later shown not to enter into marginal cost). Ricardo begins with the simplest case: the commodities are produced by one type of labor alone, working perhaps on free land (I, 12 ff.). In this simplest case the relative values of commodities will clearly equal the relative quantities of labor necessary to produce them, and will be wholly unaffected by the absolute level of wages (no matter in what unit they are measured).

Consider next, with Ricardo, the case in which only labor is required to produce the commodities, but different types of labor are used in differing proportions (I, 20 ff.). The market will establish wage differentials corresponding to the differences in skill and training of the occupations, and "the scale, when once formed, is liable to little variation." Hence a rise of wages will affect the money costs of all commodities in equal proportion, and leave relative values unaffected. Ricardo did not consider the possibility that the relative amounts of skilled and unskilled labor employed to produce a commodity might change and hence its relative value would change; he could have asserted, however, that the relative value of the commodity will change only if the "common labor" equivalent of the original labor input changed.[13]

It is evident that we can still retain the proposition that relative values of commodities are independent of the absolute level of wages (and profits) if, when each worker is equipped with fixed capital, we assume that the ratio of fixed capital to labor is the same in every industry, provided the capitals have equal durability. And this is Ricardo's next case (I, 26 ff.). At this point it is not made clear whether the fixed capital earns a

---

[13] But a closer analysis would have indicated that the wages of superior labor contain interest on the investment in acquiring skill, and therefore the relative levels of wages and interest rates enter into relative values.

net return: Ricardo views the fixed capital as previously expended labor, and says, correctly but unnecessarily, that "exchangeable value of the commodities produced would be in proportion to the labour bestowed on their production; not on their immediate production only, but on all those implements or machines required to give effect to the particular labour to which they were applied."[14] At a later point it is made utterly clear that the contribution of the fixed capital consists of not only amortization quotas but also interest on the investment.[15]

And this is as far as Ricardo could go in attacking Smith's theory. The next step, and analytically the final step, is to allow the ratio of fixed capital to labor to vary between commodities, and when this is done:

> This difference in the degree of durability of fixed capital, and this variety in the proportions in which the two sorts of capital [fixed and circulating] may be combined, introduce another cause, besides the greater or less quantity of labour necessary to produce commodities, for the variations in their relative values—this cause is the rise or fall in the value of labour [I, 30].

The variations among commodities in the productive role of capital are classified as variations in (1) the ratio of fixed capital to labor (I, 34), (2) the durability of fixed capital (I, 31, 40), and (3) the rate of turnover of circulating capital (I, 37). A rise of wage rates relative to profit rates will lead to a relative rise in the values of commodities made with little fixed capital, or

---

14 I, 24. Since the indirect ("hoarded") labor is in fixed proportion to the direct labor, exchangeable values are of course proportional to either part or the total.

15 I, 39, where the case of a virtually perpetual asset is discussed.

capital of short life, or with raw materials that turn over rapidly.[16]

This is of course a cost-of-production theory, and differs from Smith's theory only in the exclusion of rents from costs: "By cost of production I invariably mean wages and profits."[17]

Ricardo believed that the changes brought about in the relative values of commodities by fluctuations in wages and profits were very small relative to those brought about by fluctuations in the quantity of labor (direct and indirect):

> The reader, however, should remark, that this cause of the variation of commodities is comparatively slight in its effects. With such a rise of wages as should occasion a fall of one per cent. in profits, goods produced under the circumstances I have supposed, vary in relative value only one per cent.; they fall with so great a fall of profits from 6,050 l. to 5,995 l. The greatest effects which could be produced on the relative prices of these goods from a rise of wages, could not exceed 6 or 7 per cent.; for profits could not, probably, under any circumstances, admit of a greater general and permanent depression than to that amount.[18]

And so, although it would be "wrong wholly to omit the consideration of the effect produced by a rise or fall of labour

---

[16] Ricardo's measure of value, a hypothetical product made by labor working with the average amount of capital, the capital being of average durability, and having an average "period of production," leads to the proposition that profits fall (measured in this unit) when wages rise, and the actual direction of movement of the values can be predicted; see my "The Ricardian Theory of Production and Distribution," *Journal of Political Economy*, LX (June 1952), 202–4.

[17] *Notes on Malthus*, Ricardo's *Works*, II, 42.

[18] I, 36. This passage underlies the title of this paper.

[wages], it would be equally incorrect to attach much importance to it" and therefore in the remainder of the book he will
"consider all the great variations which take place in the relative value of commodities to be produced by the greater or less
quantity of labour which may be required from time to time to
produce them" (I, 36–37).

I can find no basis for the belief that Ricardo had an *analytical* labor theory of value, for quantities of labor are *not* the
only determinants of relative values. Such a theory would have
to reduce all obstacles to production to expenditures of labor
or assert the irrelevance or non-existence of non-labor obstacles, and Ricardo does not embrace either view. On the other
hand, there is no doubt that he held what may be called an
empirical labor theory of value, that is, a theory that the relative quantities of labor required in production are the dominant determinants of relative values. Such an empirical proposition cannot be interpreted as an analytical theory, any more
than the now popular view that the price level is governed by
the wage level and the productivity of labor can possibly be
defended as an analytical proposition.

This is not to say that Ricardo's analytical theory was correct, for it contained several important deficiencies. It excluded
rent from costs, and even if the supply of land were fixed the
rent a piece of land could yield in one use would be a cost to
other uses. (Ricardo's practice of assuming that land was used
to grow only corn obscured this point.) His theory was wrong
in reducing all capital to previously expended labor plus interest; except in some irrelevant day of Genesis all capital has
been made by the cooperation of earlier capital and labor and
land. This view may have fostered his empirical judgment that
labor quantities were decisive, but one could have adopted
(wisely or not) the empirical proposition even if he had a correct concept of capital. And of course if all commodities are
not produced subject to constant costs, an explanation of relative values that ignores demand is simply inadequate.

II. THE INTERPRETATION BY CONTEMPORARIES

Ricardo's *Principles* received very diverse reviews, ranging from the adulation of McCulloch to the reaction of one anonymous reviewer that the volume "contains no valuable information in point of fact, and very little good reasoning in point of doctrine."[19] This same diversity extended to the interpretation of his theory of value.

J. B. Say could find only a simple labor theory of value. In the notes he added to the French translation of the *Principles,* he observed:

> M. Ricardo does not appear to have included [in the contribution of machinery to the value of a commodity] the profits or the interest on the capital as constituent parts of the prices of commodities.

> M. Ricardo . . . teaches throughout this book that the quantity of labor necessary to produce a product is the sole element of its price, . . .[20]

Malthus, the other leading economist of the period, did not attribute a labor theory to Ricardo, but chided him for his language:

> If to this cause of variation [differences in rate of durability of capitals] we add the exception noticed by Mr. Ricardo, arising from the greater or less proportion of fixed capital employed in different commodities, the effects of which would shew them-

---

[19] *The British Critic,* N. S. VIII (1817), 354. The reviewer continued: "He holds, for example, and this is the leading principle of his system, that the price of all commodities brought to market, consists solely of the wages paid to workmen, and of the ordinary profits on the stock. . . ."

[20] *Des principes de l'économie politique et de l'impôt,* transl. by F. S. Constancio, Paris, 1819, I, 28; II, 297.

selves in a very early period of savage life; it must
be allowed that the rule which declares "that commodities never vary in value unless a greater or less
quantity of labour be bestowed on their production," cannot possibly, as stated by Mr. Ricardo, be
"of universal application in the early stages of society."[21]

It should be noticed that apropos of this discussion, Ricardo
says, "In all the observations of Mr. Malthus on this subject I
most fully concur" (II, 58). The only difference between Malthus and Ricardo in their concepts of costs of production was
that the former included and the latter excluded the rent of
land. The real dispute between them centered on the proper
measure of value, rather than on the determination of relative
values.

When James Mill wrote his primer on the Ricardian economics, *Elements of Political Economy* (1821), he restated
Ricardo's theory in substance. After stating a labor-quantity
theory, he went on to explain at length that because of differences in capital-labor ratios in various industries the fluctuations in wages and profits affect exchange values. He concluded:

It is evident, however, that though this difference
in the ratios according to which the wages of two
kinds of labour were exchanged, and the different
proportions in which they were applied in the
production of commodities, would, upon a rise or
fall in wages, alter the relative value of commodities, it would do so, without in the least affecting
the truth of the previous proposition, that quantity
of labour determined exchangeable value.[22]

---

21 *Principles of Political Economy* (1st ed., London 1820), p. 90; reprinted
in *Notes on Malthus,* Ricardo's *Works,* II, 59.

22 *Elements,* p. 76.

The brazen illogic with which this passage closes was questioned by Ricardo:

> In page 76 there is a passage ending with these
> words "without in the least affecting the truth of
> the previous proposition," etc. etc. If a watch and a
> common Jack altered in relative value without any
> more or less labour being required for the produc-
> tion of either of them, could we say that the propo-
> sition "that quantity of labour determines ex-
> changeable value" was universally true? What I call
> exceptions and modifications of the general rule
> you appear to me to say come under the general
> rule itself. [IX, 127.]

Mill forfeited all hope of entering the economist's heaven when, in the second edition, he retained the passage unchanged and then went on to compound the sin by turning the labor theory into a tautology: "If the wine which is put in the cellar is increased in value one-tenth by being kept a year, one-tenth more of labour may be correctly considered as having been expended upon it."[23]

Ricardo's other fervent disciple, McCulloch, treated him with greater kindness. He repeated Ricardo's analysis, and then, before embarking on his own argument that the increased value of wine or timber arising merely from the passage of time was due to labor, warned the reader:

> But Mr. Ricardo was inclined to modify his grand
> principle, . . . so far as to allow that the additional
> exchangeable value that is sometimes given to com-
> modities by keeping them after they have been pur-
> chased or produced, until they become fit to be
> used, was not to be considered as the effect of la-

---

23 *Elements of Political Economy* (2d ed., London 1824), pp. 97–98.

bour, but as an equivalent for the profits the capital laid out on the commodities would have yielded had it been actually employed.[24]

The final disciple we shall notice is De Quincey. His exposition of the Ricardian theory took the form of a series of dialogues between himself and Philebus, an anti-Ricardian, and Phaedrus, a neutral. The debates went better, for De Quincey, than any in which I have ever been participant or spectator: De Quincey carried every point, no really embarrassing questions were posed to him; and his adversary capitulated handsomely after every sally.[25]

The dialogues were concerned with a defense of the proposition that a rise in general wage rates will not affect the relative values of commodities. Early in the discussion De Quincey asserts:

> *The Ground of the value of all things lies in the quantity* (but mark well that word "quantity") *of labour which produces them.* Here is that great principle which is the corner-stone of all tenable Political Economy; which granted or denied, all Political Economy stands or falls. Grant me this one principle, with a few square feet of the sea-shore to draw my diagrams upon, and I will undertake to deduce every other truth in the science.[26]

---

[24] *Principles of Political Economy* (1st ed., London 1825), p. 313. The qualifications arising out of differing capital-labor ratios are summarized on page 309.

[25] "Dialogues of the Three Templars on Political Economy," which appeared as three articles in the *London Magazine* in 1824; I use the reprint in *The Collected Works of Thomas De Quincey*, ed. by David Masson (London 1897), Vol. IX.

[26] *Ibid.*, p. 55; his italics.

And again,

> It is Mr. Ricardo's doctrine that no variation in
> either profits or wages can ever affect price; if wages
> rise or fall, the only consequence is that profits must
> fall or rise by the same sum; so again, if profits rise
> or fall, wages must fall or rise accordingly.[27]

The complications raised by different ratios of labor to capital
in various industries are not considered.

There is reason for believing that De Quincey did not mean
to attribute a simple labor-quantity theory to Ricardo, despite
the explicit clarity with which this is asserted. The dialogues
were never completed, and the complications may well have
been postponed to these unwritten parts. In the later *Logic of
Political Economy* (1844), De Quincey summarized the complications which Ricardo raised with respect to differing capital-
labor ratios, and did not challenge their basic significance.[28]
Yet the reader of the *Dialogues* would have received only the
account of the first approximation, in which capital (and
various types of labor) are ignored.

Samuel Bailey's penetrating analysis of the value concepts of
Ricardo and his contemporaries revealed with admirable clarity the carelessness, ambiguity, and dubious metaphysics that
saturated this literature.[29] Yet this clarity was achieved partly
by avoiding a real problem with which these economists were
grappling: how can one measure the value of commodity A not

---

27 *Ibid.*, p. 60.

28 Sec. VII; *Collected Works*, p. 196: "In this case, it can no longer be
said that the prices of the resulting articles, according to the general rule
of Ricardo, vary as the quantities of the producing labour: a disturbance
of that law occurs."

29 *A Critical Dissertation on the Nature, Measures, and Causes of Value*
(London, 1825).

merely in comparison with commodity B (the case Bailey studies) but in comparison with all other commodities? This latter problem, of which the isolation of monetary fluctuations is one instance, was surely the rationale of most of the discussion of a measure of value.

So far as Ricardo's theory of value is concerned, Bailey makes no charge that it is a labor-quantity theory.

> Mr. Ricardo, indeed, explicitly allows the influence of other causes, such as time, differences in the proportion of fixed and circulating capital, and inequalities in the durability of capital, by which he admits the value of commodities is liable to be affected. Notwithstanding these modifications, however, his followers continue to lay down the position of quantity of labour being the sole cause of value in the most precise and positive terms; not that they deny the exceptions, but they appear to lose sight of their existence, and frequently fall into language incompatible with their admission; . . .[30]

It may be added that in substance Bailey accepts Ricardo's theory of value, including the exclusion of rent from costs of production.

We may recapitulate this brief survey. McCulloch, Bailey, and Malthus correctly understood Ricardo's theory to be a cost-of-production theory excluding rent, and De Quincey should probably be added to this group. The theory was understood as a simple labor-quantity theory by Say and Mill, and also by Torrens.[31] It is worth repeating that Ricardo ac-

---

[30] *Ibid.,* pp. 230–31.

[31] "Mr. Ricardo has pushed this principle still further, and contended, that in all periods of society, whether before or after the accumulation of capital and appropriations of land, and labour expended upon production is the sole regulator of value." *An Essay on the Production of Wealth* (London 1821), p. vi.

cepted Malthus' analysis and rejected Mill's. The theory was more widely understood in its correct sense in Ricardo's time than in later times.

III. CONCLUSION

How did the misunderstanding of Ricardo's theory arise? Although Ricardo's exposition has been often and justly denounced, the main argument stands out clearly enough: it does not require great generosity or deep subtlety to comprehend the main structure of his value theory—indeed he has suffered from overly subtle reading. The confusion over his theory has arisen from more fundamental sources.

In Ricardo's period several factors probably played a minor role in the confusion. Ricardo's two leading disciples, Mill and McCulloch, asserted a labor-quantity theory with all emphasis, although actually neither held such a theory to the extent of denying that fluctuations in wage and profit rates affected commodity values. Their expositions naturally colored the interpretation of Ricardo, even though McCulloch expressly indicated his disagreement with Ricardo. Another source was the vast confusion of the causes of value with the proper measure of value, and in Ricardo's first edition a pure labor measure of value was used.

The main source of the confusion, however, was probably the failure of economists to distinguish clearly between analytical and empirical propositions. Among economists who were not methodologically self-conscious, who did not systematically consider the necessary and sufficient conditions for an equilibrium, the distinction would seldom be remarked. Ricardo's emphasis upon the quantitative importance of labor tended to be read as an analytical proposition that labour quantities were the sole regulators of value.[32]

---

[32] The "philosophical" and "empirical" theories of value distinguished by Wieser and elaborated by A. C. Whitaker, *op. cit.*, bear only verbal

The failure to distinguish between analytical and empirical propositions has been a source of much misunderstanding in economics. An analytical statement concerns functional relationships; an empirical statement takes account of the quantitative significance of the relationships. When Marshall viewed the demand for a commodity as a function of its price, the prices of closely related goods, and of income, he was criticized by members of the Walrasian school for failing to recognize that all prices in principle influence the demand for any commodity. This is a characteristic instance of the distinction in question: No Marshallian ever denied the existence of the formal relationships that were omitted; no Walrasian ever presented an empirical example of important error resulting from their neglect.

One further source of misunderstanding of Ricardo increased through time. His exposition was much influenced by his desire to refute what he deemed to be popular and pernicious fallacies, such as that a rise in wage rates increases all commodities' values, and that high money-wage rates lead to low-profit rates. When these views dropped from sight the thrust of the chapter on value became more obscure, so the view could ultimately emerge that Ricardo was desperately trying to stave off for twenty pages the admission that labor requirements are not the only determinants of value.

Schumpeter asked why if Marshall's (and the present) interpretation of Ricardo is correct, there should have been any controversy—would it then not amount simply to the current cost-of-production theory?[33] One is inclined to reply that there was no controversy, and that the controversy was about something else. There was in fact no active controversy over the so-

---

similarity to the present distinction. In fact their "empirical" is my "analytical" theory, and their "philosophical" is either my "empirical" or a metaphysical theory of value.

[33] *History of Economic Analysis* (New York: Oxford University Press, 1954), p. 594.

called labor theory in Ricardo's lifetime. The main points of controversy were different. First, Ricardo eliminated rent from the costs of production, which was not in keeping with popular views. Second, he appeared to deny (but did not do so) that supply and demand governed value; in fact he considered this a wholly superficial view that merely postponed analysis of the real determinants of relative values, namely the factors governing supply.[34] Finally, the endless dispute between Malthus and the Ricardians concerned the measure of value, not its causes.

The basic reason Ricardo's theory is often misinterpreted is that it was often misinterpreted in the past. If a theory once acquires an established meaning, each generation of economists bequeaths this meaning to the next, and it is almost impossible for a famous theory to get a fresh hearing.[35] Perhaps one hearing is all that a theory is entitled to, but one may plead that Ricardo deserves at least a rehearing—his theory is relatively more widely misunderstood today than it was in his lifetime. One can build a strong case that the modern economist need not be acquainted with Ricardo's work, but there is no case for his being acquainted with an imposter.

---

[34] "It is admitted by everybody that demand and supply govern market price, but what is it [that] determines supply at a particular price? cost of production." *Notes on Malthus, Works,* II, 45.

[35] Very occasionally a theory, unlike a dog, has its second day, as when Keynes persuaded many economists of the error of the century-long tradition that Malthus' criticisms of the full employment assumption of Ricardo were invalid. The example is the more remarkable because the tradition was correct and Keynes was wrong.

13

Henry L. Moore and Statistical Economics[1]

If one seeks distinctive traits of modern economics, traits which are not shared to any important degree with the Marshallian or earlier periods, he will find only one: the development of statistical estimation of economic relationships. Mathematical analysis became increasingly more common after Walras's first edition; statistical descriptions of economic phenomena were expanding throughout the nineteenth century; bold pronouncements on public policy are as old as economics. But statistical economics, the name given by Henry Moore, is the one important modern development.

Henry Moore was its founder, in the sense in which most large movements have a founder. He had gifted predecessors and contemporaries; but no one else was so persistent, so am-

Reprinted from *Econometrica*, Vol. XXX (January, 1962).

1 My debts are so numerous that it hardly seems feasible to list them. I must, however, thank Roland Baughman, head of Special Collections at the Columbia University Library, for indispensable assistance in making Moore's materials available, and Claire Friedland, especially for collecting biographical materials.

bitious, or so influential as he in the development of this new approach. This essay is devoted to the man and his work.

I. BIOGRAPHICAL NOTES

Most scholars have uneventful lives, embellished at most by a tour of governmental service, a few professional chores, and a wife. Moore had only the last: an extremely nervous and sensitive man, he unfailingly avoided all of the minor entanglements of professional life, and the story of his books is the essential story of his life. So I shall briefly go over the main facts of a quiet academic career.

The main chronology of Moore's life may be set forth very easily:

1869 (Nov. 21)	Born in Charles County, Maryland, the first of 15 children.
187?–89	Attended Scheib's Zion School and Milton Academy, Baltimore.
1889–92	Attended Randolph-Macon College (B.A. 1892).
1892–94 1895–96	Attended Johns Hopkins University (Ph.D. 1896).
1894–95	Attended University of Vienna.[2]
1896–97	Instructor, Johns Hopkins University.
1897 (June 16)	Married Jane Armstrong Schaefer of Richmond, Virginia.
1897–98	Lecturer, Johns Hopkins University.
1897–1902	Professor of Political Economy, Smith College.

---

[2] He attended courses in political economy taught by Menger (whose influence cannot be detected in later work), as well as courses on the philosophy of the jurists, Shakespeare, and art.

1902–06	Adjunct Professor of Political Economy, Columbia University.
1906–29	Professor of Political Economy, Columbia University.
1929 (April 1)	Retired at own request, due to illness.
1958 (April 28)	Died, at age 88.

Although Moore was an excellent student (his grades seldom fell below 98 at Randolph-Macon), his training in mathematics (beyond trigonometry) and statistics came considerably after his formal education was complete. He became interested in mathematics, I presume, in the course of his work on Von Thünen's theory of the natural wage, which began in 1892 and culminated in his dissertation, and studied mathematics on his own.[3] His statistical knowledge was at first also self-taught, but in 1909 and 1913, he took courses both in Mathematical Statistics and in Correlation with Karl Pearson. His meticulous lecture notes still survive.

He made innumerable trips to Europe—seeking out Walras in 1903, Pareto in 1908, Bortkiewicz in 1912, and others, but maintaining correspondence only with Walras.

He taught chiefly courses in mathematical economics and in his own field of statistical economics.[4] His discomfort with undergraduate teaching was such that from 1909 through 1918 he agreed to a reduction of about half in his salary for a corresponding reduction in his teaching load.[5] There is one plaintive note in which he explained (September 1, 1918) that he

---

[3] Moore probably attended a series of eight lectures on mathematical economics given by Simon Newcomb in 1892–93. J. B. Clark was another visiting lecturer.

[4] His first series of lectures on "The Application of Mathematics to Political Economy" go back to Johns Hopkins in 1896–97.

[5] Joseph Dorfman, "The Department of Political Economy," in *A History of the Faculty of Political Science* (New York, 1955), p. 187.

had been transferred from "what was virtually a research professorship to the headship of the department of Economics and Sociology in Barnard College," and "the whole of the summer I have spent in preparing a course of lectures on the History of Feminism: Its Plans and Ideals." Not the least of the evils of war!

And this is the whole story! He was completely dedicated to his scientific work, and spurned every invitation to lecture or attend professional meetings. Aside from his admired friend, John Bates Clark (and his son, John Maurice), there is no evidence of personal intimacy, and much evidence of its avoidance. When Mitchell, for example, wrote (from Washington) a complimentary letter on *Economic Cycles,* but asked for the privilege of discussing certain points, Moore firmly declined the request on the ground that any such discussion would cost him many sleepless nights. Moore was extraordinarily sensitive to criticism, possessive of his own priorities, and quick to read disparagement in the words of others. These traits were obvious enough to his colleagues, and his correspondence reveals extraordinary displays of tact and understanding by Taussig, Mitchell, J. B. and J. M. Clark, Seligman, Alvin Johnson, Schumpeter, and by his one professed disciple, Henry Schultz. The treatment of Moore by his premier American and Continental colleagues—I shall comment on the English economists later—does them great honor.

The nervous collapse which led to Moore's retirement was the climax of lifelong illness.[6] A psychiatrist, I suppose, would find a deep lack of self-confidence in his thirst for appreciation: his careful collections of generous letters and reviews on each book, his meticulous attention to citations of himself, his extraordinary sensitivity to criticism. He was a proud and lonely

---

[6] As early as April of 1898 Moore became ill, and, on the advice of his physician, negotiated a reduction in his teaching duties (*and* an increase in salary) from Smith College, on threat of returning full time to Johns Hopkins, where he had continued to give series of lectures.

man, dedicated in almost a religious way to Pure Scholarship, devoid of a trace of humor in this area, punctiliously honorable, wholly incapable of practicing the politics of everyday life.

The final years were sad. He had lost the power of creativity, but not ambition, and he tortured himself with an immense analysis of the structure of "progressive democracy," which near the end he wisely but unnecessarily requested should not be published. The pathos of this long twenty-nine years was a poor payment by Providence for services rendered.

II. THE SCIENTIFIC WORK

Moore's earliest work was in the history of economic theory. His dissertation (published in the *Quarterly Journal of Economics*) was an interesting but inconclusive analysis of Von Thünen's theory of the natural wage rate ($\sqrt{ap}$), and his second essay was on Cournot. We find him seeking out Walras in the summer of 1903, and a year later asking for a biographical sketch.[7] In 1905 Moore attempted to get permission from one of Cournot's descendents to publish Cournot's *Souvenirs* in English. But this interest in doctrinal history waned rapidly as Moore's work in statistical economics progressed.

The program of statistical economics was embarked upon with great self-consciousness. In his private journal (one of several soon abandoned), Moore wrote on June 21, 1901:

> I have outlined a course of study that I scarcely dare to describe—so much is given and so great ability and patience is assumed. I am fairly persuaded that *pure economics* is a mathematical science to be developed only through the use of the higher mathematics. . . . With a view to contribute

---

[7] In 1905 Moore wrote to Walras promising to write an article on the genesis of Walras's theory with special notice of the work of Walras's father, Auguste. This essay was never written.

something toward this pure, mathematical economic science, I propose to go through these works:

1. De Morgan: *The Study of Mathematics*
2. Lagrange: *Elementary Mathematics*
3. Cournot: *L'Algèbre et la Géometrie*
4. Euler: *Introduction à l'Analyse Infini-*
                    tesimale
5. Cournot: *Théorie des Fonctions*
6. Newton: *Principia*
7. Lagrange: *Mécanique Analytique*
8. Clerk Maxwell: *Electricity and Magnetism, or*
                    Webster's Introduction to
                    Electricity and Magnetism

The mathematical and statistical preparation was considerably
more ambitious than this list suggests, and it culminated a
decade later in his first book.

The public announcement of Moore's program was made
in the *Laws of Wages* (1911)[1]. The stage had been set, he
argued, for a statistical complement of pure economics by
three main developments:[8]

1. "The pure theory of economic statics has reached a definite, mathematically symbolic form. . . ." Clarity and precision
of concepts and the logic of interdependent systems of relationships have been developed, and they "are absolutely indispensable to any form of quantitative work."

2. "The material for the concrete treatment of economic
questions is being supplied yearly in increasing abundance,"
because of the expansion of the state's social and economic
activities.

---

[8] *Ibid.*, Introduction. The 1908 "Statistical Complement of Pure Economics" [13] is primarily a description of statistical techniques, and the
economic part (which lacks his customary lucidity) seems to emphasize
chiefly the development of empirical uniformities which will require theoretical rationalization.

3. "The invention of a calculus of mass phenomena that will probably yield its best results when applied to the material of the social sciences."

4. "The perfection of mechanical devices for performing mathematical computations. . . ."

The exact nature of this new statistical economics was described by illustration rather than by an explicit methodological program. It consisted of three different types of study:

1. The testing of abstract theories.

2. The estimation of the quantitative magnitudes of parameters of theoretical relationships.

3. The discovery of empirical laws which provide the basis for an enlarged economic theory.

The first and third types were illustrated in *Laws of Wages:* the second type was to come three years later.

A. THE TESTING OF THEORIES

The testing of a theory by empirical evidence is an ancient custom, and Moore had no basically new contribution to make to this kind of study. His tests differed from those commonly used in only one important respect: he made extensive use of the recently developed correlation analysis. They differed also from the best work in that the theories he tested were vague and non-rigorous by the standards of 1910, even though he had asserted the necessity for theoretical precision as a condition of empirical testing. Let me first consider one of his tests before examining this difference.

The marginal productivity theory was tested in three steps. First, assuming that all workers have the same marginal product in an industry, "it follows that if an industry could be discovered in which labor played the chief role in production, the variations in the mean value of the product per laborer per day would be a close first approximation to the variations in the specific productivity of labor."[9] Moore correlated annual ratios to trend of

$$\frac{\text{Payroll}}{\text{Man-days}} \quad \text{with} \quad \frac{\text{Value of Coal Mined}}{\text{Man-days}}$$

over a 56-year period for coal mining in France; the coefficient was $r = .843$.

The second step in the test involves the proposition that "the fluctuation in the laborer's relative share in the value of the product varies directly with the fluctuation in the amount of machine power per laborer" [1, p. 55]. Here the correlation was made between

$$\frac{\text{Payroll}}{\text{Value of Product}} \quad \text{and} \quad \frac{\text{Machine Horsepower}}{\text{Man-days}} \quad ,$$

again measuring the variables as ratios to trend. The coefficient is $r = .599$.

The final step is to test the assertion that "the general trend of the laborer's relative share of the product is dependent upon the ratio in which capital and labor are combined in production" [1, p. 61]. This is converted into the proposition that between regions with similar technologies, the laborer's share increases most rapidly where capital (measured by horsepower) per laborer increases most rapidly. A comparison (between two departments of France) of trends in labor's share and in horsepower per worker over 22 years yields the positive association predicted.

Moore's standard of craftsmanship is high: the basic data are fully reported and the work was carefully done.[10] The

---

9 [1, p. 48.] The assertion that the laborers of an industry (not merely the homogeneous class of laborers of a firm) would have equal marginal products is of course Moore's, not the traditional theory's.

10 Moore's data and trend lines in Chapter III of *Laws of Wages* were verified, in a sample test of his work. Eight trend lines of the form $y = AB^t$

uncritical correlation of ratios in the first test was the only major fall from statistical grace.[11]

The economic theory, on the other hand, was extremely primitive. The first test was marred by the identification of average with marginal products, the neglect of differences between money and "real" values, and the lack of an alternative hypothesis—even the wages-fund theory would have predicted a similar finding. The second and third tests were simply wrong: the marginal productivity theory does not predict that the relative share of workers is larger, the larger the relative use of capital—the movement of the relative share depends upon the precise nature of the production function.

Such bold, grossly simplified theorizing was characteristic of all Moore's work, and in fact it was probably essential to the work. An accurate and complete statement of the marginal productivity theory would have posed demands for data (and for analytical techniques) which simply were not available. It is not accidental that a rigorous theorist like Edgeworth—or even a more empirically-minded theorist like Marshall—should have shrunk from any attempts at direct statistical verification of broad theories.

The chief attempts in Moore's first volume to establish new empirical uniformities were in the relationship of unions to the outcomes of strikes, and in the relationship of wage rates

---

are here fitted to wages, output per worker, machinery per worker, etc. In no case did Moore's estimate of log A err by as much as .001, and in no case did his estimate of log B err by more than .0001. His correlation of percentage deviations from trend of wages/output with machinery/labor was .599; the true figure was .619. This was extraordinarily careful work for the period. I am indebted to Claire Friedland for these tests. She emphasizes that Moore's statistical work was done by his wife, a fact whose implication for the verification is in dispute.

[11] K. Pearson's famous paper on this problem had already appeared in 1897; "On a Form of Spurious Correlation which may Arise when Indices are Used in the Measurement of Organs," *Proceedings of the Royal Society of London*, LX.

to size of establishment. They lack the interest of Moore's investigations of business cycles, and will be passed over.

Let us pause to notice the reception of Moore's first book. The reviews were almost universally appreciative. Taussig had many detailed (and sensible) objections but praised the work [33], and so too did Schumpeter.[12] Edgeworth was generally appreciative: ". . . this is the first time, we believe, that the higher statistics, which are founded on the Calculus of Probabilities, have been used on a large scale as a buttress of economic theory" [34]. But Edgeworth pointed out that "in the course of his splendid calculations," Moore had made a gross blunder in attempting to show that the wages of individuals varied in proportion to their ability. And indeed he had, although his rejoinder did not confess error.[13]

Marshall's opinion was communicated to Moore when the latter wrote from London asking for an interview (which was granted so ungraciously that it could not well be accepted).

> I will be frank. I have had your book on Laws of Wages in a prominent place near my writing chair ever since it arrived, intending to read it when opportunity came. It has not come; and I fear it never will come. For what dips I have made into the book made me believe that it proceeds on lines which I deliberately decided not to follow many years ago; even before mathematics had ceased to be a familiar language to me. My reasons for it are mainly two.

---

12 "If this volume has palpable errors, in the future it will be remembered as the first clear, simple, motivated presentation and exemplification of the application of the 'higher statistics' to economic problems" [37]. See also the enthusiastic review by Warren Persons [35].

13 Moore had constructed a distribution of wages by (1) dividing workers into skilled and unskilled, and (2) assuming a one-tail normal distribution of abilities for each class, and (3) showing that his distribution agreed with an observed distribution [1, Ch. 4]. Edgeworth pointed out that a similar procedure could be used to "verify the hypothesis that tallness depends on ability" [34]. The rejoinder and reply added nothing of substance [32].

(1) No important economic chain of events seems to [*sic*] likely to be associated with any one cause so predominantly that a study of the concomitant variation of the two can be made as well by mathematics, as by a comparison of a curve representing these two elements with a large number of other curves representing other operative causes: the "caeteris paribus" clause—though formally adequate seems to me impracticable.

(2) Nearly a half of the whole operative economic causes have refused as yet to be tabulated statistically.[14]

And he encloses a letter he had sent to Edgeworth which says Moore "reached results not nearly as helpful *practically* as those which he could have got by looking at the world with wide open eyes for a few minutes." It is not easy to say more for this narrow reaction than that Marshall was getting along in years.

B. THE CYCLE THEORY

We may begin the survey of Moore's work on cycles with the conclusions of *Economic Cycles:*

> The principal contribution of this Essay is the discovery of the law and cause of Economic Cycles. The rhythm in the activity of economic life, the alternation of buoyant, purposeful expansion with aimless depression, is caused by the rhythm in the yield per acre of crops; while the rhythm in the pro-

---

[14] Letter, to which "Date about 16, 1, 12" has been added, presumably by Moore.

duction of crops is, in turn, caused by the rhythm
of changing weather which is represented by cyclical
changes in the amount of rainfall. The law of the
cycles of rainfall is the law of the cycles of the crops
and the law of Economic Cycles [2, p. 135].

There are four links in this analysis, and Moore proceeds to
forge them.

1. Cycles in rainfall are calculated from data for three
weather stations in Ohio—the stations with long records (1839–
1910) closest to the great grain belt. He fits curves of the form,

$$y = a_0 + a_1 \cos nt + b_1 \sin nt ,$$

where y is rainfall, and $2\pi/n$ is the period of a cycle, with n
taking on all values from 3 to 36. By Shuster's criterion of the
amplitude $(a^2 + b^2)$ of a given period compared to the mean
amplitude of all cycle durations, he finds that there "can be
very little doubt" as to an 8-year cycle, and a lesser but high
probability of a 33-year cycle.[15] The combination of 4, 8, 16.5,
and 33-year cycles reduces the root-mean-square deviation of
Ohio rainfall only from 6.70 inches to 5.29 inches, so actually
relatively little of the fluctuation in rainfall is accounted for.
These periods are then used to fit Fourier functions to the
shorter span of Illinois rainfalls, with what was deemed on
shaky grounds to be good success. The correlation coefficient
between rainfall in the two states was .600.

2. The yields per acre of corn, oats, hay, and potatoes in
Illinois (1870–1910) are next considered. After removing an
upward linear trend in yields of corn and potatoes, Moore
locates the month in which rainfall most affects yields by cor-

---

15 The tests greatly exaggerate the probability that the observed amplitudes are not due to chance because they do not take account of the fact
that the largest amplitudes are chosen after the periodogram analysis; see
R. A. Fisher, "Tests of Significance in Harmonic Analysis," in *Contributions to Mathematical Statistics* (New York, 1950), article 16.

relating yields with rainfall in each month from March through September. This correlation coefficient is at a maximum (.589) for corn using July and August combined, and similar results are given for the other crops. To avoid the labor of computing periodograms of rainfall for the critical months, the periods already found in annual rainfall are now fitted to (1) the rainfall in the critical months, and (2) the yield per acre, for three of the crops,[16] and they seem to Moore to "flow almost congruently"—which is not surprising, since they have been forced to the same periods. The four crop yields are then combined in an unweighted average, and a similar average is made of rainfall in the critical months—the two series have a correlation of .584. Two new sets of sine curves with 33, 16.5, 8, and 4-year periods are fitted, and they lead Moore to the conclusion that "the cyclical movement in the weather conditions represented by rainfall is the fundamental, persistent cause of the cycles of the crops" [2, p. 57]. Moore does not discuss the odd fact that the cycles in rainfall lead those of yields by four years.

3. The next step is to associate the annual changes in yields with the prices of the crops, and here Moore launches the study of statistical demand curves. I shall defer discussion of this topic, and notice only that he obtains elasticities of demand for corn (—.92), hay (—1.06), oats (—.84), and potatoes (—.66). Similar relationships hold for yields per acre [2, p. 99].

4. Finally, the circle is closed. It is shown that demand curves are (irregularly) higher during a period of rising prices (1890–1911) than during a period of falling prices (1866–90)—mistakenly identified with high and low prices. An index of trade—the output of pig iron—is shown to be correlated with an index of the yields per acre.[17]

---

[16] Oats, where the correlation of yields with rainfall is poor, is omitted.

[17] Linear trends are eliminated from both series, and the deviations are correlated. With pig iron lagged one to two years a maximum correlation of .72 is obtained. The actual correlation is poor (see [2, p. 111]) but both series have downward trends to 1893 and upward trends thereafter.

And here, at the threshold of success, Moore faces a crucial problem:

> . . . if we assume that all demand curves are of the same negative type, we are confronted with an impossibility at the very beginning[!] of our investigation. Upon the assumption that all demand curves are of the negative type, it would be impossible for general prices to fall while the yield per acre of crops is decreasing. In consequence of the decrease in the yield per acre, the price of crops would ascend, the volume of commodities represented by pig-iron would decrease, and upon the hypothesis of the universality of the descending type of demand curves, the prices of commodities like pig-iron would rise. In a period of declining yield of crops, therefore, there would be a rise of prices, . . . But the facts are exactly the contrary [2, p. 112].

And here he is rescued by "a new type of demand curve"—the positively sloping demand curve for pig-iron, which will be noticed below. The fall in industrial prices (with low yields) leads to a downward shift of demands for agricultural products, and the path from rain to general prices is completed. The theory is verified by (1) correlating deviations from 3-year moving averages of general prices and crop yields, with a correlation coefficient of about .3, and (2) correlating the moving averages after removing trends—the correlation is .8 if the prices are lagged four years.

The reception of *Economic Cycles* was distinctly cooler than that of *Laws of Wages*. The positively sloping demand curve elicited generally critical reactions, as we shall see. The cycles of weather were questioned; Wright found, for example, that the 8-year cycle in "effective rainfall" (during the growing season) was negligible. Yule believed that Moore had presented "a strong case for believing that weather cycles are at least a very important contributory cause of economic cycles" but requested periodograms of general business conditions instead of a long chain of indirect reasoning [42]—a procedure Moore was to follow five years later. Persons was the only reviewer who thoroughly praised the book [40]. No one, so far as I know, embraced this theory of cycles as even a working hypothesis.

Forecasting the Yield and the Price of Cotton (1917) was Moore's most successful book, and the most entertaining. He wished to see how closely he could predict the yield of cotton,[18] but before turning to his own analysis he examined the record of the Department of Agriculture in its crop forecasts. An official description of the crop reporting service is quoted at length: how it rests upon the reports of thousands of informed observers; how the reports are kept in complete secrecy in the safe in the Secretary's office; how the personnel analyzing the data are rotated each month; etc.[19] Moore now compares their predictions in various months over a 25-year period with the actual yield, to obtain the following results:[20]

Month of Forecast	Correlation Coefficient between Actual and Predicted Yield
May	$-.049$
June	.292
July	.595
August	.576
September	.685

Apparently the need for secrecy before July was not great, and indeed even by September less than half the variance in yields could be "explained" by predictions!

Moore's own method of predictions was to relate yields to temperature and rainfall in earlier months. Judged by the

---

[18] The demand curve for cotton is discussed later.

[19] 3, pp. 52 ff.   [20] 3, p. 74.

modest standard of the official forecasts, his method was quite successful. In three of the four states he analyzed, predictions based on the weather conditions through May, June, or July left a smaller unexplained variance than official predictions two months later; only in Texas, where most economic analysis has trouble, did Moore fail to improve upon the official forecasts.[21]

A spate of articles in 1919–21 mark the revival of Moore's interest in his cycle theory—8-year cycles are now found almost everywhere [14, 16, 17, 18, 19]. *In Generating Economic Cycles* (1923) these results are brought together. The major progress beyond the 1914 volume consists, not in the improvement of the underlying statistical proofs, but in two other directions. First, the law of positively sloping demand curves is quietly replaced by "the law of competitive price," under which increases in prices of agricultural and mining products increase costs of production of manufactures.

And second, the origin of the 8-year cycles is hypothesized:

> The consequence of the long rotation period of Venus with the one face always turned towards the Sun is that the planet is in a constant state of violent meteorological commotion on a vast scale; and this planet, which is about the size of the Earth, thrusts itself at intervals of eight years almost exactly in the direct path of radiation from the Sun to the Earth. Is it not probable that the storm-racked planet creates a disturbance in the interplanetary medium which affects the Sun's radiation on its way to the Earth? If that is the case, then the cause of the eight-year generating cycle is the planet Venus in its eight-yearly periodic motion with respect to the Earth and the Sun [5, p. 102].

---

21 A less dramatic application of the same technique was made in [17].

The profession greeted this final extravagance with respectful scepticism. The most favorable reaction was apparently that of Allyn Young, who wrote to Moore.

> I confess that my first reaction to your August paper [19] was one of fairly complete scepticism. I know the elasticity of any harmonic analysis. . . .
>
> As you will gather from the enclosed memorandum, I have been able to give only the most superficial kind of scrutiny to your results. But I have gone far enough to be compelled to abandon my former sceptical position and to hold that the burden of proof is now upon your possible critics.[22]

The memorandum made clear that Young found a presumption only for a *nine*-year cycle in Sauerbeck's general price index. But the general reaction was one of suspicion, perhaps best revealed by an observation of Henry Schultz in an early article on statistical demand curves:

> Perhaps it is worthwhile to call attention, in this connection, to the fact that Professor Moore's treatment of the law of demand does not depend for its validity upon his theory of economic cycles, as is supposed by some economists [56, p. 262 n.].

I suspect that the sterility of his cycle work eventually dawned on Moore. He could not have relished his admirers. The *Herald Tribune* ran an editorial on "Naughty Venus," and he was embraced by the astrologists, of whom a typical representative wrote:

> I am well-born, a graduate A.B. of Harvard, LL.B. of Penn., and a member of the Bar of the U.S. Supreme Court and also of England.

---

[22] Letter of December 22, 1921.

As for the present financial depression [1933], I surmise and tentatively suggest that it is due in part to Uranus in Aries, square 90° ± to Pluto in Cancer, formerly aggravated by Saturn in Capricorn, square Uranus and opposite Pluto.

There is no evidence in his manuscripts of even a minor interest in the subject after 1930.

Moore's work on cycles has left no imprint on present day economics, and by this most basic of tests it must be judged a complete failure. That it did not make Moore a failure is a tribute to his efforts to provide a chain of causation. Had he attempted to relate business cycles (or cycles of general prices) directly to cosmic origins, he would have provided only exercises in fitting Fourier series. But since he sought also a chain of causation, he was driven to provide a link between quantities and prices, and thus to statistical demand curves.

C. STATISTICAL DEMAND AND SUPPLY CURVES

And now we come to the statistical estimation of economic functions, the area of Moore's work which was of permanent scientific importance. Elsewhere I have traced the evolution of empirical estimation of demand functions from "Gregory King's" law through the Italian statistician Benini and the brilliant dissertation of Marcel Lenoir.[23] Moore's basic contribution was not to invent the field (he knew Benini's work), but to make statistical estimation of economic functions an integral part of modern economics.

The first of Moore's statistical demand curves, as we noticed, were only necessary links in his theory of economic cycles. They gradually became a more important part of his work, probably in response to two facts. One was that they provided

---

[23] "The Early History of Empirical Studies of Consumer Behavior," *Journal of Political Economy*, LXII (1954), 103 ff.

a method of predicting prices on the basis of rainfalls and yields. This had obvious practical uses; rumor has it that Moore was offered a position in a commodity brokerage house after *Forecasting the Yield and Price of Cotton* appeared.[24] The second reason for the enhanced importance of his statistical demand curves was that they elicited interest from other economists—and non-economists, as we shall see.

The first demand curves, presented in *Economic Cycles,* were derived for both agricultural products and pig iron, "our representative producers good." The analysis begins with an attack on the conventional exposition of demand curves, which relates quantities of a commodity to various prices, *other things being equal.* Moore believes this approach is unworkable: no one can enumerate all the other forces which are impounded in *caeteris paribus,* and no one knows how to add them together. The method of multiple correlation, on the other hand, "inquires, directly, what is the relation [between two variables], not *caeteris paribus,* but other things changing according to their natural order" [2, p. 67].

Letting "other things change according to their natural order" sounds like a complete, bold rejection of the existence of an identification problem. The present day economist would complain to Moore that he was mixing up supply and demand relationships, and that although this was permissible for a predictive cycle theory, it did not yield the demand functions of economic theory. And we shall see that Moore is clearly guilty of this confusion in a blatant form, when he derives his "new kind of demand curve for pig iron"—in fact his methodological view was probably drafted partly as a justification for that demand curve.

But Moore's position, properly limited, is also correct and unavoidable once the economist embarks on statistical estimates of theoretical relationships. There are always a vast num-

---

[24] A cursory examination of the financial press of the times reveals no attention to either this work or the cycle studies.

ber of theoretical relationships into which any economic quantity (say, corn production) enters, and they cannot all be introduced into a statistical analysis. For example, the activities of speculators with respect to the carry-over of corn clearly affect, in principle, the relationship between output and price, yet later statistical demand studies have not introduced the numerous structural equations for commodity speculation into their estimating procedures for the demand for agricultural produce. So long as these innumerable relationships change according to their "natural order," the estimated function does serve for the theoretical function in most of its uses.

In the event, the methodological view is immediately modified: it is recognized on the very next page that "the condition of the market" will change over time. In particular, an empirical demand function will be distorted by "increasing population" and "changes in the level of prices." These disturbing factors are to be partially eliminated by correlating link relatives of quantity and of price. This is true, although it is not obvious that the procedure yields "an extremely exact formula."[25] The demand curve for corn (based on the years 1866–1911), for example, is calculated to obtain an elasticity of —1.12 (with $r = -.789$) with a linear regression, and an elasticity of —.92 with a cubic equation. Similar analyses are made of oats, hay, and potatoes.

Moore's primary test of the validity of the results was the size of the correlation coefficient; and the criterion is also used to decide on the type of function to fit: "The demand curve that fits best the data affords the best measure of the degree of elasticity of demand" [2, p. 84]. But there is no awareness of the loss in degrees of freedom.[26]

---

[25] [2, 69.] The procedure assumes that the magnitudes of secular trends (plus cycles?) are small relative to annual fluctuations.

[26] One incidental test is to predict the 1912 price of corn, given the 1912 output. The predicted price was 52.7¢ per bushel; the actual price was 48.7¢.

Moore draws from this work the lesson that pure theory had conjured up wholly imaginary difficulties in estimating demand functions.

> We have obtained the concrete laws of demand for representative commodities, have affixed the degree of precision with which the laws may be used as formulae for predicting prices, and have measured the elasticity of demand for the respective commodities [2, p. 87].

Among the many puzzling juxtapositions of vision and blindness that characterize Moore's work, the most striking is provided by Chapter V of *Economic Cycles*. Early in the chapter he calculates separate yield per acre–price regressions for the periods of falling (1886–90) and rising (1890–1911) general prices.[27] The demand curves are slightly higher in the second period, and this fact was exploited (really, vastly exaggerated) in his cycle theory as we have seen. But when he turns to the demand for pig iron, no such independent influences are recognized, and a simple correlation is made of link relatives of price and quantity produced (1870–1912), to get a demand elasticity of $+.52$. No explanation was given for the result. And so the statistical estimation of demand curves was launched in the English-speaking world.

One important modification was added in *Forecasting the Yield and Price of Cotton* (1917). A correlation of link relatives of production and price yields a coefficient of $-.819$.[28] Moore then lists the long series of conditions Marshall puts on his demand curves (amounting to constancy of other prices, fixed tastes, fixed income). Moore finds the product of these qualifications to be meager: all one has is a function $x_0 =$

---

27 His own data indicate that prices fell to 1897 [2, p. 133].

28 [3, p. 143].

$\phi(x_1, x_2, \ldots, x_n)$, unknown in form, in which only $\partial x_0 / \partial x_1$ is considered.[29]

How does the theorist know, Moore asks, that simply

$$x_0 = a + b_1 x_1 \qquad \text{or} \qquad x_0 = a + b_1 x_1 + b_2 x_2$$

will not predict with adequate precision? And why cannot one add any measurable variable the theorist proposes? He illustrates this by adding the link relative of the wholesale price index (which he tacitly identifies with "the consumer's purchasing power"), to obtain a slight improvement in the correlation coefficient ($R = .859$). Thus "theoretical difficulties disappear before a practical solution" [3, p. 161].

Two years later Moore made his last significant contribution to this area [15]. It was here that he proposed the term "flexibility of prices" for the relative change in price divided by the relative change in quantity—that is, the reciprocal of the elasticity of demand.[30] The interest of the essay lies in the extension to supply curves.

The empirical law of supply under free competition is deduced in symmetry to the demand curve. Farmers make their chief decision on supply in deciding on the acreage to plant; the yield per acre depends on unpredictable forces.

> We would suppose that one important factor leading the farmers to increase or decrease the number of acres planted is the movement of prices in the preceding years. If the price of cotton has been falling, fewer acres will be seeded in that crop; and, on the other hand, if prices have been rising, there is likely to be an increase in the acreage [15, p. 560].

---

[29] [3, p. 152]. The complaint is not wholly a fair one: Marshall does not ignore the influences of $x_2, \ldots x_n$, nor are the interrelations among them ignored, as Moore claims.

[30] The new term is justified on two grounds: some economists may wish to restrict elasticity to a "statical meaning"; and it is convenient to have names for reciprocals (e.g., the cotangent). [15, p. 556 n.]

Hence percentage change in acreage (y_t) is correlated with the percentage change in the price of the preceding year (x_{t-1}), to get $y_t = .375x_{t-1} + 2.76$ $(r = .532)$. I shall return later to this procedure.

Moore's article was addressed to the proposals of southern farm leaders to restrict cotton acreage, and he therefore presented also a second supply curve appropriate to a policy of maximizing farmers' net income. This cost function is deduced with extreme simplicity. The (1914) costs of production per pound of cotton are elsewhere given for a sample of 115 farms, classified into four yield-per-acre classes. Obviously costs are less, the higher the yield per acre. The data are converted into a particular expenses curve and a cubic parabola is fitted to the average costs. It is then found that maximum profits for cotton farmers involve a 35 per cent restriction of output.

This is in one respect a distressing piece of work. That it is improper to treat a particular-expenses (or bulk cost) curve as a supply curve is now well-known, although most of the economists of that period did precisely this.[31] The real complaint is about Moore's uncritical acceptance of yields per acre as the classification base. On his own logic, yields have a very large random component. Hence the high yield farms have on average a large positive random component, and the low yield farms the opposite, and the procedure greatly exaggerates the true difference in costs of different classes of farms (classified by long run average costs). Moreover, unless a restriction scheme withdrew all high cost farms before curtailing output of lower cost farms, his maximizing procedure was wrong.

Moore's most complete formal statement of his procedures is found in *Synthetic Economics* (1929), in the chapter (III) on The Law of Demand. There is no important change in Moore's vision: it is instructive that the empirical example (potatoes) is analysed for the period 1881 to 1913—thus stopping 15 years before the calculations were made. The reason is very probably

---

31 See Charles Hardy, *Wartime Control of Prices* (Washington, D.C., 1940).

that the World War I inflation disrupted the relationship and Moore never introduced deflated variables.

The Law of Supply (Ch. IV) is primarily a formal analogy: indeed if one carried out the instructions of eliminating trends and estimating various functions relating quantity to price, he would simultaneously be fulfilling the instructions to get a demand curve.[32] In the illustrative application to potatoes (this time for 1900–1913), we are simply told that "the price-trend ratios . . . are advanced one year" [5, p. 95], i.e., that the production data are correlated with the preceding year's price ratio. The two functions so derived are:

$$x_{dt} = 1.702 - .702 p_t ,$$

$$x_{st} = .181 + .820 p_{t-1} ,$$

where x_{dt} and x_{st} are quantities demanded and supplied in period t. Since the coefficient of price in the supply equation is numerically greater than that in the demand equation, the system is explosive on usual cobweb analysis, but Moore does not investigate its stability.

Synthetic Economics was Moore's last published work. Its title stemmed from a broad concept of economics: (1) the use of (Walrasian) systems of equations to describe the economy, (2) the extension of the functions to dynamics, whereby all variables are functions of time, and (3) giving the equations concrete, statistical form [5, p. 6]. But he did not go beyond the restatement of Walras's theory; the "dynamic" formulation consisted of replacing the variables by their ratios to trend; the statistical portion consisted of proposing simple forms for the equations. Moore's creativity had been exhausted.

---

[32] The remainder of the chapter consists of a variety of manipulations of the concept of a "coefficient of relative return," defined as

$$k = \frac{\Delta y}{y} \Big/ \frac{\Delta x}{x} ,$$

where y is total cost and x is total quantity produced [5, p. 77]. The section is very careless in mixing costs of the firm and the industry.

III. THE IMPACT OF THE WORK

Moore's statistical demand curves attracted generally favorable attention from the outset; had he not blundered into the positively sloping demand curve for pig iron, I think the reaction would have been even more favorable. As it was, Lehfeldt [39], Wright [38], and Fanno [43] all criticized him for failing to recognize that his procedures led to demand curves only if demand was relatively stable and supply fluctuated erratically.

But the general economist was not ready to take up such work, and the early applications were made by agricultural economists. They began on August 20, 1915, when the obviously intelligent associate editor of *Wallace's Farmer* wrote to Moore:

> Dear Sir:
>
> I have read with much interest your book, "Economic Cycles; Their Law and Cause." Never having studied however, calculus or the method of least squares, I am unable altogether to follow this. Can you refer me to some book which explains in a simple arithmetical way the manner of applying the method of least squares. I want to derive the law of demand as you have done for cattle, hogs and sheep.
>
> The demand laws as derived in your book indicate to me that the farming class as a whole is penalized for over-production and rewarded for under-production. It is of course right and reasonable that the units of a high acre yield should sell for less per unit than the units of a low acre yield, but is it right and reasonable for the total value of a high acre yield to be less than the total value of the low acre yield? In order for truly permanent agriculture to be established would you not regard it as necessary for some price mechanism to be established

which would reward farmers the country over for a
high acre yield and penalize them for a low acre
yield?

I trust that you will continue to publish books
such as your Economic Cycles. If you publish anything further along this line in magazine or book
form I would be very glad to know it.

Sincerely,

H. A. Wallace

The inquiry was not idle: in 1920 Henry Wallace wrote a
most intriguing volume, arguing that chaotic short run price
fluctuations should be eliminated from markets in agricultural
products, by having powerful combinations of farmers and
marketers set equilibrium prices established by mathematical
studies.

I may say, also, that I hold to no particular
philosophy of economics unless a very firm belief in
the utility of thoro mathematical price studies
might be considered as constituting the basis of a
philosophy [51, preface].

In the study he established the long run stability of the corn-
hog ratio as the basis for rational pricing, and calculated a
demand curve for hogs. Three years later he gave lectures at
Iowa State College (now University) on correlation methods
that culminated in his monograph with George Snedecor [54].

This was one clear line of influence by Moore on statistical
demand analysis; the second was through Henry Schultz.
Schultz was Moore's only real disciple, in the full sense of an
active exploiter of his techniques [56, 63, 64, 65, and numerous
articles]. Moore not only supervised Schultz's dissertation but
also was a frequent critic of manuscripts and proofs until 1929.

So much for the direct connection Moore had with subsequent work on statistical economics. When one seeks to go be-

yond direct communication to the more extensive influence of a man's work,[33] there is no more elusive quarry. Who can specify today the differences that would exist in economics if Walras or Edgeworth had never lived? The problem is no easier in Moore's case.[34]

That there was a very extensive development of statistical studies of demand, and to a lesser extent of supply, in the 1920's, is well-known. Beginning with Holbrook Working's fine study of potatoes in 1922 [52], a series of studies emerged in agricultural economics: Fred Waugh on potatoes [53]; Hugh Killough on oats [57]; Bradford Smith on cotton [58]; Sewall Wright on corn and hogs [60]; Chelcie Bosland on wheat [61]; Haas and Ezekiel on hogs [62]; etc.

Presumably it is no coincidence that all of these men (except Henry Schultz, who worked only with agricultural products) were agricultural economists. The existence of a "farm problem" in the postwar period was perhaps a contributing factor to the interest of the economists. But the pioneers themselves emphasize that their interest in quantitative work was partly due to its potential usefulness in agriculture, and O. C. Stine actively recruited a group of able young men at the Bureau of [61]; Haas and Ezekiel on hogs [62]; etc.

The channels of intellectual influence are too often subterranean to deny or attribute all this work to Moore's influence. Holbrook Working, for example, derived his interest in the subject from Marshall, and was influenced by Allyn Young, who was quite possibly influenced by Moore. In general one

---

[33] It may be of interest to report the lifetime sales of Moore's books (which was kindly supplied by the Macmillan Company):

Law of Wages	584 copies
Economic Cycles	907 copies
Forecasting the Yield and Price of Cotton	858 copies
Generating Economic Cycles	831 copies
Synthetic Economics	873 copies

[34] I have benefited greatly from correspondence with O. C. Stine, Frederick Waugh, and Holbrook Working in the material that follows.

can say that Moore was as much the founder of this movement as any one man is likely to be the founder of a great movement toward which a science has been steadily moving.

REFERENCES

PUBLICATIONS BY MOORE

[1] *Laws of Wages; An Essay in Statistical Economics.* New York: Macmillan Co., 1911. Pp. viii+96.

[2] *Economic Cycles: Their Law and Cause.* New York: Macmillan Co., 1914. Pp. viii+149. [Japanese translation, Tokyo, 1926.]

[3] *Forecasting the Yield and Price of Cotton.* New York: Macmillan Co., 1917. Pp. vi+173.

[4] *Generating Economic Cycles.* New York: Macmillan Co., 1923. Pp. xi+141.

[5] *Synthetic Economics.* New York: Macmillan Co., 1929. Pp. vii+186.

[6] "Von Thünen's Theory of Natural Wages," *Quarterly Journal of Economics,* IX (April, July, 1895), 291–304, 388–408.

[7] "Antoine-Augustin Cournot," *Revue de métaphysique et de morale,* XIII (May, 1905), 521–43.

[8] "The Personality of Antoine Augustin Cournot," *Quarterly Journal of Economics,* XIX (May, 1905), 370–99.

[9] "Paradoxes of Competition," *Quarterly Journal of Economics,* XX (February, 1906), 211–30.

[10] "The Variability of Wages," *Political Science Quarterly,* XXII, (March, 1907), 61–73.

[11] "The Differential Law of Wages," *Journal of the Royal Statistical Society,* LXX (Dec., 1907), 638–51.

[12] "The Efficiency Theory of Wages," *Economic Journal,* LXIII (Dec., 1907), 571–79.

[13] "The Statistical Complement of Pure Economics," *Quarterly Journal of Economics,* XXIII (Nov., 1908), 1–33.

[14] "Crop-Cycles in the United Kingdom and in the United States," *Journal of the Royal Statistical Society,* LXXXII (May, 1919), 373–89.

[15] "Empirical Laws of Demand and Supply and the Flexibility of Prices," *Political Science Quarterly,* XXXIV (Dec., 1919), 546–67.

[16] "Crop-Cycles in the United Kingdom and in France," *Journal of the Royal Statistical Society,* LXXXIII (May, 1920), 445–54.

[17] "Forecasting the Crops of the Dakotas," *Political Science Quarterly*. XXXV (June, 1920), 204–35.

[18] "Generating Cycles of Products and Prices," *Quarterly Journal of Economics*, XXXV (February, 1921), 215–39.

[19] "Generating Cycles Reflected in a Century of Prices," *Quarterly Journal of Economics*, XXXV (August, 1921), 503–26.

[20] "The Origin of the Eight-Year Generating Cycles," *Quarterly Journal of Economics*, XXXVI (Nov., 1921), 1–29.

[21] "Elasticity of Demand and Flexibility of Prices," *Journal of the American Statistical Association*, XVIII (March, 1922), 8–19.

[22] "An Eight-Year Cycle in Rainfall," *Monthly Weather Review*, L (July, 1922), 357–59.

[23] "Economic Cycles," *Geographical Review*, XIII (Oct., 1923), Sup., 662.

[24] "A Moving Equilibrium of Demand and Supply," *Quarterly Journal of Economics*, XXXIX (May, 1925), 357–71.

[25] "Partial Elasticity of Demand," *Quarterly Journal of Economics*, XL (May, 1926), 393–401.

[26] "Pantaleoni's Problem in the Oscillation of Prices," *Quarterly Journal of Economics*, XL (August 1926), 586–96.

[27] "A Theory of Economic Oscillations," *Quarterly Journal of Economics*, XLI (Nov., 1926), 1–29.

[28] Review of H. Cunynghame, *A Geometrical Political Economy* in *Political Science Quarterly*, XX (1905), 346–47.

[29] Review of D. H. MacGregor, *Industrial Combination* in *Political Science Quarterly*, XXII (1907), 337–39.

[30] Review of A. C. Pigou, *Protective and Preferential Import Duties* in *Political Science Quarterly*, XXIII, (1908), 143–44.

[31] Review of E. R. A. Seligman, *The Currency Problem and the Present Financial Situation* in *Economic Journal*, XIX (1909), 253–55.

[32] "A Reply to Professor Edgeworth's Review of Professor H. L. Moore's 'Laws of Wages'," *Economic Journal*, XXII (1912), 314–17; with a rejoinder by Edgeworth, 317–23.

REVIEWS OF MOORE'S WORK

Reviews of *The Laws of Wages:*

[33] F. W. Taussig, *Quarterly Journal of Economics*, XXVI (1912), 511–18.

[34] F. Y. Edgeworth, *Economic Journal*, XXII (1912), 66–71.

[35] Warren M. Persons, *Journal of Political Economy*, XX (1912), 524–29.

[36] H. G. Brown, *American Economic Review,* II (1912), 875–77.

[37] J. Schumpeter, *Archiv für Sozialwissenschaft,* XXXVI (1913), 256–58.

Reviews of *Economic Cycles:*

[38] Philip G. Wright, *Quarterly Journal of Economics,* XXIX (1914–15), 631–41.

[39] R. A. Lehfeldt, *Economic Journal,* XV (1915), 409–11.

[40] W. M. Persons, *American Economic Review,* V (1915), 645–48.

[41] James D. Magee, *Journal of Political Economy,* XXIII (1915), 514–17.

[42] G. U. Yule, *Journal of the Royal Statistical Society,* LXVIII (1915), 302–5.

[43] M. Fanno, *Giornale degli Economisti,* 3d. series, LII (1916), 151–54.

Reviews of *Forecasting the Yield and Price of Cotton:*

[44] G. U. Yule, *Economic Journal,* XVIII (1918), 216–18.

[45] W. M. Persons, *American Economic Review,* VIII (1918), 405–6.

Reviews of *Generating Economic Cycles:*

[46] F. A. Hayek, *Zeitschrift für Volkswirtschaft, Sozialpolitik, und Verwaltung,* N. F. IV (1924–25), 387–90.

[47] P. G. Wright, *Journal of the American Statistical Association,* XIX (1923–24), 103–8.

[48] M. K. Ingraham, *Journal of American Statistical Association,* XVIII (1922–23), 759–65.

Review of *Synthetic Economics:*

[49] Philip G. Wright, *Journal of Political Economy,* XXVII (1930), 328–44.

[50] Mordecai Ezekiel, *Quarterly Journal of Economics,* XLIV (1929–30), 663–79.

EARLY STATISTICAL STUDIES OF DEMAND AND SUPPLY

[51] Henry A. Wallace: *Agricultural Prices* (Des Moines, 1920).

[52] H. Working: *Factors Determining the Price of Potatoes in St. Paul and Minneapolis,* University of Minnesota Agricultural Experimental Station, Technical Bulletin 10 (1922).

[53] F. V. Waugh: *Factors Influencing the Price of New Jersey Potatoes on the New York Market,* New Jersey Department of Agriculture, Circular 66 (1923).

[54] Henry A. Wallace and G. Snedecor: *Correlation and Machine Calculation,* Iowa State College Bulletin 35 (1925).

[55] HENRY A. WALLACE: "Forecasting Corn and Hog Prices," in *The Problem of Business Forecasting*, (ed. by Warren M. Persons, W. F. Foster, and A. J. Hettinger, Jr. (New York, 1924).

[56] H. SCHULTZ: "The Statistical Measurement of the Elasticity of Demand for Beef," *Journal of Farm Economics*, VI (1924), 254–78.

[57] H. KILLOUGH: "What Makes the Price of Oats," U.S. Department of Agriculture, Bulletin 1351 (1925).

[58] B. B. SMITH: "Forecasting the Acreage of Cotton," *Journal of The American Statistical Association*, XX (1925), 31–47.

[59] H. WORKING: "The Statistical Determination of Demand Curves," *Quarterly Journal of Economics*, XXXIX (1924–25), 503–43.

[60] SEWALL WRIGHT: *Corn and Hog Correlations*, U.S. Department of Agriculture, Bulletin 1300 (1925).

[61] C. C. BOSLAND: "Forecasting the Price of Wheat," *Journal of The American Statistical Association*, XXI (1926), 149–61.

[62] G. C. HAAS AND M. EZEKIEL: *Factors Affecting the Price of Hogs*, U S. Department of Agriculture, Bulletin 1440 (1926).

[63] H. SCHULTZ: *Statistical Laws of Demand and Supply* (Chicago: University of Chicago Press, 1928).

[64] H. SCHULTZ: "Henry L. Moore's Contribution to the Statistical Law of Demand," in Stuart Rice, ed., *Methods in Social Science* (Chicago: University of Chicago Press, 1931).

[65] H. SCHULTZ: *The Theory and Measurement of Demand* (Chicago: University of Chicago Press, 1938).

14

Notes on the History of the Giffen Paradox

For more than half a century economists have recognized the possibility of a positively sloping demand curve. They have desired a real example, probably to reassure themselves of the need for discussing the possibility, and almost invariably they have used Marshall's Giffen paradox as this example. The present note arose out of curiosity as to the nature of the evidence for the paradox—a curiosity that was and is far from satisfied.

Marshall introduced the paradox in the third edition of his *Principles* (1895),[1] with a paragraph that was not changed in essentials in later editions:

> There are however some exceptions. For instance, as Mr. Giffen has pointed out, a rise in the price of bread makes so large a drain on the resources of the poorer labouring families and raises so much the

---

Reprinted from *Journal of Political Economy,* Vol. LV (April, 1947).

[1] This and all subsequent works of Marshall to which reference is made are published by Macmillan & Co., Ltd., London.

marginal utility of money to them, that they are forced to curtail their consumption of meat and the more expensive farinaceous foods: and, bread being still the cheapest food which they can get and will take, they consume more, and not less of it. But such cases are rare; when they are met with they must be treated separately (p. 208).

One suspects that the paradox was a last-minute addition to the *Principles,* for it stands in bold conflict with the law of demand:

> There is then one *Law of Demand,* which is common to all demands, viz. that the greater the amount to be sold, the smaller will be the price at which it will find purchasers . . . (p. 175).
>
> Thus the one universal rule to which the demand curve conforms is that it is *inclined negatively* throughout the whole of its length (p. 175 n.).

Already in the fourth edition of the *Principles* (1898), the law of demand was stated more cautiously:

> There is then one general *law of demand,* viz. that the greater the amount to be sold, the smaller the price at which it will find purchasers . . . (p. 174);

but the footnote stating the universal rule of negative slope persisted in all later editions.

The paradox is stated again in the *Memorandum on Fiscal Policy of International Trade* (1903),[2] with somewhat more detail for the parliamentary audience to which it was addressed:

---

2 Reprinted in *Official Papers of Alfred Marshall* (1926); the passage is on p. 382. The essay was written in 1903 and revised for publication in 1909.

It is, indeed, an almost universal rule that a tax
on the importation of a commodity lessens its consumption more or less; and the consequent diminution of demand tends to induce foreign producers
to offer it on terms which are lower, although not
always perceptibly lower. Wheat has conformed to
this rule throughout all history, so far as is known,
until about forty years ago. But now nearly the
whole of the English people can afford to buy as
much bread as they want, and yet have money
enough left to buy some more expensive foods: and,
as Sir R. Giffen seems to have been the first to observe, a rise in the price of wheat still leaves bread
the cheapest food, which they will consent to eat in
any quantity; so that, having to curtail their purchases of more expensive foods, they buy, not less
bread than they would have done, but more.

In 1909 Edgeworth commented upon the paradox in the
course of a review of Russell Rea's *Free Trade in Being*.[3] Rea
had stated that "a rise in the price of wheat would increase
rather than decrease the consumption in this country,"[4] and
Edgeworth expressed disbelief on grounds of "a priori unveri-
fied probability"—which this time he defines as "general experience and common sense":

Even the milder statement that the elasticity of
demand for wheat *may* be positive, although I know
it is countenanced by high authority, appears to me

---

[3] *Economic Journal*, XIX (1909), 104–5.

[4] *Free Trade in Being* (London: Macmillan & Co., Ltd., 1908), p. 126.
The remark occurs in a letter to Pigou (reprinted from the *Westminster
Gazette*). Pigou replied: "I agree that it is possible that the elasticity of the
English demand for wheat may be positive. This certainly *used* to be the
case; but I doubt if it is appreciably the case now" (Rea, *op. cit.*, p. 131).

so contrary to *a priori* probability as to require very
strong evidence.

There could be little doubt of the identity of the "high authority," and Marshall rose to the defense of the paradox:

> I have just noticed your review of Rae [*sic*] in
> the *Ec. J.* [XIX (1909), 102]. I don't want to argue.
> But the hint that a rather rash and random guess
> has been made by those who suggest that a (mod-
> erate) rise in the price of wheat might increase its
> consumption in England (not generally) provokes
> me to say that the matter has not been taken quite
> at random.
>
> When wheat was dear and men were cheap, the
> estimate of consumption of wheat per head in Eng-
> land was one quarter: now it is, I believe, between
> 5 and 6 bushels. And thrifty Frenchmen with all
> their cabbages are said to consume more than a
> quarter now. Ever since I saw Giffen's hint on the
> subject, I have set myself to compare the amounts
> of bread (and cake, wheaten biscuits and puddings)
> eaten at first class dinners in private houses and ex-
> pensive hotels, with the consumption in middle
> class houses and second-rate hotels; and again with
> the consumption in cheap inns, including a low
> grade London hotel: and I have watched the baker's
> supplies to cottagers. And I am convinced that the
> very rich eat less than half as much bread as the
> poorer classes; the middle class coming midway.
> This proves nothing conclusively: but it is a fair
> basis, I think, for a surmise as to a probability.
>
> In America the waste of cereals is said to be pro-
> digious: I think a rise in price would check that;
> also all cereals, including even wheat, are some-
> times fed to stock. In Germany it is known that dear

wheat and rye increase the always enormous consumption of potatoes. I have never seen evidence that dear wheat has a considerable effect in that direction here.

With bad world harvests for two or three years in succession, I suggest that part of English wheat consumption would come from American and Australian waste. If not, then bread might become so dear that our consumption of wheat would diminish. I don't say I am right: but I am not random.[5]

We do not know Edgeworth's reply; in his rejoinder, Marshall merely reaffirms what is not in dispute—that a positively sloping demand curve can exist.[6]

So far as I know, these are Marshall's only writings on the paradox.[7] The original statement of the paradox in the *Prin-*

---

[5] *Memorials of Alfred Marshall* (1925), pp. 438–39.

[6] "I am even more perplexed by what you say about elasticity of demand. . . . I object to the phrase negative elasticity, because I think it tempts people to carry analytical mathematics beyond their proper scope. In this case, for instance, it suggests a paradox. And I submit that there is no paradox at all. Take a parallel case. I believe that people in Holland travel by canal boat instead of railway sometimes on account of its cheapness. Suppose a man was in a hurry to travel 150 kilos. He had two florins for it, and no more. The fare by boat was one cent a kilo, by third class train two cents. So he decided to go 100 kilos by boat, and fifty by train: total cost two florins. On arriving at the boat he found the charge had been raised to $1\frac{1}{4}$ cents per kilo. 'Oh: then I will travel $133\frac{1}{3}$ kilos (or as near as may be) by boat, I can't afford more than $16\frac{2}{3}$ kilos by train.' Why not? Where is the paradox? What but needless perplexity can result from calling this negative elasticity, on the abstract ground that that name is in harmony with mathematical symbols, which are being pushed beyond their proper scope?" (*ibid.*, p. 441). Apparently Edgeworth was not convinced, for he reprinted the disputed review without change in his *Papers Relating to Political Economy* (London: Macmillan & Co., Ltd., 1925).

[7] But it is worth noticing that in his *Industry and Trade* (2d ed.; 1919), the demand for wheat is described as follows:

". . . Tooke convinced the Commission on the Depression of Agricul-

ciples is modified in two respects by these subsequent writings: first, the letter to Edgeworth states that the paradox holds only for moderate variations of price;[8] and, second, the parliamentary *Memorandum* implies that the aggregate demand curve for wheat, and not merely that of the poorer classes, will have a positive slope.

A fairly extensive search has not uncovered any explicit statement of the phenomenon by Giffen, or even a hint of it. But I cannot pretend exhaustiveness: Sir Robert was extremely prolific—author of many and long articles; director of many Board of Trade studies; witness before many Royal Commissions; and member of many committees. There are three reasons for believing that, when the hint is found, no detailed evidence for the paradox will be found with it. First, Marshall—who is famous for the generosity of his acknowledgments—re-

---

ture, 1821, that an exceptional 'principle' applies to staple grain; because a fall in its price cannot generally increase its consumption as human food; and, when it becomes dear, people will still buy enough of it to keep them alive so long as they have any means of purchase: in modern phraseology the demand for it is exceptionally inelastic" (p. 794).

"It is of course true that when wheat is scarce, inferior grains, potatoes, etc., may be taken from livestock and used as human food: but Tooke had collected evidence, which has been enlarged recently, that an exceptional cheapness of wheat does not cause the well-to-do working classes to eat more bread; though some wheat is lost through negligent treatment on the farm and in the kitchen and some is fed to cattle, and some stands over for future consumption" (p. 794 n.).

8 This interpretation also conforms with the other discussion of the demand for wheat in the *Principles* (8th ed.):

"The case of necessaries is exceptional. When the price of wheat is very high, and again when it is very low, the demand has very little elasticity: at all events if we assume that wheat, even when scarce, is the cheapest food for man; and that, even when most plentiful, it is not consumed in any other way. We know that a fall in the price of the quartern loaf from 6*d.* to 4*d.* has scarcely any effect in increasing the consumption of bread. With regard to the other end of the scale it is more difficult to speak with certainty, because there has been no approach to a scarcity in England since the repeal of the corn laws" (p. 106).

fers only to Giffen's "hint." Second, when Marshall was meeting Edgeworth's challenge for evidence, he relied upon facts of personal observation when more objective evidence would have been most useful. Finally, Giffen continued to treat the demand curve for wheat as negative in slope after 1895.[9] The following passage is the closest approach I have found to the paradox, and it is hard to believe that Giffen would have written it if he had once gone to the trouble of proving the paradox:

> Fears are expressed that this rise in wheat will affect the consumption of the working classes seriously, and be bad for trade, but this is certainly contrary to long experience. Until 30 years ago wheat was always thought cheap when it was anywhere under 50*s.*, and no particular bad effects on consumption were experienced from fluctuations below that figure. It remains to be seen whether there will be any different effect now from an advance to near 50*s.* when people have become so long accustomed to much lower figures.[10]

It may be added that Marshall was wrong in his conjecture that Giffen was the first to allege a positively sloping demand curve for wheat; Simon Gray had done this shortly after the Napoleonic Wars.[11]

---

[9] See "City Notes," *Economic Journal*, XII (1902), 435. In the foregoing and following references, he spoke of the inverse relationship between harvest and price. Earlier examples are reprinted in *Economic Inquiries and Studies* (London: George Bell, 1904), I, 135–37 (first published in 1879), 215 (1888), and 394 (1883).

[10] "City Notes," *Economic Journal*, XIX (1909), 334.

[11] See the article on Gray in R. H. I. Palgrave's *Dictionary of Political Economy* (London: Macmillan & Co., Ltd.). I am indebted to Professor Viner for this reference.

Let us turn now to the empirical evidence. Two tests of the paradox are worth investigating: first, whether observed quantities and prices of wheat indicate a positively sloping demand curve; and, second, whether the income elasticity of demand for wheat is negative, which is a necessary condition for a positively sloping demand curve.

The annual per capita consumption of wheat and its price between 1889–90 and 1903–4 are given in Table 1. One is struck by the narrow range of fluctuation of consumption, which certainly argues for an unusually inelastic demand. But the data do not reveal a positive relationship between quantity and price; in fact, there is a small, statistically non-signifi-

TABLE 1*

PER CAPITA CONSUMPTION AND PRICE OF
WHEAT IN THE UNITED KINGDOM
1889–90 TO 1903–4

Crop Year (September–August)	Per Capita Consumption (In Pounds)	Price of British Wheat (Per Quarter)	
1889–90.	347	31s.	2d.
1890–91.	343	35	5
1891–92.	357	33	4
1892–93.	347	26	8
1893–94.	344	25	5
1894–95.	357	21	5
1895–96.	332	24	10
1896–97.	333	28	8
1897–98.	324	36	2
1898–99.	344	26	0
1899–1900.	340	26	4
1900–1901.	334	27	1
1901–2.	341	28	4
1902–3.	350	26	5
1903–4.	363	27	2

* Source: *Report of the Royal Commission on the Supply of Food and Raw Material in Time of War*, Vol. I (1905), Cmd. 2643, p. 14, for prices and aggregate consumption; and *Statistical Abstract of the United Kingdom* for population. Consumption equals domestic production plus net imports minus increase in firsthand stocks (those in the ports) minus seed and grain unfit for milling. The quarter contains 480 pounds of wheat. The rank correlation referred to in the text was computed from consumption data before rounding off to the nearest pound.

cant negative coefficient of rank correlation between quantity and price (—.15). We should like also to have information on income and other-than-port inventories, but it is not available. All that we may state is that the evidence does not confirm the paradox.

If we interpret Marshall to mean only that the working classes have a positively sloping demand curve for wheat, a direct analysis of prices and quantities is not possible. But it is known that the elasticity of demand for wheat equals

$$- k\eta - (1-k)\sigma ,$$

where k is the proportion of income spent on wheat, η is the income elasticity of demand for wheat, and σ is the weighted average of all elasticities of substitution between wheat and other commodities (the proportions of income spent on the commodities being the weights) and is necessarily positive.[12] Therefore, it is a necessary, although not a sufficient, condition for a positive demand elasticity for wheat that the income elasticity (η) be negative.

The findings of the Board of Trade's 1904 study of workmen's budgets are summarized in Table 2. Consumption is virtually independent of income except in the highest income class; the income elasticity is small and positive. Again the data are defective (income and consumption expenditure are for only one week), but later English budget studies reveal larger positive income elasticities for wheat.[13]

In this connection, however, it should be mentioned that the first, very unsatisfactory study of workmen's budgets made by

---

12 J. R. Hicks, *Théorie mathématique de la valeur* (Paris: Hermann et Cie, 1937), p. 21.

13 See R. G. D. Allen and A. Bowley, *Family Expenditure* (London: P. S. King, 1935), pp. 34 ff. In view of the emphasis Marshall placed upon the high percentage of income spent by laborers on wheat in explaining the paradox, it is curious that he did not attribute the paradox to an earlier period when this proportion was much larger—he sets it at more than 50 per cent at the beginning of the nineteenth century (*Principles* [8th ed.], pp. 189–90).

the Board of Trade for the year 1887 displays a very large negative income elasticity for wheat in the lowest income classes,[14]
and we know that Marshall thought enough of this study to
reproduce one of its tables in the second edition, and this edition only, of his *Principles* (1891, p. 173). It should also be

TABLE 2*

INCOME AND EXPENDITURES ON BREAD AND FLOUR
BY URBAN WORKMEN'S FAMILIES
UNITED KINGDOM, 1904

WEEKLY INCOME (IN SHILLINGS)	AVERAGE FAMILY INCOME	PURCHASES OF BREAD AND FLOUR	
		Expenditures	Quantity (In Pounds)
Under 25............	21s. 4½d.	3s. 0½d.	28.44
25–30..............	26 11¾	3 3¾	29.97
30–35..............	31 11¼	3 3½	29.44
35–40..............	36 6¼	3 4¼	29.99
40 and more........	52 0½	4 3¾	37.76

* Source: Board of Trade, *Cost of Living of the Working Classes*, Cmd. 3864
(1908), p. xxvi. The study covered 1,944 families who reported income and expenditures during one week in the summer of 1904.

14 *Returns of Expenditure by Working Men* (1889), Cmd.-5861. Only 34
families of different size, occupation, and location were included. To ascertain food expenditures, the families were asked to report expenditures on
17 foods (including pickles and treacle, but excluding potatoes), and the
Board of Trade then computed total expenditure on the assumption that
the list was exhaustive. The pertinent table (IV, p. 28) contains the following averages:

Income Class (In Pounds per Year)	No. of Families	Average Expendi- ture on Bread and Flour
28– 40..............	4	£10 13s. 9¼d.
40– 50..............	2	5 4 0
50– 60..............	7	6 14 7¾
60– 70..............	3	8 16 2½
70– 80..............	3	9 10 8
80– 90..............	5	8 18 1¼
90–100..............	4	13 8 8
100–110..............	4	7 6 3
125.................	1	10 8 0
150.................	1	9 2 0

mentioned that Giffen had a very low opinion of budget studies, as Marshall knew.[15]

We must all agree with Edgeworth that experience and common sense are opposed to the idea of a positively sloping demand curve and that the burden of proof rests on the person who claims to have found a real example. Our investigation does not uncover any attempt at a systematic empirical demonstration of the validity of the example of wheat and casts some doubts on the possibility of making such a demonstration. We shall have to find a new example of the positively sloping demand curve or push our discussion of it deeper into footnotes.[16]

---

[15] When testifying before the Labour Commission on Jan. 24, 1893, Giffen explained at length his misgivings with such studies, and concluded: "Beyond the fact that the proportion spent for food out of income diminishes as income increases, and that the proportion spent for rent and clothing increases, very little, it seems to me, has been really ascertained by means of these budgets which can be of great utility." (*Minutes of Evidence Taken before the Royal Commission on Labour*, Cmd. 7063-I ["Sessional Papers," XXXIX (1893), p. 482].) Marshall, a member of the Commission, was present that day, and, indeed, caused Giffen some anguish with his questions on other subjects.

[16] A possible source of the Giffen paradox is debated by Professor A. R. Prest and me in *Journal of Political Economy*, LVI (1948), 58–62. [Note added, 1964.]

Index